MANAGEMENT
IDEAS AND ACTIONS

MANAGEMENT
IDEAS AND ACTIONS

W. Jack Duncan

NEW YORK • OXFORD
OXFORD UNIVERSITY PRESS
1999

Oxford University Press

Oxford   New York
Athens   Auckland   Bangkok   Bogotá   Buenos Aires   Calcutta
CapeTown   Chennai   Dar es Salaam   Delhi   Florence   Hong Kong   Istanbul
Karachi   Kuala Lumpur   Madrid   Melbourne   Mexico City   Mumbai
Nairobi   Paris   São Paulo   Singapore   Taipei   Tokyo   Toronto   Warsaw

and associated companies in
Berlin   Ibadan

Published by Oxford University Press, Inc.
198 Madison Avenue, New York, New York 10016

Library of Congress Cataloging-in-Publication Data

Duncan, W. Jack (Walter Jack)
    Management : ideas and actions / W. Jack Duncan.
        p.   cm.
    Includes bibliographical references and index.
    ISBN 0-19-511846-4 (alk. paper). — ISBN 0-19-511847-2 (pbk. :
alk. paper)
    1. Management.   I. Title.
    HD31.D8377   1998
    658—dc21   98-15512
                                                                 CIP

9 8 7 6 5 4 3 2 1

Printed in the United States of America
on acid-free paper

To Judy

Who Always Has Faith and Encouragement

CONTENTS

IN BRIEF

Preface xiii

PART I   AN INVITATION TO MANAGEMENT 1

Chapter 1   Why Management? **3**

Chapter 2   Management and Managers **18**

PART II   CHALLENGES OF MANAGEMENT **45**

Chapter 3   The Challenge of Efficiency:
Doing Things Right **47**

Chapter 4   The Challenge of Change:
Doing the Right Things **69**

Chapter 5   The Challenge of Leadership **94**

PART III   COORDINATING RESOURCES **117**

Chapter 6   Goal Setting and Decision Making **119**

Chapter 7   Coordination and Authority **144**

Chapter 8   Motivation and Management **162**

PART IV   RESPONSIBILITY AND CULTURE **185**

Chapter 9   Managing Responsibility:
Obligations and Values **187**

Chapter 10   Managing Culture and Quality **206**

Chapter 11   Lessons for Management: Prescriptions,
Enigmas, and Paradoxes **226**

References 245

Index 263

Preface xiii

PART I AN INVITATION TO MANAGEMENT 1

Chapters in Part I are designed to provide an introduction to management (Chapter 1) and the nature of managerial work (Chapter 2).

Chapter 1 Why Management? **3**

This chapter defines what management is and why it is important. It also sets the stage for the forthcoming chapters by discussing some important contributions prior to scientific management.

Chapter 2 Management and Managers **18**

This chapter examines what managers do and the various attempts to study the nature of managerial work. Not only the traditional studies are included (i.e., Mintzberg and Kotter) but more recent developments regarding CEOs and "real managers." Discussions are also included regarding management at different levels of the organization.

PART II CHALLENGES OF MANAGEMENT **45**

Part II includes chapters that discuss the challenge of efficiency and doing things right (Chapter 3), the challenge of change and doing the right things (Chapter 4), and the challenge of leadership (Chapter 5).

Chapter 3 The Challenge of Efficiency:
Doing Things Right **47**

Much of management is paradoxical. This chapter examines the first element in a complex management paradox: how to build efficiency and order into an organization. In other words, how to do things right.

Chapter 4 The Challenge of Change:
Doing the Right Things **69**

The second element in the management paradox is how to facilitate change in organizations that must be relatively efficient just to survive. The focus of this chapter is doing the right things.

Chapter 5 The Challenge of Leadership **94**

Ultimately change is about leadership, and the discussion of change in this chapter provides the natural bridge to an examination of leadership.

PART III COORDINATING RESOURCES **117**

Part III examines some of the most basic concerns of management as a discipline and how these concerns have evolved over time. Chapter 6 deals with goal setting and decision making. Chapter 7 examines authority and coordination. Chapter 8 is about motivating and coordinating human resources.

Chapter 6 Goal Setting and Decision Making **119**

Goal setting is the first and most essential component in effective coordination of individuals and groups. Goals also provide the markers upon which decisions are made and evaluated. If, as some believe, decision making is the heart of executive activity, goal setting is the necessary ingredient in giving this activity direction.

Chapter 7 Coordination and Authority **144**

Successful organizations have been designed in different ways. All structures, however, depend to a greater or lesser extent on the managerÕs ability to influence behavior.

Chapter 8 Motivation and Management **162**

Coordination of human resources is a critical aspect of management and an issue that has attracted much attention throughout the development of systematic management thought. It remains as important as ever today.

PART IV RESPONSIBILITY AND CULTURE **185**

Management is a social institution and as such it must be responsive to the larger community. It must also conduct itself in a way that is consistent with the values of society. The management of obligations and values is the subject of Chapter 9. Chapter 10 addresses the management of organizational culture and Chapter 11 summarizes ten recurring themes and lessons for management.

Chapter 9 Managing Responsibility:
Obligations and Values **187**

This chapter is a discussion of the evolving view of management as a social institution. Management must be responsive to the larger society, as illustrated by this chapter.

Chapter 10 Managing Culture and Quality **206**

Organizational culture and quality are not entirely new topics in management. This chapter deals with these two important topics in the management of relationships.

Chapter 11 Lessons for Management: Prescriptions, Enigmas, and Paradoxes **226**

This chapter lists ten recurring themes and lessons of management. The themes are provided in bipolar terms.

References 245

Index 263

Management is serious business. The seriousness of this enterprise is demonstrated by the way decisions made by individuals entrusted to run large and small organizations affect our world, our nation, our cities, and our lives. When managers make good decisions, or get lucky as some believe, the environment is protected, jobs are created, corporate profits soar, and employees are satisfied with their jobs and their pay. When managers make bad decisions, or get unlucky as others believe, the environment suffers, downsizing takes place, corporate profits drop, and labor strikes occur. Indeed, management is serious business.

Unfortunately, for those who do it and those who study and write about this complex field, managers and management seem almost irrelevant in the minds of the general public. Except for the attention given to a relatively few high-profile executives and consulting gurus, little attention is given to the people who ensure that plans are made for the future, goals are set to focus our behavior, team members are recruited, payrolls are met, and the "wheels of industry" keep turning. Indeed, management is a worthy occupation that seems to never quite get "what it is due." Management is one of our best kept secrets.

Many people, if they think about management at all, think about fads and fashions. People jokingly say this or that program is "our CEO's management flavor of the month or year" and attempt to become as immune as possible to the latest management virus infecting their organizational world. Indeed, organizations are full of management fashions—those "relatively transitory collective beliefs, disseminated by management fashion setters, that a management technique leads to rational management progress" (Abrahamson, 1996, p. 257). This book, or any other single book, will not eliminate management fads, fashions, folklore, and myths. In fact, one could argue that banishing fads, fashions, and folklore might not be a good idea since they perform positive functions such as building culture and improving teamwork.

It is important to recognize, however, that many of the most successful "fashions" in management are "new spins on old ideas." The fact is that the contingency theory of management and leadership, management by objectives, organizational culture, employee empowerment, and so on are not revolutionary ideas that have emerged in the past half-century. It is safe to say that much of what is true in modern management theory is not new, and much of what is new is not true! The roots of the most successful contemporary management ideas run deep into the history of administrative thought.

The primary goal of this book is to demonstrate this fact. Even experienced managers will likely encounter individuals and ideas in this book that have escaped their diligent search. One might hear a mention of Frederick Taylor and maybe even Elton Mayo. Almost certainly there will be enthusiastic exchanges about Peter Drucker, Rosabeth Moss Kanter, Tom Peters, Michael Porter, and Peter Senge in boardroom musings, but the ideas of Ordway Tead, Henry Dennison, and Harrington Emerson will likely escape the discussion. My intent is not to diminish the value and importance of modern management thought but to frame it—to put it in its proper perspective. Why is this important? Because origins and evolutions add something of importance to our understanding of management concepts.

Throughout the revision of this book, knowledgeable and conscientious reviewers have provided exceptionally useful insights and suggestions. I am extremely grateful for the recommendations of the following reviewers: Richard Hodgetts, Ken Eastman, David J. Lemak, Arthur G. Bedeian, Robert Gephart, and David Jamieson.

For more than two and a half decades I have been fortunate to receive support and encouragement from the administration, faculty, and students at the Graduate School of Management and the School of Pubic Health at the University of Alabama at Birmingham. In fact, the support has been so available that I hesitate to acknowledge individuals for fear of overlooking someone of particular importance. The risk, however, must be assumed.

In the Graduate School of Management, former dean M. Gene Newport has supported every project with enthusiasm and resources. Associate Dean Robert A. Scott has relentlessly tested materials in the classroom and provided regular and insightful feedback. Students in the MBA, MPH and Ph.D. programs have allowed me incredible freedom to test materials and have been unbelievably tolerant of all attempts to improve the manuscript at their expense.

In the School of Public Health, my colleagues in the Department of Health Care Organization and Policy and the Lister Hill Center for Health Policy have been unusually supportive. Peter M. Ginter, chair of the department, coauthor on many other projects, and partner in consulting ventures, has provided support, constructive criticisms, and sage advice. Stuart A. Capper, former chair of the department, provided encouragement for more years than either of us care to remember. Michael A. Morrisey, professor and director of the Lister Hill Center of Health Policy, continues to make my presence in the school and the center both a rewarding and an enjoyable experience, as do my other colleagues Janet M. Bronstein and Stephen T. Mennemeyer. Finally, Dean Eli I. Capilouto continues his unqualified support. On this project there was even a new supporter—Provost Peter V. O'Neil, who agreed to be patient as this project took precedence over other demands and responsibilities.

The support of colleagues and friends can never be underestimated, even though writing a book is ultimately a solitary endeavor. Perhaps the only ones who really understand the time and energy required are family members who pay in terms of opportunities foregone and good times wasted. This has been particularly true of this project. For this reason and many others too numerous to count, I dedicate this book to my wife and friend, Judy, who has shared yet another publishing experience faithfully and with a good sense of humor.

Birmingham, AL   *W. J. D.*

AN INVITATION TO MANAGEMENT

In one afternoon last week I had three similar conversations. The first was with a physician who wanted to enroll in an MBA program and "learn something about business." It was a field, according to her, that she never studied in medical school and frankly was something she would never expect to need. The second conversation was with a dean of an engineering school who informed me that 75 percent of the students graduating from his school were not "doing engineering" five years later. "What are they doing?" I asked. His reply startled me: "They are managing!" The third meeting was with the head of a research laboratory. The question was the same. Do you have any business courses that do not require all those prerequisites? "I have a group of very talented scientists who run multimillion dollar labs, but they have never seen a balance sheet or income statement and they are atrocious managers of people. They are brilliant scientists but they need some business skills."

Times have changed I thought. It was not long ago that no self-respecting physician, engineer, or scientist would go into a business school, much less enroll in a business course. Now they can hardly wait until the next class is admitted, and they pursue the subject with a passion. Management is suddenly a very "in" thing to do and learn.

We could smugly say, "we told you so" or, choosing to be less egotistical, we could simply enjoy our good fortune and capitalize on the opportunity managed care in medicine, profit seeking in engineering, and efficiency consciousness in science have provided. That, however, in my opinion, would be a mistake. Instead, we have a unique opportunity to share the truly valuable subject of management with new and enthusiastic groups of people who are willing to listen. We should do all we can to share our appreciation of management in the interest of better functioning health care, business, educational, and political systems.

This book attempts to contribute to the appreciation of management by illustrating how our understanding of modern management is connected to more than a century of prior thinking and discovery. The first part of the book consists of two chapters. Both are designed to introduce the reader to the nature of management and managers. Chapter 1 attempts to set the stage for modern management thought by discussing important developments that provided the foundation for contemporary advances in the field. This chapter introduces the most fundamental principle of industrial society—division of work or specialization of labor.

Specialization of labor enabled astounding increases in human productivity and made management a necessity. Management was simply not required in great measure when most people lived on a farm, owned their own property, and could do any job demanded. The factory system, however, was a very different reality. Factories required specialists such as tool and dye makers, machine operators, and mechanics, and specialists became very good at the work they performed. Unfortunately, they usually knew very little about what others were responsible for doing. Without someone to coordinate their efforts, little coordinated action would occur. Coordination required management.

Chapter 2 examines the nature of managerial work. Interest in what managers do can be traced to the early days of management research. However, one cannot help but be impressed by the lack of systematic studies of actual managers throughout the early history of management. Fayol reflected on his career and pictured a manager as a rational problem solver. Mintzberg observed a few CEOs over a short period of time and concluded that they were anything but rational. Others attempted to study managers at different levels, including CEOs, but we continue to know very little about the true nature of managerial work.

These two chapters provide an introduction to management and managers. This is where we must necessarily begin our quest to understand managers' actions today in light of the experiences of past managers and previous researchers in the field.

Why Management?

"But history, as they say, is comprehended backward though it must be lived forward, and when we examine our predecessors we bring our own lamps."

Timothy Ferris
Coming of Age in the Milky Way (1988)

Henry Ford believed that history was "more or less bunk" and that the only history that mattered was what we make today. The philosopher George Santayana thought otherwise and argued that those who do not remember the past are condemned to repeat it. As a practical matter, Burke (1978) says it best when he asks why we should look to the past in order to prepare for the future. The answer is simple: "because there is nowhere else to look" (p. 287).

Management actions, not ideas, concern managers. Their lives are too busy to spend time reflecting on the advice of thinkers who lived a century ago (Kantrow, 1986). Certainly, I know of no one who would argue for management scholars what Lord Keynes argued for economists—that practical managers, who believe themselves quite exempt from such influences, are ruled by some defunct management writer. Or, that there are few things more powerful than the "gradual encroachment of [management] ideas" (Heilbroner, 1967, p. 12). For obviously self-serving reasons, I wish we could convincingly draw the parallel. But I cannot. At the same time, anyone who has spent much time in organizations knows that ideas and writers do have their devotees. CEOs regularly circulate copies of Drucker's writings as required readings for vice presidents, and quality gurus such as Deming, Juran, and Crosby have been essential readings for managers in some organizations for the past decade.

The purpose of this book is not to argue that evolving management ideas should be required reading for present and prospective managers. Such a discussion, in the end, would be of little value. Understanding the rich legacy of management thinkers is, after all, a matter of choice. Besides, mastering the ideas of management cannot ensure that mistakes of the past will not be repeated. There will always be J. C. Penneys and IBMs who continue to insist that the "old ways are best" until radical change becomes the only alternative. Companies such as A. C. Gilbert will neutralize and even reverse years of success with a series of successive bad decisions (Hartley, 1991). These things will happen in spite of the vast stores of ideas and experiences available to managers today.

Henry Ford's disdain for history, however, did not serve him any better. The Ford Motor Company remains an economic miracle, and some of the innovations introduced by the man and the company changed America and the world forever. A disregard of history, however, does not account for the success. At times Ford was close to financial ruin and the Edsel is one of the lasting business "bad jokes" of all times (Lacey, 1986). Burke's advice is sound. We should learn from history because it is the only thing we have to teach us about the future. Maybe it will prove useful, maybe it will not. But is this any different from any other forecast? The perceptive manager cannot afford to ignore good advice regardless of its source. Management ideas contain valuable lessons and guidelines for action only for those who are wise enough to listen and learn.

Peck (1993) reminds us that the sign of a healthy body is not that it is free from disease. Healthy people catch colds and stomach viruses. Healthy bodies, however, possess the special capacity to heal themselves with and without the aid of a physician. In the same sense, the healthy organization is not free from problems. Excellent managers make mistakes, formulate inappropriate strategies, and fail to inspire employees. Healthy organizations and excellent managers, however, address problems actively and effectively and facilitate healing. A good dose of tried and proven experiences from the past may be an effective elixir—just what the doctor ordered. To ignore ideas and experiences is unwise and irresponsible.

Ideas and Actions

This book is organized around some of the most frequently discussed and debated ideas in management. Actions of real managers and experiences in real organizations have been inserted to illustrate how the ideas have been used and the benefits derived from using them. Examples have also been included to illustrate the ill effects of ignoring sound management experience. In the interest of objectivity, illustrations are included to demonstrate the inappropriateness of some ideas and how experience has refined issues that were inaccurate, outdated, or both.

All of the ideas included are alive today and just as important and controversial as when they were first presented. They have been selected from a search of the "classic" books on management and chosen from literally hundreds of important ideas and concepts that were candidates for inclusion. Since selections were made, explanations and justifications are needed for the choices.

Each chapter focuses on an important idea in management. Each idea is discussed by analyzing what specific management writers had to say with respect to the subject. The writers included are not the only important ones who pondered and discussed the idea. Selectivity, again, was necessary, even essential. Rather than merely cite the many comments all the classical writers made about the idea, details are given with regard to only a few. The idea is then traced to modern times to illustrate, using experiences and actions of actual organizations, that the topic remains important today. Throughout each chapter, "boxes" are included to provide backgrounds on key individuals and actions taken by real managers that represent applications of the idea being discussed.

The array of writers assembled in this book is an interesting mix. The composition of the sample reflects a mysterious characteristic of management literature. For example, until the Hawthorne Studies, which will be discussed in detail in Chapter 8, most of the significant books in the field of management were businessmen and women who either ran business firms or acted as consultants to those who did run companies. Frederick Taylor, Frank Gilbreth, Henry Gantt, Henri Fayol, Lyndall Urwick, James Mooney, Chester Barnard, Mary Parker Follett, and Henry Dennison were all actively engaged in the day-to-day management of businesses or as consultants. Even though Hugo Munsterberg and Lillian Gilbreth were exceptions, most of the writers during the first 30 years of management's development were never college professors.

Professors entered the picture with the events surrounding the Hawthorne Studies. Elton Mayo, Fritz Roethlisberger, Herbert Simon, Rensis Likert, Fred Fiedler, Paul Lawrence, Jay Lorsch, and others illustrate how completely the development during the last six decades has been dominated by academics. A possible exception is what some consider the "best seller" phenomenon of the past two decades. Even I will not speculate about what it means when the business best seller list for a typical week includes two books written by a cartoonist (*The Dilbert Future* and *The Dilbert Principle*), one is by a coach (*Success Is a Choice*), and one is coauthored by a physician (*One Minute Manager*).

A balance of the writings of both practicing managers and academics has been provided in this book because it is important to see how similar at points and how different at others the ideas of the two groups have been. Fortunately, the contributions of both groups are significant, and collectively they account for the profound modern institution known as management. Because of this there is no reason to attempt to evaluate the relative importance of the two groups' ideas. They are both important and add to our knowledge of organizations and people at work.

There are many other writers whose ideas could and should have been analyzed if space allowed. The goal of this book has been to include representatives from the major streams of thought that comprise modern management ideas and relate them to recommended management actions. In this manner ideas are discussed that find their origin in a period of scientific management but are as modern as yesterday's newspaper. Specific representatives from each period were selected because of the thoughts they had on the topics selected for discussion. The logic of the selection will be more apparent as the issues are introduced and discussed.

English Factories and the American System of Manufacture

Tracing the origins of modern management ideas requires that we "begin before the beginning." Management is a young discipline by intellectual standards. Most agree that, as a formal discipline, it is less than a century and a half old. However, the curiosity that spawned it can be found much earlier.

As with so many other things, our search for beginnings requires an international focus. It was in Great Britain that the Industrial Revolution began in the mid-18th century. For the inquiring mind, Great Britain at the time must have been an exciting place. However, the excitement and the reality took almost 100 years to reach the shores of the new world. There were, to be sure, only a few attempts during the Industrial Revolution to commit management ideas to paper with the ultimate effect of developing principles. The necessary conditions for the eventual evolution of management thought were, however, firmly established during this time.

Steam power created the potential for the Industrial Revolution, but mass markets made it necessary. Nowhere was this more evident than in mid-19th-century America. Immediately following the war between the states, America was "railroadized" through a sixfold increase in the miles of track in the last half of the 19th century. The population increased and headed west, demanding more and more products and machines along the way. A mass market developed, transportation facilities were in place, and workers discovered strength in numbers, thereby accelerating union activism and militancy. It was clear to industrialists that merely adding more laborers would not solve production problems (Duncan, 1971). With stronger unions it might not even have been possible. It would certainly be expensive. Large-scale operations were a necessity, and that required greater specialization and larger factories. Factories, however, required investment of capital, specialized machines, and machine operators. That is where and why management entered the picture.

▲ Box 1-1

EARLY MASS PRODUCTION IN AMERICA

It is true that the Industrial Revolution took almost a century to move from England to America. It is also true that mass production in the United States has been associated primarily with the automobile industry. However, in the late 18th and early 19th centuries mass production textile factories were emerging in New England. Samuel Slater opened "America's first factory" using a business format in 1790 and Francis Cabot Lowell opened another in 1814.

Both of these factories harnessed technologies that led to the development of complete textile manufacturing systems. These entrepreneurs adapted existing technologies to their special needs, obtained the capital needed to build and operate their factories, developed management hierarchies and personnel practices necessary to run them, and marketed their products. Interestingly, these two industrialists shared the same resistance to the economic and technological changes that took place. In terms of both receptiveness and resistance to change, these early factories had much in common with today's organizations.

Source: Combs (1995).

The expansion of the railroads presented opportunities and challenges for American enterprise which had not existed previously. This practical and efficient form of transportation also created the necessity of organizing and managing large-scale businesses. Daniel McCallum, for example, worked for the New York and Erie Railroad Company even before the Civil War and pioneered many progressive managerial efforts (Wren, 1994).

Management is the coordination of human and nonhuman resources toward the accomplishment of organizational goals. When machines and human beings began moving to progressively greater levels of specialization, management became necessary to coordinate diverse tasks and operations. Two individuals, Charles Babbage and Andrew Ure, were instrumental in advocating important ideas that, along with mass markets, made factories inevitable and the emergence of management as a discipline inescapable.

Division of Labor and the Economics of Specialization

Babbage was born in 1792, the son of a wealthy English banker. If it had not been so, he would likely have died in childhood. He was ill much of his life. However, the weaknesses of his body accounted for the strength of his mind. He was curious, inventive, and more intelligent than most children. It may have been his illness that made him cranky and impatient.

It was not uncommon for him to blow horns outside his home to drive away organ grinders who disturbed his work. One person said of Babbage that "he spoke as if he hated mankind in general, Englishmen in particular, and the English government and organ grinders most of all" (Moseley, 1964). In spite of his disposition, he was interested in how things worked, an interest that led him to study mathematics at Cambridge. His mathematical talents aided him in inventing his famous "analytical engine"—the forerunner of the digital computer (Froehlich, 1985). His broader interests in science led him around Europe for over 10 years, observing and studying factories, before returning to Cambridge and settling down in a mathematics professorship in 1828 (Moseley, 1964).

One of Babbage's most lasting contributions was the publication of his book*, On the Economy of Machinery and Manufactures* (1832). Ten years of visiting factories clearly influenced the content of the book, as evidenced by the enormous range of topics discussed. A sample of the contents reveals discussions of the importance of tools, plant location, unions, and the use of calculating machines operated by punched cards. It was, however, Babbage's discussion of *specialization, or the division of labor*, that aids us in understanding the nature and importance of the factory.

Babbage was not the first to discuss the virtues of division of labor. Half a century earlier Adam Smith (1776) published his famous *Wealth of Nations*. The first three chapters dealt with the importance of the division of labor, complete with an example of its use in making pins. Babbage's debt to Smith is obvious, although he was able to extend and improve on the ideas. In fact, all the management writers from the beginning to the most modern times who have seriously examined the issue of specialization trace the origins of their ideas to Adam Smith.

One of the most important distinctions presented by Babbage had to do with the division of physical and mental labor. If specialization worked so well for factory workers, Babbage asked, why not for mathematicians? In our society specialization is easy to appreciate and understand. We are used to doctors who work only on ears or bones, lawyers who concentrate solely on real estate, and accountants who deal exclusively with taxes.

That was not the case in 18th-century England. Specialization was not so obvious to the farmer or worker in a cottage industry. Before factories and assembly lines, people were generalists who plowed the land, planted the seeds, fertilized, and harvested the products of their labor. Babbage was quick to recognize the potential of specialization. In fact, he stated that the division of labor was the most important principle among all the people who performed work.

To Babbage the virtues of specialization were numerous. Specialization reduces the time needed for learning a job. Moreover, the time required to master a job depends on its difficulty and the number of distinct processes it requires. Therefore, the more difficult the task and the more processes it involves, the greater the benefits of specialization. Specialization also reduces waste. Waste is reduced when people "confine their attention to one task" and learn faster through specialization. Specialization reduces the time consumed in changing from one job to another. Carpenters do not lose time doing electrical work.

▲ Box 1-2
WHERE WILL IT END?

The Mizushima Works of Kawasaki Steel had a problem with the traditional method of production planning. It had accumulated computer programs of over 30 million steps in an attempt to integrate and control its entire operations. Coal blending and coke making remained an area requiring a great deal of expensive human judgment and decision making. To be successful, however, an expert system capable of replacing human judgment would have to manage a coal yard with 25 coal beds composed of 20 types of coal, selected from over 40 types, and standardize a planning system that required 2 days for experts to develop a 40-day plan. The challenge was formidable. No one knew whether an expert system could tackle such a complex problem successfully.

Today, with the use of expert systems, the company's Compass-88 system has reduced the planning time from 2 days to 3 hours. In fact, a 90-day plan can now be produced in 3 hours with a level of accuracy that equals or exceeds the work of human experts.

Source: Kunitoshi (1995).

Skills are developed to higher levels through specialization, and, at least in principle, quality is improved because repetition leads to rapidity and excellence. Specialization also encourages labor-reducing innovation. Like Smith, Babbage believed that the specialist who became an expert in performing a single task would be more likely to invent or create a tool or process to improve work. Finally, specialization allows a more careful matching of people and tasks. If workers are expected to do everything, each person must be capable of doing the heaviest or most demanding subtask in the complete job. With specialization, skills and stature can be more easily matched to the subtask. Babbage thought that, as a rule, the higher the skill required by a job and the less time the skill is actually employed, the greater will be the advantage of specialization.

Without the division of labor, learning would require time, waste would increase, and inefficiencies would result. As we might guess, it was inevitable that Babbage would ask: "Should mathematicians perform the lowest processes of arithmetic?" Of course not! That was precisely why he developed the analytical, or difference, engine to relieve talented people of the chore of routine calculations.

Babbage was a dreamer, but he was not altogether unrealistic. He knew that there must be mass markets for the "product" of the specialist's labor, and capital would be required in greater amounts if specialization were practiced on a grand scale. A consideration of capital brings us to another important Englishman.

Substituting Capital for Labor

Andrew Ure was older than Babbage. He was born in Glasgow, Scotland, in 1778, just 2 years after Adam Smith published his *Wealth of Nations*. Ure earned a degree in medicine and embarked on a career as a scientific writer and chemist. What led to his interest in factories no one knows. It might have been the popular scientific lectures, the first of their kind, he prepared and delivered to the working people of Glasgow. Factories were what his audiences understood best, and perhaps his search for meaningful examples enlightened the teacher as much as the pupils. How he became interested is not important; that he became interested is the critical point.

Ure was particularly concerned about the progress of British textiles. He made careful studies of factory districts and actually tried to "eat, sleep, think, and feel" like a factory worker. He talked to workers, observed them, and finally wrote about them in his book, *The Philosophy of Manufactures* (1835). Ure's book has been called many things, including the "railings of a frustrated mechanic" and a "defense of manufacturing and manufactures." It was both and more. It is one of the most important books we have about the factory system of England during the Industrial Revolution.

Probably because of the demands of his scientific nature and the fact that he was a physician, Ure began his book with tremendous amounts of demographic and public health data. He documented the average age of the British industrial worker, divided employment figures into males and females, reviewed their health status, repeated their complaints, and observed their habits away from work.

Important elements of Ure's philosophy were formed as he attempted to refute a report by a Mr. Sadler, who accused Britain's industrialists and their factories of being too harsh on workers, abusing children, and generally allowing a variety of poor working conditions. "Not so!" argued Ure. The real culprit was the lack of automation. Data showed that the best work was done entirely by machines, thus relieving humans of heavy and boring tasks. Workers in automated factories with steam engines were more satisfied, according to Ure, because they were relieved of physical labor and could produce enough to achieve more than a mere subsistence level of existence.

The Sadler Report blamed machines for worker misery and child abuse. Ure blamed the conditions on the way factories were operated. Children in textile factories were ruled by spinners and the men who operated "slubbing" machines. These slubbers supervised children and were paid on the basis of how much work the children accomplished. Any mistake or failure to work hard led to a beating. Most of the cruelty "complained of in the factories takes place between the slubber and his pieceners" (Ure, 1835, p. 179). It had nothing whatsoever to do with machines.

The most basic principle for reforming the factory system, as Ure viewed it, was to "substitute mechanical science for hand skill." In other words, substitute machines for manual labor. Machines reduced tiring work and boredom, and promised a higher standard of living. *The Philosophy of Manufactures* was nothing more than an exposition of the general principles on which productive industry should be conducted by self-acting machines. The essence of the factory system was to "substitute mechanical science for hand skill, and the partition of a process into its essential constituents" (p. 20). The mechanic in Ure is easy to infer from his writings. Where Babbage had called for specialization, Ure seconded the call and extended it with a plea for machines as well.

At this time, the fascination with machines was making its way to the New World. In this new and exciting place, the government encouraged western settlement with cheap land. Many of the men headed west and left large numbers of relatively unskilled women to run the farms or to move to the city in search of work. The entrepreneurs in the textile and other manufacturing industries took seriously the advice of Ure and opted for machines. The relatively low skilled workers could tend the machines even if they could not operate them. At the same time, military men in Europe had discovered the value of interchangeable parts for muskets and handguns. When the idea of interchangeable parts and the automated factories were combined, a new phenomenon known as the *American system of manufacture* resulted (Rosenberg, 1969). The industrial world, again, was changed forever. The power of interchangeable parts has not been lost in modern manufacturing. For example, the Toyota RAV4 multipurpose vehicle was designed to share 40 percent of its parts with other Toyota models. It even uses a Cambry engine that has 30 percent fewer parts than the original model.

Mass Production and Economies of Scale

The significance of the *American system of manufacture* was far-reaching. Machines worked fast, and people with relatively low skills could tend them. At the same time, schemes for making things would be developed whereby interchangeable parts could be used in a variety of goods from sewing machines to bicycles. Eventually, and most significantly, the automobile would be produced in large numbers because of advances in this concept of manufacture. Manufactured goods could at last be produced in the quantities demanded by a growing market with increased transportation capabilities. Mass production and mass consumption are closely interrelated, even though we can rarely determine which is cause and which is effect.

Once the process begins, the management problem is one of how to respond efficiently to the opportunities and needs that mass consumption and production create. The substitution of machines for manual labor and the resulting specialization signaled the death of the mom and pop manufacturing business. When products were needed in large numbers, the conditions for the large-scale factory were created. The size of manufacturing facilities in modern times illustrates just how far economies of scale can be taken. At peak employment in the 1970s, the General Electric Company's Major Appliance Group in Louisville, Kentucky, employed over 20,000 workers. Single factories employing thousands of workers are commonplace. Even retailing operations have sought economies of scale with mega discount stores and large no-haggle pricing at new- and used-car superstores. While it is true that downsizing has occurred and in some industries small "focused" factories have been successful, large-scale operations remain the rule rather than the exception in manufacturing.

The trend toward mass production and the accompanying economies of scale began in the American automobile industry. Oldsmobile was the first to introduce the "nonmoving" assembly line. After a fire destroyed its Detroit plant in 1900, local machine shops were contracted to make component parts and deliver them to the new factory, where they were carried from one worker to another to be assembled. Using this technique, output was increased from slightly over 400 cars in 1901 to 5,000 in 1903. Even though the Oldsmobile sold for about $650 and became a very popular car in America, the company was not able to make an automobile for a mass market. The genius of that belonged to Henry Ford.

Henry Ford's objective was to build a car that people from all occupations could afford. That goal was accomplished in 1913 with the installation of the first moving assembly line. Just 5 years earlier, Henry Leland of the Cadillac Automobile Company impressed the world with the practicality of perfectly interchangeable parts. The experiment was simple. Prior to Leland's vision, parts for cars were made for a specific automobile, and the parts had to be matched with considerable accuracy. This consumed large amounts of time. In 1905, Leland sent three Cadillacs to England, where they were disassembled and their parts were mixed with other parts from dealers' warehouses. They were then reassembled into three workable Cadillacs. What military leaders discovered about muskets, automobile makers discovered about cars. Great speed and economies can be achieved through the use of interchangeable parts.

In 1913, Henry Ford combined all the previous ideas of Oldsmobile and Leland into his famous moving assembly line. The frame of the automobile moved through the plant on a conveyor belt while workers on each side of the line placed parts on the frame. In 1908, before the installation of the moving assembly line, a Model T cost about $850. This was more expensive than the Oldsmobile and beyond the reach of most industrial workers. After the installation of the line, workers could build a Model T in less than 2 hours for a cost of about $400. The concept was so successful that for almost 20 years, between 1908 and the late 1920s, half the cars sold in the United States were Fords (Bryant and Dethloff, 1983).

The moving assembly line accomplished several things and set the stage for a number of others. First, the assembly line combined both the desire for specialization championed by Babbage and the substitution of machines for manual labor envisioned by Ure. The result was a production process that consisted of a series of relatively simple tasks organized in a continuous flow along a long, moving line. Each piece of equipment and all required materials, at least in theory, arrived at the right place at precisely the right time. The theory of the assembly line was to break each job down into a series of simple sequential tasks. The point where work was actually done demanded little thought. Good work habits, it was hoped, would lead to more habitual and higher quality products. The craftsman and the apprentice and their caring but relatively expensive way of doing work virtually disappeared over night when the factory arrived on the scene. Friedman (1961) illustrated the extent to which division of work was carried out by showing how the relatively simple task of making a man's waistcoat was broken down into 65 different units of work.

The savings were incredible. Lacey (1986) stated that the output at Ford in 1911–1912 was over 78,400 cars with 6,867 employees. The following year, production and the number of workers more than doubled. In 1913, with the installation of the moving assembly line, production almost doubled again, but the number of employees actually dropped by about 1,500. The refinement of the moving assembly was perfected in time to become a major element in the Allied victory in World War II. Ford Motor Company applied its mass production techniques to airplanes, and industrialists like Henry Kaiser were able to apply innovative prefabricating techniques to constructing Liberty ships. During peak operations an entire ship could be welded together in only $8^{1}/_{2}$ hours (Bailey, 1977).

Mass production and the search for economies of scale were the answers to the problem of supplying mass markets composed of relatively affluent shoppers. The assembly line, in fact, so revolutionized our lives that Burke (1978) listed it along with seven other innovations, including the atomic bomb, telephone, computer, television, plastic, airplanes, and guided rockets, as things that "may be most influential in structuring our own futures and in causing a further increase in the rate of change to which we may have to adapt" (p. i). By the 1970s, changes brought about by the moving assembly line were under way that would have surprised even Babbage and Ure. The most significant of these changes was the industrial robot.

Robotics and Specialization

What manager would not like to have an employee who could insert over 7,000 components into a printed-circuit board in less than an hour; tighten 16,000 screws a day and never get bored; and paint, weld, and operate in the midst of toxic fumes and never take a day of sick leave? You are right if you say "no human can work like that." However, robots can, and those manufactured by companies like Matsushita Electric can do even more. A robot made by Hitachi, for example, called the "visualtactile sensing robot," has multiple arms, seven cameras for eyes, and can independently assemble home appliances such as vacuum cleaners. The company's motto is: "We believe robots free the minds to create by freeing bodies from toil." Babbage and Ure would have been proud!

In the mid-1990s, robot sales worldwide increased almost 30 percent to over 75,000 units. It was estimated that sales would increase 15 percent per year throughout the decade ("Robotics: Artificial Workers," 1996). Interestingly, 70 percent of the world's robot population resides in Japan. At the Fujitsu Fanuc robot factory in Japan, 100 humans supervise and maintain robots who make robots (Donleavy, 1994). It is unlikely that the demand for robots will decrease because they perform predictable, redundant tasks better than humans.

For example, over 1.3 million patient injuries or ill effects result from drug therapy annually, and two-thirds of these involve human error. Automated Healthcare's RxOBOT uses bar coding and advanced technology to dispense, stock, track, and manage inventory for medicines in hospitals. Since 1993, RxOBOT has dispensed more than 25 million doses of medications in hospitals in 20 states without a single error ("Robotics: Right Rx," 1995). In an unmanned satellite laboratory at the University of Virginia Medical Center, cost savings through the use of robots in areas of sample transportation, labor costs, and improvements in test turnaround time have been significant. It was estimated that the system paid for itself in 3 years through cost savings and test turnaround time. For example, formerly it took from 17 to 72 minutes for a doctor to receive a lab report after it was requested. Robots reduced the time to 7 minutes (Felder, Savory, Margrey, Holman, and Boyd, 1995).

▲ Box 1-3
ROBOTS AT NISSAN

Robots work longer and harder than humans, but like all machines, as they wear out, they become less accurate in doing what they do. Nissan has developed an intelligent body assembly system (IBAS) to overcome this problem. The IBAS instructs robots to perform 68 spot welds, which assemble the automobile shell from eight basic unpainted parts. The welds made by the robots are accurate to within half a millimeter.

Accurate welds are, in themselves, not particularly impressive innovations. The real innovation in IBAS comes from the fact that the system uses the information obtained from each shell assembly to adjust when the next set of eight pieces is sent to it along the assembly line. Moreover, when new models are placed in production, expensive production line retooling can be made by software changes. Before IBAS, retooling for new models could take 11 months and cost millions of dollars. Today it takes one-fourth of the time and involves only about one-third of the cost.

Source: "Factory Robots" (1990).

Economies of scale, moving assembly lines, and increased mechanization created new possibilities. The more predictable and programmable work became and the more interchangeable the parts used in manufacturing, the more easily it could be performed by machines. The prospect of automation offered solutions to several of the primary problems faced by businesses in the mid-20th century. Automated factories, for example, could be located in lower cost areas since large supplies of human resources were not required. Moreover, industrialists observed an interesting phenomenon. Often workers were more willing to accept the startup of a completely automated factory in a new location making new products than they were to accept the conversion of old facilities for the production of an old product in a more automated manner where workers were displaced (Diebold, 1952).

The developing industrial society observed by Babbage, Ure, and people in the United States 100 years later depended on capital as the critical resource. The most competitive automobile plants were those that were backed by the capital necessary to remain at the edge of industrial technology, and not many people had such storehouses of funds. Today, however, information has displaced capital as the scarce resource of modern times, as Naisbitt (1984) illustrates. This is no less true in manufacturing than it is in space exploration. Capital is necessary, but information is essential. This makes the case for robots even stronger.

Computers process information rapidly. When the information processing capabilities of computers were directed toward the control of artificial limbs in precise and predictable ways, the industrial robot became a reality. With the birth of the industrial robot people began to look forward to the day when machines, especially robots, would perform all routine, boring, and repetitive work (Maccoby, 1981).

Serious interest in the use of industrial robots started in this country in the late 1960s, but most of the applications have taken place in the past decade. Industrial robots are predictable extensions of the automated machine, which were made possible by specialization. The difference between a robot and an automated machine is that the robot is capable of relatively free motions, much like the human arm or hand. The robot is automatic, but capable of much more flexibility. That is why it is sometimes called a programmed manipulator or programmed automater. Almost all robots used today are employed in manufacturing operations such as appliance assembly and automobile production. In the early 1980s, the majority of industrial robots performed material handling or spot and arc welding. Painting and finishing operations also made extensive use of robots (Wheelwright and Hayes, 1985). Robots have been successful in relieving human beings from dangerous and boring work.

The growing popularity of industrial robots is primarily a matter of economics. In 1964, Robot Systems, Inc., estimated that the average hourly factory wage was $2.53 while the average hourly cost of operating an industrial robot was about $5.00. By 1984, the situation had reversed. The average hourly wage for factory workers had climbed to over $8.00 while the average operating cost per hour of a robot was only $6.50. It is not hard to see why American companies have become increasingly aware of the need for and promise of robotics.

Information and estimates like this help us understand why General Motors paid billions of dollars for H. Ross Perot's Electronic Data Systems Corporation. The move into electronic data processing along with purchases of interests in artificial intelligence companies, a joint venture with Fanue, Ltd., one of Japan's leading robot manufacturers, and the subsequent formation of GMFanue Robotics Corporation makes GM's strategy understandable. General Motors, Nissan, Caterpillar Tractor, John Deere, Apple Computer, and ASEA of Sweden are betting on a technology-driven future in their respective industries and plan to be ready when the changes occur. Perhaps they can even direct some of the changes.

It is, of course, computer technology that has made all this possible. The economics of replacing today's high-cost skilled worker earning $20 or more per hour makes robots an appealing alternative to human labor. As one observer noted, American industry has few choices, it must "automate, emigrate, or evaporate" (Halberstam, 1983, p. 19). With advancing computer technology, robots are becoming more practical. It has been said that if "the price of cars had come down like the price of computers over the past fifteen years, the price of a new Cadillac today would be $19.95" (Halberstam, 1983). Advances of this nature could make robots and the computers that drive them even more appealing in the future.

Specialization and the Future

It is a long way from the "servomanipulators" of Hitachi to the analytical engine and steam operated factories of Babbage and Ure, but the connection is clear. What started out as a means of improving efficiency through the development of expertise in performing a task has all but eliminated the skilled craftsperson. In a very real sense, much of the meaning was taken away from work. The factory made the apprentice a tender of machines; the moving assembly line made the journeyman a machine operator; and the automated factory of today places the robot at center stage while the human designs, repairs, and maintains this loyal servant, which requires little more than an occasional tune-up. There is no doubt that advances in specialization and automation, the most basic of all lessons of the factory system, have freed human beings to do more creative work. The discovery of interchangeable parts made possible not only large quantities of muskets but Model T Fords as well.

Mass production responded well to the demands of mass consumption (Whitsett and York, 1983). Unanticipated problems were created by the division of labor and machines, which complicated the problem of motivation. As specialization and automation have increased, small parts of total products and services are produced at ever-increasing rates. The manager's job is to coordinate the diverse specialists and ensure that something of value results. This is no small responsibility, and the management challenge is clear.

Summary and Conclusions

It is a long way from the steamy textile factories of New England and the noisy production lines of Detroit to the robotic assembly operations in Spring Hill, Tennessee. Who could have imagined such a thing? To some these changes are frightening and signal the beginning of an unwanted world where people mutate into weaklings who do no physical work or where mindless people spend too much time in leisure pursuits. A more likely, but equally scary scenario to others is a future characterized by a class system based on technological know-how. Those who understand and master technology accumulate wealth while people without education and training are able to acquire even less than is possible today. Doomsday predictions notwithstanding, technology will be an important part of the future of all economically developed nations.

Will robots eliminate meaningful work? Not likely. It has been suggested that robots would have to possess four important characteristics if they are to displace human beings and evade our control. They would have to be able to: (1) create new ideas; (2) possess complete self-monitoring capabilities; (3) reconcile conflicting data; and (4) have the ability to change their own structure (Donleavy, 1994). Will they ever possess these capabilities? Most cautious people would "never say never." Few could have imagined the changes that have taken place over the past century. Again, the most appropriate response is probably, "not likely but stay tuned."

Regardless of the direction of change, managers should appreciate the way in which things have evolved and where all this might take us. A few of the more important things to remember about this discussion are:

1. Specialization or the division of labor is an important economic principle that has made much of our prosperity today possible and sustainable.
2. Division of labor played an important role in the emergence of modern management. In fact, it made it necessary because of the need to coordinate the work of diverse specialists toward the accomplishment of organizational objectives.
3. The progressive specialization of labor also made automation and computerization of work possible because more specialized tasks, in many cases, were more programmable.
4. Specialization of work, however, is not without its problems. To this point, we have focused on the brighter side of specialization. Later in the book we will examine its darker side.
5. The future world of work will be technologically centric. Managers in this world of the future will have to be comfortable with technology and those who make their living using it.

Questions for Discussion

1 In the development of management theory, the domination of real managers prior to the 1930s and the equally evident domination of academic researchers after the 1930s remain a mystery to many. How would you explain this phenomenon?

2 Were specialization of labor and mass markets really the primary drivers in the emergence of modern management thought? What other reasons could explain why and when modern management emerged as an occupation and field of study?

3 Why did it take so long for the Industrial Revolution to reach America?

4 Is the division of mental labor really equivalent to the division of physical labor? Can mental labor be specialized in the same way as physical activities, and can the continuity of thinking be maintained?

5 Why has Japan been the world leader in the use of robots? What types of implications does this hold for her own economic future and that of the remainder of the industrialized world?

Management and Managers

"It is this ability to act with a knowledgeable sense of risk and reward that separates both the business executive and the wise individual from a bureaucrat or a gambler."

Peter Schwartz
The Art of the Long View (1991)

What is happening to organizations and the people who manage them? For one thing, organizations are becoming smaller and managers are becoming fewer. More than a few executives have boasted about their companies' becoming "leaner and meaner" and the elimination of "entire levels" of middle managers.

There are, of course, corporate giants like General Electric and IBM, massive government agencies, colossal universities, and even churches and synagogues with thousands of members. It is also true that managerial and professional employees account for one-third of the civilian workforce in the United States. But is this simply an artifact of times gone by? Who will deny that the composition and the character of organizations are changing radically? We trust our financial resources to *virtual* banks, our health to *virtual* hospitals, our appearance to *virtual* retailers, and our information processing needs to *virtual* computer companies without ever seeing and frequently without even talking to a real person. One can easily imagine a world where our ability to work our way through a labyrinth of electronic menu selections will be more important to survival than interpersonal communication. The obvious question, then, is: "If organizations are changing radically, what is the role of management and managers in this new organizational world?"

Why Management Matters

Organizations functioned for thousands of years without managers—at least, without people called managers. However, functioning without managers is one thing while functioning without management is quite another. Ever since human beings began hunting and working together, someone performed the management function.

▲ **Box 2-1**

MANAGING VIRTUAL REALITIES

Managers are action-oriented people. However, we are increasingly faced with virtual realities. Managers in many organizations are coping quite well with these new challenges. One of the more interesting ways of coping is through *virtual alliances* or fluid partnerships, where organizations share their best practices and core competencies in order to take advantage of unique opportunities. Take, for example, Nintendo of America, Inc., and Silicon Graphics, who formed a *virtual alliance* with the goal of creating a 64-bit video game system called Nintendo 64. Silicon Graphics viewed the collaboration as a way to gain knowledge of the video game market and an understanding of cost leadership strategies. Prior to the alliance, Silicon Graphics competed strictly on the basis of technological superiority without significant regard to price.

Nintendo 64s have been very successful. Some project that sales will exceed six million units within 4 years. These same observers thought that Sega and Sony would be lucky to sell a combined total of six million units with their top-of-the-line systems during the same period. Both companies have slashed prices of comparable systems in order to compete with the new Nintendo 64.

Source: "Nintendo Wakes Up" (August 3, 1996); Noaker (1994); Myers (1995).

Managers and Management Ideas

Everything has a beginning and, so far as we know, everything has an end. In 1986, the Academy of Management observed the Centennial of Management and thereby declared the beginning of management as the 1886 meeting of the American Society of Mechanical Engineers. Of course, no one seriously suggests that management is only a little more than 100 years old. In a telecast shown around the nation, Peter Drucker stated that he thought the best managers in history were those responsible for building the pyramids of Egypt. They had limited transportation and scientific resources, yet they built one of the great wonders of the world. Unfortunately, they told us little about their techniques and shared almost none of their know-how. Therein lies the difference between knowing how to do management and contributing to the development of a field of knowledge that others can learn and practice.

The emergence of this "systematic field" of management is what is traced to the 1886 meeting of the American Society of Mechanical Engineers. At this meeting Henry Towne, cofounder and president of the Yale and Towne Manufacturing Company, read a paper titled "The Engineer as Economist (1886)." In it he called for the recognition of the "management of works" as a practical art similar to engineering.

Essential to this recognition was the development of literature and the formulation of normative principles.

Towne's paper was not profound. Presentations at academic societies rarely are. Its effects, however, were revolutionary. His plea that engineers should be concerned with more than technical efficiency even to the point of considering costs, revenues, and profits was new. No major change took place in the society or its charter, but the presentation was attended by Frederick W. Taylor—the "father of scientific management," and his ideas *did* alter the nature of industry, not only in the United States but around the world. However, before we go too far, we should examine an important object of study in management—the manager.

There may be a very few people living today who were alive when Towne presented his landmark paper that, at least according to the Academy, ushered in the era of systematic management. However, none of us alive today will likely witness the end of management as a social institution. In fact, management has never been more popular. Managers like Jack Welch at General Electric and Bill Gates at Microsoft are folk heroes, and books written by managers actually make the best seller list (Gates, 1996). People are interested in management because they recognize that decisions made by managers affect their lives and the lives of people around them.

What Is Management?

There are almost as many definitions of management as there are people who write on the subject. Therefore, a general definition is preferred. We can add the specifics of each application and discussion as we proceed. Management is the coordination of human and nonhuman resources toward the accomplishment of organizational goals in a way that is acceptable to the larger society. The essential elements in the definition are:

1. *Coordination:* Management is about coordination. Without managers organizations would be little more than so many individuals working by and for themselves. When machines and human beings began moving to progressively greater levels of specialization, management was necessary to coordinate diverse tasks and operations.
2. *Organizational goals:* The focus of management is on organizational goals. Goals, however, are not always given, so the development of mutually agreed-upon goals is also a role of mangers (Drucker, 1989).
3. *Society:* Management takes place in a larger cultural matrix, and, like all social institutions, it must be accomplished in a manner that is acceptable to the culture and society in which it occurs (Duncan, 1986; Wren, 1994).

Management ideas are not new. When managers practice their trade, it is expected that some will inevitably try to share what they have learned with others. As they share their experiences and ideas, articles are written and books are published that serve as useful information for present and future managers.

Origins of Management Ideas

Books by managers are not new, only our interest is novel. Thoughtful and instructive books have been written by managers like Chester Barnard, President of the New Jersey Bell Telephone Company; Henry Dennison, President of the Dennison Manufacturing Company; and Henri Fayol, President of the Commentary-Fourchambault Company. None of these books ever made the best seller list and, for the most part, they have been seriously read and studied by only a few management historians. This is unfortunate because the advice and the insights of these writers are practical, to the point, and useful to managers who regularly make decisions in large corporations and small businesses. Their wisdom deserves wider circulation than it can be given by professors in management classes. The benefits of their experiences need to be applied at the "cutting edge" of organizational life.

One of the best kept secrets of management according to Drucker (1986) is that the first systematic application of management theory principles did not occur in business enterprises but in the public sector. He goes further to note that the first time a senior executive was actually referred to as a *manager* was also in the public sector—the *city manager* of Staunton, Virginia, in 1908. Perhaps this bit of trivia is important only to academic historians, but one should not deny the importance of the

---

▲ **Box 2-2**

MANAGEMENT—"THE PRIMARY ORGAN OF MODERNIZATION"

It has been said that the 20th century is the American century. If this is true, and it very likely is, then management has played a major role in making it so. Yet, management as a discipline and managers as a group are rarely heard from except in discussions of excessive pay and ethical transgressions.

Like it or not, managers run America! The organizations they manage and the decisions they make affect everyday American life more deeply and directly than media celebrities, professional athletes, or even politicians. Along with this power a managerial class has developed in America and around the world that has unprecedented power. This class needed legitimacy, and the idea that evolved to legitimize them was that of the guardian. Managers became the guardians and thought of themselves in terms of competence, moral integrity, and stewardship.

Management has passed through many stages and has been thought of in many ways, but no one can deny the importance of managers in everyday organizational life. In fact, to understand fully the world in which we live, we must understand the managerial state.

Source: Scott (1992).

history to any practitioners of a profession. This understanding of the history of their trade does not ensure better practitioners, but it does provide a useful and common bond.

Becoming a Manager

Becoming a manager is the goal of many, and becoming a better manager is the goal of many more. Helping in this pursuit are managers who share their experiences, professors who study organizations and people in them, and consultants who make their living marketing their expertise. The fact that management knowledge is for sale is not surprising. It is a valuable commodity. What is surprising is how this knowledge has evolved.

Who can imagine a discussion of anatomy without observation of a real body? At least, the "scientist" would be expected to examine an occasional cadaver. Ironically, the earliest theories of management were developed with few, if any, observations of real managers, except for the personal, limited experiences of the manager proposing the theory. In fact, formal theories of managerial behavior were quite advanced before observations of managers became a focus of research. Well into the decade of the 1960s, what we knew about administrative behavior and what managers actually did was based more on commonsense impressions and mythology than on observations and facts (Sheriff, 1969).

The fact that academic researchers paid little attention to how real managers behave is as alarming as it is confusing. Management is an applied art, and its emphasis has been on developing guidelines and recommendations to aid in accomplishing operational efficiency. The goal of most management research and theory has never been to understand administrative behavior. As a result, most of the early attention was directed toward the results hoped for not the activities performed.

Andrew Grove, CEO of Intel, illustrates the point. According to him, one problem in understanding managerial behavior is the distinction that must be drawn between the activities and the outcomes of management. Activities are what managers do while outcomes are what managers achieve. To many, perhaps most, the latter seems significant while the former appears trivial. Of course, the same is true of surgery. When we see outcomes such as cured patients and lives changed for the better through successful surgery, the importance of the healing art is obvious. The significance of "less important" activities such as scrubbing and suturing is more difficult to appreciate (Grove, 1985).

In the same sense, the existence of a strategic plan for a company or a new and innovative organization structure appears significant when compared to answering telephones, business lunches, and frequent staff meetings that constitute much, perhaps most, of a manager's day. Yet, the activities are not unimportant because, as Stewart (1984) notes, "we need to understand what it is that managers do before we can decide what managers should know and how they can best acquire this knowledge" (p. 323).

Management: A Functional View

We often attempt to understand a particular thing by examining the functions it performs. Business firms attract customers, provide them with products or services, and maintain relationships in an effort to encourage repeat business. Understanding the functions provides an incomplete understanding of business firms, but it is an important first step. Henri Fayol (1949) developed the first comprehensive picture of managers by the functions they perform—planning, organizing, coordinating, and controlling. This has become known as the functional or process view of management.

Industry or business, in Fayol's way of thinking, consisted of six types of activities. These were: *technical* activities, including manufacturing and production; *commercial* activities such as buying, selling, and exchanging; and *financial* activities, including the search for the best sources of capital. Good technical, commercial, and financial operations built the resources that required protection and safeguarding. This made three additional types of activities necessary: *security* activities to guard against fire, theft, floods, and social disorder; *accounting* activities involving data gathering and the presentation of financial statements and statistics; and *managerial* activities, which involved forecasting, organizing, commanding, coordinating, and controlling.

▲ **Box 2-3**

HENRI FAYOL (1841–1925)

Fayol was a mining engineer who spent his career at the Commentry-Fourchambault mining company. Fayol worked his way to higher positions in the firm and became instrumental in saving the company from financial ruin in the late 1880s. His experiences as an executive began to define his views of the nature of and the need for good management. He isolated what he observed were the activities performed by managers, the importance of management abilities relative to technical expertise, and some fundamental principles of management. Fayol was the first to focus on the manager's importance in achieving organizational success.

Fayol's ideas were translated into English but did not make a significant impact on American managers for more than 30 years. Even in France his views were not completely appreciated. Controversy developed between the advocates of Fayol's executive perspective on management and Taylor's scientific management which focused primarily on work and the worker. No doubt these different perspectives could be accounted for by the diverse careers of these two men. However, in the end, many came to see the ideas of these two pioneers of management as more complementary.

Sources: Breeze (1982, 1985); Breeze and Bedeian (1988); Wren (1994).

More specifically, Fayol stated that "to manage is to forecast and plan, to organize, to command, to coordinate, and to control" (p. 6).

Although Fayol was concerned with the development of guidelines for improving management practice and assisting in the understanding of management as a process, his more fundamental concern was for the development of a theory of management. He was particularly disappointed by the fact that there were no schools where people could go to learn management. Such schools did not exist, according to him, because there was no general theory that could be taught within their walls. Without a theory no teaching of management was possible. His presentation of principles and concepts was part of his strategy to build a theory of management that would make possible the training and development of present and aspiring managers.

This training, in his view, was the responsibility of schools, businesses, the family, and the state. If the family emphasized the principles and procedures of home life, management concepts would "penetrate naturally" the child's mind and form the foundation for later learning in school. Even though postsecondary education should be general in the sense of providing exposure to the liberal arts and sciences, it should also offer courses on management. Organizations should offer workshops and encourage all types of management study by employees, and the state should offer a good example by adding management to the curriculum in state schools. Clearly, Drucker (1986) was not the first to argue the virtues of management as a liberal art.

In the first part of *General and Industrial Management* (1949), Fayol sought to establish the case for the necessity of teaching management. In the last part he tried to indicate what the teaching should include (p. 110). Management historians regret that Fayol's book represents only half of what was to be an integrated four-part work but was not completed before his death. As it stands, however, it is an unequaled argument for the importance of management education and training (Carter, 1986).

Managers as Reflective Calculators

The view of managerial action presented by Fayol is consistent with classical economic theories and scientific approaches to decision making. If we are to approach any problem scientifically, including the management of organizations, we should first define it, develop an action plan, itemize, analyze, select the best approach, and follow up to ensure the goal is properly accomplished. Fayol believed management should be approached in the same way and carefully outlined the steps involved in a systematic technique of administration and management. These steps were logical and straightforward. Under the heading of administrative operations he included the following activities.

To plan is to study the future and arrange a way of dealing with it. Actually, Fayol proposed a unique concept by stating that planning should be considered only one part of a broader function called "prévoyance." Prévoyance consisted of forecasting or foreseeing the future, but it was more. It included preparing systematically for the future discovered in the process of forecasting. In the scheme presented by Fayol the result of planning is more than a formal plan. The result of the process of prevoyance includes ways of accomplishing the plan. In contemporary terms we think of the outcome as a series of goal statements as well as the strategies for goal accomplishment. Prévoyance is an action-oriented approach to planning.

To organize involves the development of a design for the business that will effectively relate human and nonhuman resources. Organizing means developing a structure to assist in goal accomplishment. *To coordinate* is to unite all activities taking place in the organization. Coordination and organization allow the manager to "orchestrate" the resources of an organization toward goal accomplishment. *To command* is the function that ensures that the organization is operating as it was intended to operate. In the most general sense, command includes attempts to motivate employee action toward organizational goals and leadership. Finally, *to control* involves ensuring that everything is carried out in accordance with the plan "that has been adopted, the orders that have been given, and the principles that have been laid down" (Urwick, 1947, p. 119). When all these functions are properly conducted, the manager achieves a unity within the organization that allows for efficient and effective operations (Wren, 1990).

Building Unity through Management

Fayol's review of each of the functions in the final chapter of *General and Industrial Management* (1949) leaves no doubt as to how he viewed the unity of the management process. Managers were logical, well informed people who had a goal, a plan, and a will to ensure that results were achieved. This was possible when the manager approached problems in the following manner.

First, successful organizations must have foresight, and it is the responsibility of management to provide the futuristic view through planning. Plans should be unified vertically with those at the bottom levels of the organization, flowing logically from plans at the top. In other words, the goals of the departments should directly reinforce overall organizational objectives, and work group goals should reinforce those of the departments.

Horizontal unity is also essential if groups are to be properly coordinated. There should be a close relationship among all the goals of production units and marketing departments. At the same time, financial plans and objectives in purchasing and credit departments should facilitate rather than hinder the accomplishment of goals in line departments like production and sales. This underlines the importance of interdepartmental communication and coordination. Plans should be precise enough to provide direction but flexible enough to allow for changing conditions. The best plans in Fayol's thinking evolved from experience and stressed unity.

Organizing a business ideally results in providing it "with everything useful to its functioning; raw materials, tools, capital, and personnel" (p. 53). Fayol directed a great deal of his attention toward the human organization, used the military analogy of the chain of command, and quoted Taylor when arguing that many people possessed the potential for success in management and should be given the opportunity to manage through decentralization of the organization structure. On the matter of organization, however, Fayol stopped short of endorsing Taylor's functional foremanship because of his fear that the "Taylor system," as he called it, negated the unity of command principle (pp. 66–70). As a manager and a theorist, Fayol appeared unable to recommend an organizational system where employees reported simultaneously to more than a single boss.

The calculating manager, having planned and organized effectively, must now "get things moving." At this point command enters the picture. The manager's command goal is to get the most return possible from all the workers under her supervision. This was to be done under the watchful eye of the supervisor, but Fayol cautioned that initiative would develop and be maintained only if employees had the freedom to make mistakes.

Harmonization of all aspects of the organization is achieved through coordination. Well coordinated businesses build units that operate in harmony, and weekly meetings of department heads may be useful in building this relationship. Finally, control verifies that everything conforms to the plan. Control of commercial activities requires checks on quantities, qualities, and prices. Control of technical operations involves operational progress, and financial controls are directed toward cash and other assets through financial records and reports.

Advocates of the work of Fayol extended the logic of his view of management behavior and gave us two concepts that are supported by many and rejected by others. These concepts are: (1) the universality of management functions; and (2) the transferability of management skills. Since Fayol argued that all the functions he itemized applied to the governing of organizations in all industries, support grew for the idea of the universality of management functions. All managers, including the president of General Motors, generals in the army, chancellors of universities, and even the Pope, planned, organized, coordinated, commanded, and controlled. Thus, the functions of management were universal.

Second, as the person moved higher in the organization to more purely managerial jobs, less technical functions were performed so that the job became predominantly managerial. In view of these arguments, it was suggested that the person doing strictly managerial functions should be able to transfer these talents to other industries and even different careers. The business executive might transfer managerial expertise and become a successful hospital administrator or dean of a business school. The general in the army, because the job is essentially managerial, should find success in civilian jobs at similar organization levels. Dwight Eisenhower's service as General of the Army, President of Columbia University, and President of the United States provided some support for the argument as well as Robert McNamara's success as a management scientist during World War II, a Ford Motor Company "whiz kid," President of Ford, Secretary of Defense, and President of the World Bank.

Of course, not everyone agrees with either of these logical extensions. Many people continue to insist that health care management and public administration are fundamentally different from the management of business firms. Yet, when we look for evidence of successful people who have found success in more than a single industry or company, the examples are not hard to find. In recent times, General Norman H. Schwarzkopf, Jr., "the hero of the Gulf War," became a much sought-after speaker to business groups, advisor, and candidate for corporate board membership because of his managerial expertise in effectively waging war.

The image of managerial work created by Fayol was that of a demanding job and one that required unusually qualified people to measure up to the task. The reflective

▲ **Box 2-4**

APPLYING PRINCIPLES THAT WORK

Robert S. McNamara is used by many as a primary example of the transferability of management skills. McNamara himself notes that one of the first things he did when he was appointed Secretary of Defense was to significantly change the posture statements used as reports to Congress. The change was designed to improve decision making in the Department of Defense through the application of tested and tried management principles. He stated that even though many in the State Department objected to the new way of doing things, it was all part of "an approach to organizing human activities" that he developed on the faculty at Harvard and used during the war and in his leadership at Ford Motor Company.

The approach was based on the following principles: (1) clearly defining objectives for whatever organization he was leading; (2) developing a plan to achieve the objectives; and (3) monitoring progress against the plan. If actual accomplishments did not measure up to the plan, corrective action was taken. The management principles that he conceived as an academic and used successfully in government service and private industry were used again in his leadership of one of the most complex of all areas of government.

Source: McNamara (1995, p. 24).

calculating manager was a person who possesses "all the requisite knowledge for settling managerial, technical, commercial, and financial questions before him and also has sufficient physical and mental vigor and capacity for work to be able to melt all of the weight of business contracts" (p. 71). Is it really possible in our increasingly complex organizational world to be a reflective calculating manager? For that matter, was it ever possible? Should we think of Fayol's image of management as fact or folklore? In the words of Herbert Simon, do managers really have the "wits" to be reflective calculators?

A Changing Stereotype of Management Behavior

Is the reflective calculating manager folklore or fact (Mintzberg, 1975)? Levitt (1991) argued that the work of managers is much less structured than visualized by Fayol. Indeed, according to him, managers do many different things, but there are three things they must do well. They must: (1) think about the purpose of the organization and the direction in which it should be going; (2) foster and manage change; and (3) conduct operations in an effective and efficient manner. These activities are important. But how do managers accomplish these demanding tasks?

Although late in coming, attempts have been made to study managers and thereby gain insights into what managers actually do and how the managerial tasks are actually achieved. One of the most comprehensive summaries of these findings is that of Hales (1986). In this review, several of the issues that seem to be avoided by other writers are confronted "head on." For example, managerial behavior and managerial work are not considered synonymous so that mere observations of managers, it is argued, are not a sufficient basis for dealing with the complex question of what managers do. Also, the effectiveness question is addressed.

That is, to what extent does what managers do match what managers ought to do in order to maximize organizational performance? Hales' study was particularly comprehensive because an attempt was made not just to look at the activities managers perform but to "shed light on five major areas . . . about managerial work" (p. 90). These areas are:

1. The *elements* of managerial work (what managers do)
2. The *distribution* of a manager's time between work elements (how managers work)
3. The *interactions* of managers (with whom managers work)
4. The *informal* elements of managerial work (what else managers do)
5. The *themes* that pervade managerial work (the qualities or characteristics of managerial work)

After reviewing many studies on the subject, the following "body of facts" was said to exist. First, management work combines managerial elements with specialty and professional elements. Managers almost always perform some nonmanagerial functions in the course of doing their jobs. Second, the substantive elements of management work entail providing liaisons, managing human behavior, and assuming responsibility for getting work done. Next, the nature of a manager's work varies by duration, time span, and unexpectedness. It is difficult, perhaps impossible, to predict the variety of a manager's work during a given period. Managers spend a great deal of time with every-day troubleshooting and solving *ad hoc* problems.

The communication patterns managers employ vary according to what the communication is about and with whom it is taking place. Managers do a lot of persuading and engaging in brief face-to-face communication encounters. As a result, there is little time to spend on any particular activity or in the formulation of systematic plans. A great deal of the manager's time is spent accounting for and explaining what they want, and engaging in informal "politicking" and in conflict resolution. It was also noted that managers are able to exercise considerable choice in terms of what they do and how they do it. These generalizations summarize much of the research on managerial behavior and work. However, other writers have suggested different ways of looking at what managers do (Mintzberg, 1973).

Roles Managers Perform

Although Mintzberg used an extremely small sample, his view of the manager's job has been quoted often in the management literature. Mintzberg viewed the manager's job as a series of roles assumed throughout the process of achieving organizational goals (Mintzberg, 1993). In presenting his argument, three major categories of roles were identified. Each had a series of subcategories. The three main categories included interpersonal, informational, and decisional roles.

The *interpersonal roles*, as the name implies, involved the manager in developing relationships with other people and groups. This category of roles directly influences the status and the authority of the manager. Frequently managers are called on to perform as *figureheads* and to render ceremonial and symbolic acts. On a 5-day trip to India and South Africa, for example, Microsoft's Bill Gates spent much of his 16-hour days holding press interviews, submitting to photo sessions, and making speeches (Schlender, 1997).

Managers, in their interpersonal relations, are also expected to function as *leaders* and to motivate others as well as providing for effective staffing and training activities. Lee Iacocca's success as a leader during his crafting of Chrysler's recovery is illustrated by the fact that security guards were needed to protect him from dealers when he appeared at their meetings, and from the chants of Lee! Lee! Lee! by rank-and-file union members when he came to Chrysler's Sterling Heights, Michigan, assembly plant to roll out a new line of sports sedans. The manager frequently needs to fill a *liaison* role in forming communication links with individuals and groups outside the organization who are likely to provide favors. During Gates' trip to India and South Africa time was also devoted to customer meetings, audiences with government officials, and appearances before other potentially influential groups.

The *informational* roles of managers involve receiving and transmitting information. Sometimes the manager is seen as the *monitor* or nerve center of information flow in the organization. In this role the manager is a dispatcher, routing information to different internal and external groups. Sometimes the role is more that of the *disseminator* of information. Once the manager receives the information, it must be selectively shared with people in the organization, and choices must be made about who will benefit from the sharing of information most directly. In *High Output Management* (1985) Grove provides a diary of "a day in his life" as the chief executive of Intel. One 2-hour block of time in Grove's day was spent lecturing to the employee orientation program. This program was designed to afford senior managers an opportunity to provide new professional employees with information on company objectives, history, and expectations. Information is disseminated in this way to a select group of employees.

A final information role is that of *spokesperson*. Managers are regularly asked to represent the organization to various outside groups. Sometimes this role is nothing more than the standard "canned" speech to a local civic club. At other times it may be an extremely stressful interview before live television cameras at the scene of a serious industrial accident. One of the more interesting developments relative to this role is the manner in which chief executives such as Victor Kiam of Remington Products and Frank Borman, before the demise of Eastern Airlines, successfully took to the air waves as spokespersons for their own products and services in the 1980s (Poindexter, 1983). However, consumer tastes change and even though Dave Thomas of Wendy's and Ben and Jerry can still attract an audience, the appearance of the CEO on television pushing a product is no longer a recommended promotional strategy. In recent years, funny commercials or those featuring children, pets, and product demonstrations have been more successful than hidden-camera testimonials, company CEOs, celebrities, and brand comparisons (Robinson, 1997).

Mintzberg's final category is that of *decisional* roles. These roles are diverse and far ranging. They can include everything from scheduling one's own time to negotiating with the labor union. When the manager acts as an *entrepreneur*, she searches the environment for new and challenging opportunities. The entrepreneurial role involves taking the risks necessary to succeed in a competitive industry. The role of *disturbance handler* is assumed as the manager attempts to correct or fine-tune the organization's progress toward goals when things knock the operations off course. Frequently managers are expected to function as *resource allocators* and make decisions concerning whether or not to commit organizational resources to alternative uses. In one case, Grove (1985) made a decision not to grant a manager a pay increase that would have placed him outside the normal salary range for such a job. This was a resource-allocating decision. Finally, managers assume the role of *negotiator* when they bargain with employees, their bosses, or outside groups such as the labor union.

Myths about Management Work

Mintzberg (1975) states that there are four "myths" about managerial work that do not hold under careful examination. The first is the view of the manager as a reflective calculator, as pictured by Fayol. Instead, the five CEOs in Mintzberg's sample seldom spent more than 9 minutes on any task, and only 10 percent of the activities of these high-level executives required more than 1 hour to complete. Studies of foremen show that they engage in as many as 583 activities in an 8-hour shift. That is an average of one activity every 48 seconds (Guest, 1956). Rather than being the careful planner as seen in Fayol's view, the real-life manager is seen "jumping" from issue to issue, continually responding to the demands of the moment with little apparent concern for the future.

The next myth is the image of the manager who has properly planned and delegated and can concentrate on exceptions while efficiently spending most of his or her time doing the important things required by the organization. In addition to handling exceptions, most managers feel an obligation to engage in ritualistic and ceremonial duties and information processing activities. Even in high-level government positions it has been shown, for example, when Cyrus Vance was Secretary of State that he arrived at work before 7:00 a.m. and over 40 meetings and telephone calls later, he arrived back at home after 7:00 p.m. While much of this work was important, some work required of high-level officials is insignificant and foolish. At the top of an organization and in high level political positions power and influence have as much to do with symbols and appearances as with substance and reality (Adams, 1979). Managers, like politicians and public servants, feel an obligation to do those things required of their position, even if at times they could easily be done by others.

The third myth is that managers need and use information that is systematic and well documented. In reality managers prefer verbal media or information that is obtained fast, usually by telephone calls and meetings. Mintzberg noted that most man-

▲ **Box 2-5**

LEARNING ORGANIZATIONS

Organizational researchers and managers refer to two types of organizations with a particular type of excitement. The first is the organization that can "organically adapt" to changing situations without the need for massive and radical reorganizations. The ideal is an organization that adapts to change very much like living systems adapt and thereby reduce resistance. The other organizational form that fascinates today's managers and researchers is the organization that can learn—learn from others and learn from itself.

Peter Senge identifies 5 disciplines that are important to the learning organization:

1. *Personal mastery:* The discipline of personal growth where individuals are continually pushing to create the kind of organization they want. Personal mastery is the spirit of learning.

2. *Mental models:* The way people view the world, the people, and the relationships in it. These are the assumptions by which we make reality meaningful. The discipline to change our mental models is essential for learning.

3. *Shared vision:* If there is to be a learning organization, there must be a pull toward a deeply shared goal. This is the energy of the learning organization.

4. *Team learning:* The alignment of the learning organization whereby individuals function as a single unit. Team learning allows group performance to improve through reliance on individual excellence.

5. *Systems thinking:* The fifth and most important discipline of the learning organization. Systems thinking includes, but is not limited to, the ability to see the whole as distinct from the individual parts, synergies, and complex interactions.

Learning organizations are fundamentally different from ordinary hierarchies, and their management requires fundamentally different types of thinking.

Source: Senge (1990).

agers consider mail a burden. One of the CEOs he observed came in on Saturday and processed over 140 pieces of mail in 3 hours. His managers responded to only 2 of the 40 routine reports they received during the period of the study and in 25 days of observation, the managers initiated (excluding responses to other correspondence) only 25 pieces of mail.

The final myth may be one of the most damaging and disappointing if we believe what Mintzberg tells us about managerial behavior and work. This myth is that management is rapidly becoming a science and a profession. Yet all the evidence points to the fact that most of what managers do remains locked "deep inside their brains." Intuition and judgment have more to do with management than objective data, hard facts, and precise science. Although today's managers are competent by any standard, Mintzberg voiced surprise in the fact that most of the way managers act is "fundamentally indistinguishable" from the way their counterparts acted a 100 or 1,000 years ago. In his words: "The information they need differs, but they seek it in the same way—by word of mouth. Their decisions concern modern technology, but the procedures they use to make them are the same as the procedures of the 19th-century manager." Even the computer "has apparently had no influence on the work procedures of general managers" (Mintzberg, 1975, p. 54). Controversies seldom answer questions such as "who is right, Fayol or Mintzberg?" Instead they cause additional questions to be asked, more research to be conducted, and eventually at least we understand more about the phenomenon under consideration. This is certainly true with regard to managerial work and behavior.

Additional Attempts to Understand Managers

Once the interest in managers developed, it accelerated and numerous writers investigated different questions about managers and what managers do. Two of the most important areas of study include management at different organizational levels and managerial effectiveness. Each of these areas will be examined in the concluding section of this chapter.

Management at Different Organizational Levels

Fayol and Mintzberg had one thing in common—they both restricted their discussion of managerial behavior to the highest level of executive leadership. Fayol was a CEO and Mintzberg structured his sample to include only CEOs. Interestingly, this focus on the top level of management has continued, and today there is a body of literature on the subject. In fact, the literature is so expansive that in the following discussion we have devoted special attention to what we know about CEOs. First, however, it is important to deal with the other levels of management.

The most popular description of what managers do at different organizational levels was provided by Katz (1955). Katz based his model on the skills managers need for success. Skills are abilities that can be developed and are actually manifested in performance. Katz argues that there are three types of skills that are important to managers. First, there are *technical skills*, which involve knowledge of a specialized or professional nature. Technical skills in areas like engineering and accounting require analytical abilities and some, as in the field of medicine, require the use of the techniques of the specialty. *Human skills* are those that enable a person to work as a member of a group and to build cooperative effort that can be directed toward efficiently accomplishing common goals. *Conceptual skills* involve the ability to "see the big picture." This type of skill enables a person to see the interdependencies that exist among different parts of an organization and how changes in one part will influence changes in other parts.

Skills of this nature are needed to appreciate the relationships that exist between business and its constituents in different economic, political, and social environments. All three types of skills are important to managers. However, the relative importance of these skills changes with the level of the organization.

Consider the foreman in a manufacturing plant, the sales supervisor, or any other type of first-line supervisor. In this capacity the supervisor continues to perform many technical skills required by his or her former nonmanagerial jobs. The foreman spends time in actual production operations and the sales supervisor makes a number of sales

---

▲ Box 2-6
MANAGERIAL MUSCLE BUILDING

How does an organization make itself stronger managerially when the opportunities for managerial promotions are limited? Greyhound Financial Corporation (GFC) developed something known as "muscle building." The program was designed to provide fast-track executives with opportunities for new experiences and new challenges without the necessity of waiting for traditional job openings. Basically, it involved job swapping. For example, an assistant vice president in treasury might swap with an assistant vice president in marketing. Each person thus gained experience in an area outside their expertise and created new managerial expertise in GFC. The program, however, was not without its risks. There is no "safety net." If jobs were swapped and a manager was not successful at the new task, there was no place to go but out because the old job had been filled.

GFC believes that the muscle building program has minimized problems of individual career plateauing, organizational creativity, and management succession. The adverse effects of plateauing are minimized because opportunities are created in areas where expertise did not exist. Creativity and innovation were stimulated because people placed in different and unfamiliar jobs often display increased creativity. Finally, the broader managerial skill base created by the lateral job swapping resulted in larger numbers of highly qualified applicants for new jobs.

Source: Northcraft, Griffith, and Shalley (1992).

throughout the day. Both are required to develop human skills and to use them in motivating their employees to perform well, communicating effectively what is expected, and providing the kind of leadership expected by the organization. Their technical skills require that they work with things while their human skills are concerned with people (Katz, 1955, p. 34). As supervisors they are now also expected to learn certain conceptual skills and see how their area of responsibility relates to and is dependent upon other areas in the organization. Not much of their time and energy, however, is consumed by such lofty concerns.

When foremen or sales supervisors are promoted into middle-level management, they do not exercise their technical skills as often as they did as first-line supervisors. Their human skills are no less important at this level because middle managers spend a great deal of time leading, motivating, and communicating. The organization now demands much more development of their conceptual skills. The success of middle managers demands that they be able to work successfully with heads of other functional units. There can be no excuse at this level not to have a focus on and a proper appreciation for a picture larger than that outlined by the manager's own department.

Finally, when the manager arrives at the top of the hierarchy, technical skills are seldom used. The general manager who is trained as an engineer will do little engineering and the accountant will rarely do accounting. These upper level executives will continue to require human skills, and they will be no less important than they were the day he or she first became a manager. At this level, the tremendous challenge, however, relates to the use of conceptual skills. The interdependency of all units is the factor that demands so much of the chief executive's time. It is this manager's job to ensure that the activities of production, sales, finance, and personnel are mutually reinforcing and working toward the same goal. Also, it is up to the top executive levels to ensure that the organizations interact favorably with the larger social, political, and economic systems. In addition to Katz, a number of researchers have attempted to deal with managerial work at different hierarchical levels. In doing so, a variety of methods have been used, and a number of interesting findings have been presented. We will review some of this research next.

Supervisors and Middle Managers

Radical adherents of the principle of the universality of management functions argue that "a manager is a manager is a manager" regardless of where she practices her skills or the level of the organization at which she functions. To them, only the mix of the functions varies. While this argument has satisfied some, most researchers have treated it with a degree of skepticism. Few accept it literally without need for verification.

In a large-scale survey of 1,412 managers, Kraut, Pedigo, McKenna, and Dunnette (1989) asked respondents to rate the relative importance of seven managerial tasks on their jobs. The seven tasks, which were extracted from a larger list of 57, were: (1) managing individual performance; (2) instructing subordinates; (3) planning and allocating resources; (4) coordinating interdependent groups; (5) managing group performance; (6) monitoring the business environment; and (7) representing one's staff. Different levels of management rated various managerial tasks as most important for the achievement of their jobs.

First-level supervisors indicated that managing individual performance and instructing subordinates were the tasks most important to their success. The relative importance of these two tasks decreased as the level of management increased. Middle-level managers indicated that their most important tasks involved "linking groups" of people. They rated planning and allocating resources, coordinating interdependent groups, and managing group performance higher than either first-level supervisors or top-level executives. The top-level executives rated monitoring the business environment higher than either of the other two groups. Interestingly, the only managerial task that did not vary significantly with any hierarchical group was the "ambassador function," or the importance of representing staff. This was ranked high by all groups included in the study.

Hill (1992) described the transition of 19 individuals (14 men and 5 women at Fortune 500 companies) from worker to manager and, in the process, provided some important insights into the trials and triumphs of this transition. The first assignment in management, she argues, is the most demanding and a pivotal point in a manager's career because it requires a transformation—a fundamental change in outlook and identity. One of the most revealing findings of the study was how new managers conceptualized and eventually learned to deal with the sometimes conflicting expectations of bosses, employees, and peers. At first, new supervisors focused on task-related activities such as making job assignments, developing schedules, and so on. Increasingly, however, they recognized that both their bosses and their employees were evaluating them on the basis of their people orientation. Over time, the new managers created their own ways of diagnosing and dealing with human problems and with the symbolic separation their new position caused relative to other members of the work group. The advice and example of former bosses and mentors was invaluable in creating their own, and sometimes unique, philosophy of management.

Middle-level managers, perhaps because their ranks have been reduced the most by downsizing or because of the unique nature of the place they occupy in organizations, have also been examined in some detail. As the number of middle managers has decreased (it has been estimated that 20 percent or more of the job losses over the past decade have taken place among middle managers) their strategic role has increased (Floyd and Wooldridge, 1994). In the past, the middle manager's job has been thought of primarily as involving operational or tactical activities such as developing budgets, monitoring group performance, and taking corrective actions when plans deviate from expectations. However, research has suggested that increased middle management involvement in strategy formulation is associated with higher financial performance (Wooldridge and Floyd, 1990).

Another analysis (Johnson and Frohman, 1989) examined the "gap" that developed when more negative views regarding organizational issues existed at one hierarchical level when compared to the levels above and below. Of particular interest was the fact that middle managers frequently held more negative views regarding their commitment to the organization's mission and strategy, their understanding of the business plan, efforts to improve decision making, communication, and teamwork. All too often there seems to be a significant "voltage drop" in the energy and enthusiasm among top managers and rank-and-file employees regarding organizational improvements of all types. Frequently, the disconnect takes place at the middle management level. Reducing the gap and minimizing the disconnect requires rethinking and conscious actions by middle managers.

Middle managers should to be thought of more as integrators of diverse groups and less as technical or functional specialists. The functional orientation has encouraged a more internal focus on the part of middle managers as contrasted to the external focus of top leadership (Duncan, Ginter, and Capper, 1994). Overcoming this limitation will require that middle-level jobs and rewards recognize the value of integration and the need for lateral as well as vertical networks. Finally, middle managers need to be given the information to think beyond their particular organizational silo and see the larger picture.

The transition from middle- to top-level management is in some ways not as radical as the transition from employee to manager. One of the important attempts to examine the role of the *general manager* was provided by Kotter (1982). In this investigation fifteen general managers were studied using interviews, questionnaires, archival records, and more than 500 hours of direct observation. General managers (GMs), for purposes of his study, were defined as individuals who held positions with multifunctional responsibilities for a business (p. 2). In other words, they operated at higher organizational levels than typical middle managers with responsibility for a single function such as marketing, finance, or operations. However, they were not, in all cases, top-level executives.

The general managers who participated in this study displayed twelve similar patterns of behavior. They spent most of their time with other people. About the only time the participants spent alone was on airplanes or commuting to work. Most spent about 70 percent of their time with other people, and some spent as much as 90 percent. Time was spent with many people other than the manager's direct boss and subordinate. Some of the time was spent with the subordinate's subordinates, the boss's boss, customers, and suppliers. The formal chain of command was frequently isolated. An extremely wide range of topics was discussed with other people. Virtually everything that remotely related to their business or industry was discussed.

When interacting with others, general managers asked a lot of questions. Literally hundreds of questions could be asked in a short conversation and important decisions were rarely made in the course of these conversations. The interactions and conversations with others contained a considerable amount of joking, kidding, and non-work-related issues. In a large number of cases the substantive issues discussed were recognized as unimportant to the business or the organization. These general managers regularly engaged in activities that "even they regarded as a waste of time."

General managers seldom gave orders or told people what to do in these encounters. In spite of this, general managers frequently attempted to influence others. Instead of telling people what to do, however, they tended to request, persuade, and intimidate. In allocating their time, the participants tended to behave in a "reactive mode" with few of the encounters being planned. Most of the time spent with others was consumed by short and disjointed conversations, and all the general managers worked long hours. Looking over this list confirms that Kotter's view of successful management behavior has more in common with Mintzberg than with Fayol.

The effective managers Kotter studied did not approach their jobs by planning, organizing, motivating, and controlling in a formal sense. They relied on continuous, informal, and more subtle methods in approaching the complex demands of the management task (p. 127). In completing the task of management they produced agendas and networks rather than long-range plans and organization charts. The agendas they developed were not in conflict with formal plans but were less numerical, covered wider time frames, dealt with more people-oriented issues, and were, in general, "less rigorous, rational, logical, linear" than one would expect of formal planning.

In the same manner, the networks the general managers built were not in conflict with the formal structure of their organizations, but they did include more people inside and outside the firm. The cooperative relationships developed went far beyond the regular formal roles required by the organization. Grove (1985, p. 45) indicated in his diary of "a day in my life" that early in the morning of the day in question he received a call from a competitor that was "ostensibly about a meeting of an industry-wide society." In reality, the competitor was feeling him out on business conditions and, in his words, "I did the same." This is the nature of the network general managers built and relied on for valuable information that can be gathered quickly and may not be readily available within one's own organization. Admittedly, this type of managerial behavior appears quite "unmanaged."

Kotter (1982), however, objected to this conclusion and argued that strangely, substantial efficiency resulted from this apparent inefficiency. The agendas allowed managers to react efficiently and opportunistically to the flow of events around them while knowing that they were doing so within a larger, more rational framework. The network allowed for "terse and efficient" conversations. Together, agendas and networks made it possible for the managers to achieve efficiency and cope with the extreme demands of their jobs. These demands, by the way, consistently resulted in work weeks that averaged 59 hours.

Top Level Management and the Special Case of CEOs

Top-level leaders have held a special fascination, not only to Fayol but to management researchers and managers as well (Jackofsky, Slocum, and McQuaid, 1988). One particular series of studies of CEOs involved 24 executives in Cleveland, Ohio (Jonas, Fry, and Srivastva, 1989). A number of interesting things were discovered about the CEOs included in the study and the nature of their work.

First, it was noted that most of the executives had similar experiences in their ascent to the top of their respective organizations. The authors used the analogy of the "drama of the CEO as hero" and illustrated how the executives went through a period of *search* in their quest for leadership. The also faced a *test* of their capabilities, obtained assistance from a *helper,* received the *reward* for their labor and determination, and were all *transformed* into individuals who are acknowledged as *different* from the person who began the quest.

The second issue addressed was the various ways in which CEOs approached their tasks. CEOs were asked to describe how they approached their jobs and how

▲ **Box 2-7**

CEOS AND ORGANIZATIONAL SUCCESS

The way CEOs approach their business environment can be instrumental in orga-nizational success or failure. One study of 163 top executives found that these top executives matched their companies to the environment using 4 approaches:

1. *Strategic approach:* Systematic, deliberate, and structured analysis of mis-sion, strengths and weaknesses, and opportunities and threats. Most suc-cessful when environment is complex and volume and pace of change are high.

2. *Human assets approach:* Corporate staff adds value through hiring, reten-tion, and development. Most successful when strategic business units are better positioned to make strategic decisions than corporate staff.

3. *Expertise approach:* Programs are designed and implemented around spe-cific expertise in marketing, technology, or so on. Most successful when the expertise is the clear source of competitive advantage.

4. *Box approach:* Corporate headquarters adds value primarily by the imple-mentation of control systems. Most successful in highly regulated environ-ments where consistency of behavior is critical determinant of success.

Source: Farkas and Backer (1996).

they thought they differed from other leaders. The differences emerged along two di-mensions, as illustrated in Exhibit 2-1. Some CEOs possessed a very close identity with the organization; in particular founders and entrepreneurs thought of themselves as the organization and the organization as a reflection of themselves. Other CEOs visualized themselves as playing an important role in the organization but maintained their own identity. In addition, some CEOs were very optimistic about their organi-zation and saw the task of leadership as an opportunity, whereas others were more pessimistic and saw the task of leadership more as problems to be solved. Various combinations of these two perspectives resulted in the following stereotypes of CEO personal leadership theories.

The CEOs who were completely invested in the organization and saw decisions as problems to be solved were the *strategists.* They tended to use metaphors like "bat-tle" and talked in terms of winning and competition. *Analysts* also conceptualized de-cisions as problems but were less passionate about their identity with the organiza-tion. They tended to approach decisions more objectively and scientifically. *Stewards*

Exhibit 2-1 Personal Leadership Theories of CEOs

Organization as Problem or Opportunity	*Executive as Organization and Oganization as Executive*	*Executive in Organizational Role but with Personal Identity*
Organization as Problem	Strategist	Analyst
Organization as Opportunity	Artist	Steward

Source: Adapted from Jonas, Fry, and Srivastva, 1989, p. 210.

also had less personal identity with the organization but saw decisions as opportunities. The metaphor they used most often was "the family" and the need to respect the public trust, maintain continuity, and promote interpersonal relationships. Finally, the *artist*, like the strategist, is highly invested in the organization but views decisions as opportunities to be capitalized on through creativity and innovation.

In the end, it was concluded that the primary role of the CEOs is to take the complex forces impacting on the organization and *make sense* of them for themselves, employees, stockholders, and other constituencies. This sense making begins with the CEOs (Levinson, 1993). A deep understanding of themselves—their life stories, their personal experiences, philosophy, and connection to the organization—is essential before one can make sense of complex reality for others. The CEOs in this study indicated that ultimately they believed they were most essential to their organizations when they created an effective context for change, assisted key people in the organization in feeling commitment and ownership to the organization, and balanced the equally important needs for stability or efficiency and innovation or change (Harper, 1992; Jonas, Fry, and Srivastva, 1990).

Managerial Effectiveness

Management, as noted at the beginning of this chapter, is an applied discipline. Understanding the behavior of managers, while it is interesting in its own right to academic researchers, has as its ultimate goal the improvement of managerial effectiveness. Luthans, Hodgetts, and Rosenkrantz (1988) defined *successful* managers as those who have been promoted quickly while *effective* managers, according to them, are those who have satisfied and committed employees and high performing organizational units.

Luthans, Rosenkrantz, and Hennessey (1985) observed and recorded the behaviors of 52 managers in a state department of revenue, a medium-size manufacturing plant, and a campus police department. This study confirmed that networking activities such as interacting with outsiders and internally oriented socializing and politicking behaviors were positively associated with success in management. In another study Luthans (1988) observed 44 managers from a variety of organizational levels in different industries (primarily service delivery).

These studies illustrated that successful (those promoted fast) and less successful (those not promoted as fast) managers behaved differently. Managers who were promoted fast spent significantly more of their time socializing, politicking, and interacting with outsiders than did their less successful colleagues. Even though Mintzberg's roles were all observed, they did not occur with equal frequency, and the successful managers described here were observed to engage in activities similar to the planning and coordinating functions described by Fayol. Stewart (1984) came to a similar conclusion when she noted that the occurrence of variations among the activities of managers in similar jobs raises questions about the existence of a common core of management activities found in all firms and industries.

Effective managers (satisfied employees and high performing work groups) also behaved differently than their less effective counterparts. Effective managers spent relatively more of their time exchanging information and communicating and engaging in human resource management activities such as motivating and reinforcing, managing conflict, and training and developing (Wren 1992). Luthans (1988) observed that traditional management functions like planning, decision making, and controlling as well as networking were less important activities to the effective managers. Duncan, Ginter, and Capper (1994) had similar findings in a study of 40 health care managers.

Can We Reconcile the Diversity?

In this relatively brief chapter we have presented a number of different views of management work. Is it possible to reconcile these in a manner that will help us understand what management work is really like for those who do it every day? Initially, as far as the technical skills are concerned, we can state that all the models and findings on management work we reviewed concede that managers do need technical skills and use them on occasion. Kotter (1982) gives a little more emphasis to this in his discussion of management success by observing that the managers in his sample thought of themselves as general managers and as capable of managing almost anything well. Yet each was, in reality, highly specialized. Each specialized set of interests, skills, knowledge, and relationships allowed them to behave in ways that fit the demands of their specific situations (p. 8).

Human skills represent no problem of reconciliation. All the views of management behavior recognize the importance of this type of skill. One of Mintzberg's major categories of roles was labeled "interpersonal"; Fayol's functions of coordination and command particularly relate to human factors; and Kotter emphasized how much time managers spend with others, communicate frequently, and seek information from those around them. In the area of conceptual skills there is also reasonable agreement. Managers must conceptualize situations if they are to be effective planners. Certainly when we include the action orientation that was such a critical part of Fayol's view of planning, conceptual skills are critical. From the perspective of Mintzberg, the be-

---

▲ **Box 2-8**

SUCCESSFUL, EFFECTIVE, AND DERAILED EXECUTIVES

Discussions of successful (rapidly promoted) and effective (satisfied employees and high performing units) real managers can benefit from studies of derailment (when managers on the fast track jump the track and do not achieve what appeared to be their potential). Managers seem to get derailed for 4 reasons: (1) problems with interpersonal relations; (2) failure to meet business objectives; (3) failure to build and lead effective teams; and (4) inability to change or adapt during a transition.

Derailment has been a subject of concern in management research for almost 3 decades. While the reasons for derailment appear to be essentially the same as in previous periods, there do appear to be some changes taking place over time. First, managers agree that the ability to adapt and develop in the face of change is more important today than ever. Second, overdependence on a boss or mentor is less often cited as a reason for derailment in recent studies. Third, as with the ability to change, the necessity of building and leading effective teams has increased in importance as a determinant of management success. Proactively dealing with change and effective leadership skills appear to be the best safeguards against derailment for today's managers.

Source: Van Velsor and Leslie (1995).

---

haviors required to fulfill certain informational and decisional roles require an ability to conceptualize. The behavior of Kotter's sample of executives indicated an equal amount of conceptual abilities. Even though the general managers were not observed making "big" decisions, they were constantly gathering information, asking questions, and holding brief encounters designed to increase their knowledge of relevant circumstances. However, the agendas these managers constructed contained ideas that involved commitments far into the uncertain future and were complex in the sense that they required the coordination of different units to succeed. The networks of the general managers also extended beyond their immediate subordinates and bosses—even to the extent of reaching far outside the boundaries of their own organizations.

It is not essential that managers study the research on managerial work to be successful at their jobs. The important point for managers to remember is that they are responsible for doing certain things that others in their organizations cannot do. Managers must provide a sense of direction and offset uncertainty.

Managers also "must" coordinate diverse organizational units and ensure that each makes its unique contribution to the organizational mission. Managers must also make sure things are working as they should. These are the unique tasks of management. These are the roles no one else performs. In some organizations direction is well understood, groups willingly cooperate, and individuals assume the responsibility for their behavior. In such organizations, it is argued, managers are not needed because groups manage themselves (Manz and Sims, 1993). This may be, but such organizations are rare so that for the present and the foreseeable future the job of managers seems secure.

What All This Means to Managers

When researchers understand better what managers do, they can assist by providing the kind of information that will be most relevant and useful to those charged with managing. When managers understand better precisely what they do, it will be easier to compare actual behavior with the behavior that is required of managers if their organizations are to function effectively and efficiently. Luthans (1996) confesses that one of the things that led him to engage in his study of real managers was "lingering doubts" about the nature of managerial work as reported in textbooks (p. 179).

This review of administrative behavior provides an overview of selected aspects of managerial work. The following list summarizes some of the more important conclusions.

1. Managers spend relatively little of their time engaging in the traditional functions of planning, organizing, and controlling.
2. The functions of management are convenient categories for understanding the complex nature of managerial work and important tools for developing normative guidelines for management action.
3. In reality, managerial work is fragmented, too often unfocused, and reactionary.
4. The activities accomplished by managers vary significantly as they move up the organizational hierarchy.
5. Competence in a technical area and industry-specific knowledge diminish as the level of management responsibility increases.
6. Human relations skills appear to be the only competences that are equally important at all levels of management.
7. Managers are sometimes successful without being effective. However, managerial success without effectiveness is self-limiting.

Questions for Discussion

1 After reading this chapter, how would you define the term "management?" What, in your opinion, are the essential elements of a useful definition of management?

2 How would you explain the changing view of the CEO as spokesperson for the organization? Why were some chief executives so successful in this role and now caution is suggested when using this approach to promoting the organization? Is it a matter of personalities or changing times?

3 Is there really anything unique about Mintzberg's view of the manager in terms of roles when compared with Fayol's functional view? Is Mintzberg an improvement or merely repackaging?

4 Based on your experiences as a manager or your observations of managers at work, briefly evaluate each of Mintzberg's four myths. Which do you think are accurate and which, in your opinion, are inaccurate?

5 Evaluate the research we have reviewed on the changing nature of managerial work relative to the organizational level. What do you think are the essential changes that take place as a manager moves up the organizational hierarchy?

6 Do you agree with the statement: "The transition from employee to first-level supervisor is more radical than the transition from middle to upper levels of management?" Why or why not?

7 Why would managers engage in activities that "even they regard as a waste of time?"

8 There appears to be substantial agreement that the relative importance of technical and conceptual skills varies with the level of responsibility in an organization. Only human skills seem to remain equally important regardless of the level of management. Is this, in your opinion, true? Why or why not?

CHALLENGES OF MANAGEMENT

Part II of this book is about challenges—challenges of efficiency, challenges of change, and challenges of leadership. Management is, when all is said and done, a series of challenges. Management, like life itself, is ultimately an attempt to deal with scarcity and the dismal science of economics. If organizations and individuals had all the resources they needed to meet their needs, there would be no need for management and managers. There would be no need to allocate resources if they were not scarce. Scarcity is a reality, however, and management is here to stay. Resources must be used efficiently to ensure that we obtain the most we can from the limited resources we are able to acquire.

Chapter 3 examines the issue of efficiency. Efficiency was the earliest theme of scientific management, and many people think of efficiency when they think of management. Efficiency, doing things right, continues to be an important topic and challenge (F. Gilbreth, 1912 and L. Gilbreth, 1973b.). The quest for cost containment in health care and organizational downsizing in all industries illustrate that efficiency continues to be an important topic.

Interestingly, efficiency is not enough to ensure survival. Long-term survival also requires effectiveness, or doing the right things. This topic is discussed in Chapter 4. Frequently, managers are expected to destroy, for the sake of change, the very "efficiency equilibrium" they have tried so hard to create. Doing the right things is often thought of as effectiveness. Organizational success and survival require "doing the right things right."

The final chapter in Part II, Chapter 5, discusses the challenge of leadership. Leaders and managers are sometimes the same people, but they perform very different functions and add very different things to organizations. If management is about efficiency and order, leadership is about effectiveness and change. These differences as well as the nature of leadership are the subject of Chapter 5.

Part II provides us with some additional insights into the extremely complex world of management. It is a world of paradoxes and uncertainties. Order demands efficiency, but effectiveness is about change. Efficiency demands that we build structures to minimize deviations from the norms, but innovation insists that we take risks and charge ahead in the face of uncertainty.

The Challenge of Efficiency: Doing Things Right

"Efficiency and good came closer to meaning the same thing in these years [of scientific management] *than in any other period of American history."*

Samuel Haber
Efficiency and Uplift (1964) [Insert added]

The turn of the 20th century was an exciting time to be alive. Impressionism was revolutionizing art, literature, and music, and the human voice was being transmitted by radio waves, Mars had been fully and accurately mapped, Freud was rewriting psychology, and the first Zepplin had taken to the air. It must have seemed a time of incredible possibilities to people who were, for the most part, farmers, laborers, and traders. Things were about to change even more!

In the previous chapter we attempted to illustrate the reality of managerial work—an occupation characterized by fragmentation, stress, and difficulty focusing on important things. One of the reasons for this apparent lack of focus is the fact that managers are expected to accomplish two important but sometimes mutually exclusive challenges. The first challenge is short term and relates to efficiency and getting the most productivity from limited resources. To be successful, managers have to do things right and ensure efficient operations by developing goals, establishing policies, formulating procedures, evaluating performance, and so on. However, merely doing things right will not guarantee success in today's highly competitive environment. Organizations must also do the right things. They have to be effective as well, and this is the challenge of change. The focus of this chapter is efficiency. Effectiveness and change will be discussed in Chapter 4.

If there is one word that more people associate with management than any other it is "efficiency." The scientific management movement, upon which much of modern theory and practice is based, was almost called "efficiency management." This should not be surprising since scientific management was the product of engineers. As the introductory quote indicates, efficiency was the gospel, the "good news," of scientific management and assumed an almost evangelistic zeal to those who believed in it. There "was no such thing as efficiency independent of values" (Sowell, 1980, p. 361).

The Unveiling

The new industrial world, the factories made possible by specialization, and the agrarian society that preceded it shared a similar problem—the problem of continuity, or how successive generations of farmers, skilled workers, and artisans should be trained. The answer in both societies was apprenticeships. The aspiring farmer worked with an experienced planter and observed successful behavior; the prospective merchant signed on with a person trained in accounts; and future lawyers willingly served as clerks to those already practicing law. Factory workers were trained the same way. Even today, journeymen machinists, bricklayers, tool and die makers, and welders are expected to serve apprenticeships.

Learning by doing was the official teaching method, and the accomplished worker was an adequate teacher. It was an interesting system when viewed from the biases of today. We, for the most part, teach theory and delay practice. Historically, by contrast, theory was inferred from successful practice. Since practice preceded theory, the skilled and observant barber could learn enough anatomy to perform routine although rarely successful surgery; the literate and ambitious student could read independently enough books to pass the bar examination; and the well-intentioned minister and school teacher could preach a sermon or teach reading with little understanding of theology or psychology.

It was not until science was applied in medicine that the surgeon became a physician. It was not until the "science of jurisprudence" was widely accepted that the practice of law became a learned profession, and it was not until the scientific method was used in engineering that engineers gained significant social status. Science, perhaps, was the answer to the problem of inefficiency. It was worth a try.

Science and Scientific Management

Any mention of science in management requires immediate reference to Frederick Winslow Taylor. Babbage, as we noted in Chapter 1, was a mathematician and Ure was a doctor. Both were trained in science and appreciated its potential power in improving management practice. Neither, however, was concerned about the power of science to improve management's reputation. This distinction was reserved for Taylor and a few engineers.

Before beginning the discussion of Taylor, perhaps a word of justification is in order. Frederick Taylor is the most frequently discussed individual in the annals of management. Some believe the attention given to him is excessive and others believe his ideas are irrelevant to the service-oriented and knowledge-based industries of today. Some believe Taylor has been inappropriately criticized as one who freely used the ideas of others without proper credit and as someone unconcerned about the welfare of workers. Clearly Taylor has been criticized and even condemned for many reasons. People who revolutionize the thinking of any field are rarely popular and are often the object of scorn.

It would be, however, a serious mistake to underestimate or ignore the importance of Taylor. We need only look at contemporary writings to see how pervasive his influence has been not only on management thought (Kanigel, 1997) but on quality management (Knouse, Carson, and Carson, 1993) and on American society in general (Banta, 1993). Few would argue that no one can hope to understand the origin of management ideas without an understanding of Taylor and his ideas and philosophies.

Taylor's purposes in writing *The Principles of Scientific Management* (1914) were: (1) To show through simple illustrations the loss taking place in this country through inefficiency. (2) To convince the reader that the remedy for this loss lies in systematic management not in a futile search for extraordinary workers. (3) To prove that the best management is a true science resting on defined laws, rules, and principles. (4) To further prove that the principles of scientific management are applicable to all human activities and, when used correctly, will result in astounding results (p. 7).

If we are to appreciate the importance of science in Taylor's system, several things should be understood. First, Taylor believed that the legitimacy of management rested on its ability to maximize simultaneously the prosperity of both employers and employees. This, he believed, was necessary for success because the self-interests of the two groups were mutually reinforcing. Over the long run it was impossible to have one without the other. If, however, workers were to achieve their maximum productivity,

---

▲ Box 3-1

FREDERICK W. TAYLOR—THE FATHER OF SCIENTIFIC MANAGEMENT

Taylor was born in Philadelphia in 1856. He was fortunate to be born into a relatively wealthy family and have the leisure to theorize about the factories that were so much a part of his surroundings. His inclination toward mechanics was evident early in life by his fascination with taking things apart and putting them together again—Taylor sounds a lot like Babbage. Taylor planned to attend Harvard, but eye problems forced him to leave school after completing the 11th grade. He chose instead a career in industry and set about learning the trades of pattern maker and machinist.

For a period of almost 20 years Taylor was engaged as an apprentice, gang boss, foreman, and chief engineer at Midvale Steel Company. Later he became manager of the Manufacturing Investment Company, consultant to Bethlehem Steel Company, and the best known spokesperson for the scientific management movement.

Source: Wrege and Greenwood (1991); Kanigel (1997).

they must perform work in the best way possible, and this required that managers scientifically study work and train laborers in the optimum way of accomplishing jobs.

Even though Taylor believed the interests of workers and employers were mutually reinforcing, he was a realist. He knew that years of doing work the same old way would make change difficult. Workers believed that it was in their own self-interest to "soldier" or work at less than their maximum pace and, in fact, existing management systems made it in the worker's best interest to soldier.

Procedures used in most trades were based on inefficient rules of thumb rather than on scientifically determined methods (Taylor, 1914, p. 16). The most effective management systems of Taylor's day, or the *finest type of ordinary management*, were those that provided an incentive for the greatest personal performance. Taylor called this *management of initiative and incentive.*

The problem with these systems resulted from the fact that the responsibility for productivity was placed almost exclusively on the worker. In Taylor's view, managers should share this responsibility (Taylor, 1895). It was the manager's job to gather, tabulate, classify, and, through the use of science, reduce this information to principles, rules, laws, and formulas that summarize all the workers' experiences and could be used as guides for better performance of daily tasks. The practical guidelines developed from this activity of management should then be taught to workers and measures taken to ensure that the proper principles were followed. Managers, under Taylor's system, were expected to perform a new, vital, and highly respectable task—to develop a science of each element of human work and replace old rules of thumb. In the process they were to scientifically select, train, teach, and develop workers to their maximum potential.

It would have shocked, but probably not surprised, Taylor that in the early 1980s in one of Ford Motor Company's *better plants* it took a workforce with 200 job classifications, an inventory backlog of 3 weeks, and 800 square feet of floor space to support one worker in making two engines per day. At the same time in a Toyota plant in Japan, one worker could produce more than four times as many engines a day with half the floor space. There was a 1-hour backlog of inventory and a supporting workforce composed of only 7 job classifications (Murrin, 1984). The difference had to be more than the Japanese worker.

Scientific Management as Philosophy Rather than Technique

Taylor advocated the scientific approach as the solution for this type of productivity problem because he respected its power in improving industrial efficiency. He also recognized the dangers that the mechanistic application of science could entail. Taylor was emphatic in stating that the "mechanisms" of scientific management should never replace its philosophy. The philosophy was a scientific attitude demanding data collection, tabulation, and the application of knowledge to problems of an industrial society. The mechanisms were techniques such as time study, functional foremanship, instruction cards, differential piece rates, and cost systems.

Scientific management was a "mental revolution" that advocated an entirely new way of managing work. An earlier book by Taylor, *Shop Management* (1903), dealt with the techniques or mechanisms. In *The Principles of Scientific Management* the goal was to present the elements required by the mental revolution.

Taylor knew that if his system was to be widely practiced, success stories were essential. His quest for such illustrations began early in his career. However, it was not an easy road for Taylor as he attempted to prove the superiority of "science-based" management. Industry had functioned for centuries without the application of science, and not many people seemed interested in or willing to try something new.

An Opportunity for Exposure

Taylor was not the only one who advocated the application of science to problems of management. This became clear in the summer of 1910, when the railroads north of the Ohio and Potomac rivers and east of the Mississippi River filed a request for a rate increase with the Interstate Commerce Commission. From September to November of that year hearings were held to determine the wisdom of granting the request. Louis Brandeis, later Justice of the Supreme Court, a leading attorney, objected to the increase. He had read some of Taylor's papers and discussed the concepts of management with others who agreed with Taylor's conclusion that wages could be increased and labor costs reduced simultaneously if operations were more efficient. However, his recollection was vague and until the rate cases developed, there was little reason for him to occupy his attention with matters of management. Now he needed expert witnesses to make the case convincing, and according to Drury (1922), Brandeis held a meeting at the apartment of Henry Gantt, one of Taylor's close associates.

The meeting was attended by Gantt, Brandeis, Frank Gilbreth, and a few other people. Brandeis wanted to make sure that testimonies followed a similar logic and used a common language to describe the elements of this new management system. The system needed a name, and some of the "labels" the group considered for this revolutionary way of looking at the problems of industry were "Taylor system," "functional management," "shop management," and "efficiency" (p. 38). There was even an "Efficiency Society" incorporated in New York with the expressed purpose of applying the principles of efficiency to all aspects of life.

Taylor himself testified 2 years later before a special committee of the House of Representatives and illustrated why efficiency was such a compelling label and why his system had such appeal. At Bethlehem Steel, for example, his studies on pig iron loading were reported to increase labor productivity by almost 400 percent with a 60 percent increase in wages (Taylor, 1914, pp. 46–47), and it was his belief that through the application of scientific management principles, freight rates and labor costs could be reduced while at the same time wages of workers could be increased. He made his points even though his performance under questioning revealed emotional problems and dogmatic attitudes. The surviving label did not include efficiency, but efficiency has always been associated with scientific management.

Doubts and Reservations

Taylor was committed to science and the system he developed. As with most zealots, perhaps he was too committed. Psychoanalytical assessment of Taylor is not our goal, although such studies are available and at least a passing understanding of Taylor's personality is helpful in understanding his obsession with efficiency, time, and order (Kakar, 1970).

Taylor's solution to the problem of inefficiency (he called it the "greatest evil" of his time) was the application of scientific methods to the study and improvement of work. The recommendations came at a particularly critical time, and in spite of successes, he attracted more than his share of critics. Some of the criticisms were directed at his character and personality while others focused on his work.

Hoagland (1957), for example, argued that experiments on shoveling can be traced to 1699 and that Charles Babbage conducted experiments of this nature long before Taylor. Hoagland listed 20 people who studied shoveling between the end of the 17th and the early 19th centuries. None were acknowledged by Taylor, even though he stated in *The Principles of Scientific Management* (1914, p. 54) that he had hired a college graduate to review all the works on shoveling in English, French, and German.

Wrege and Perroni (1974) were even more severe in their criticism of the pig iron shoveling experiments. They contend that the entire experiment was "more fiction than fact" and present examples of how different accounts of the details of the study were inconsistently presented. The discovery of the "law of heavy loading" and the pioneering works on rest periods were, according to these authors, largely a hoax. It is confusing when we read the criticisms of Taylor, especially those that reflect adversely on his character and integrity (Wrege and Stotka, 1978). His obsession with his reputation and his Quaker heritage seem to preclude the actions for which he was frequently criticized. We cannot, however, disregard the criticisms as unfounded since they are, for the most part, well documented (Bluedorn, Keon, and Carter, 1985).

Taylor also has his allies. Copley's (1923) two-volume work on Taylor as the "father of scientific management" is largely complimentary. Boddewyn (1962) maintained that most of the criticisms of Taylor result from quotations made out of context and the overzealousness of his followers. The most systematic defense of Taylor, however, comes from Locke (1982), who stated that many of the criticisms have been "invalid or involved peripheral issues, and his [Taylor's] ideas and contributions often have gone unacknowledged" (p. 14). When we really look at what has been used by managers, it is evident that many, perhaps most, of Taylor's ideas have stood the test of time (Frey, 1976).

The Essence of Efficiency

Although there are precise definitions, the word "efficiency" has a number of connotations. To some it means "getting more for less." To others it means keeping costs low and profits high. There is some truth to both of these popular connotations. In an economic and, ultimately, the management sense, efficiency means maximizing the output with a minimum amount of inputs. In the case of automobiles it means producing as many cars as possible while carefully keeping the inputs of land, labor, capital, and management to a minimum. In doing so, costs are controlled and profits, if maintained at reasonable levels, are sufficient while allowing for prices that make it possible to sell cars without being underpriced by competitors.

It was efficiency that led Adam Smith and Charles Babbage to advocate the division of labor or specialization. It was the same motivation that has driven German automobile makers such as Opel Eisenach to develop new ways of competing. German workers are considered among the most pampered employees in the world. They work relatively short hours, get paid twice as much as their European counterparts, and receive 10 weeks paid vacation per year. The result is obvious—at Volkswagen's Wolfburg plant each employee produces an average of 24 cars per year, compared to 60 at selected American and Japanese automakers. Opel Eisenach decided to change all that with a new approach to improving efficiency.

At Opel, a system was developed to provide increased job control using team structures and skill-based pay to reward maximum worker flexibility and quality. Today, the plant is recognized as one of Europe's most productive. About 200 teams of six to eight people operate in the plant and virtually manage their own work. The system seems to be working. In the first year of the experiment, production has increased by 20 percent (Slocum, 1996).

Management's High Priest of Efficiency

Taylor was concerned with the virtues and possibilities of efficiency along with Gantt and the Gilbreths (1917), but no one devoted himself so completely to the subject as Harrington Emerson. The editor of *Engineering Magazine* once stated that Emerson's "efficiency system was large enough to become a philosophy, hopeful enough to be called a gospel." In fact, the final chapter of Emerson's first book was titled "The Gospel of Efficiency."

Emerson's experience consulting for railroads placed him in a unique position to become one of the primary witnesses in the Eastern Rate Case. When Mr. Brandeis called, Emerson quickly and effectively responded. He claimed that the use of scientific management would save the railroads a million dollars a day! His fame grew and his talents were sought by industry and government. He was aware of the work of Taylor's group and the contributions of the Gilbreths even though Taylor never really trusted Emerson's new breed of efficiency engineers or welcomed him as an insider (Wrege and Greenwood, 1991). Therefore, Emerson's contributions were, to a great extent, independent of the other champions of scientific management, even though he did share many, if not most, of their commitments.

Of particular importance to Emerson was the need to justify the concepts of scientific management to the worker. In 1921 he was appointed a member of the Hoover Committee for the Elimination of Waste in Industry (Urwick, 1956). This membership was shared with another important contributor to the efficiency movement, as we will soon discover.

▲ **Box 3-2**

AN UNLIKELY ENGINEER

Looking back, it is difficult to understand what there was about efficiency that could have so completely captured the attention of a man like Emerson. He was born in Trenton, New Jersey, in 1853. His father was a professor of English literature and a Presbyterian minister. The younger Emerson studied in Germany, England, France, Italy, and Greece. It is said that he could speak 19 languages, so it should be no surprise that he became the head of the modern foreign languages department of the University of Nebraska when he was only 23 years old. After little more than 5 years, however, university life held little excitement for him, and he resigned to pursue business interests. Over the next 20 years he engaged in economic and engineering research for the Burlington Railroad and was a consultant to firms around the world. As a consulting engineer, he completely reorganized the Atchison, Topeka, and Santa Fe Railroad, where he introduced a number of cost accounting, record keeping, and bonus systems. These types of contributions earned him the distinction of the first "efficiency engineer."

Source: Wren (1994).

Fundamentals of Efficiency

Emerson wrote *Efficiency as a Basis for Operations and Wages* in 1908. He began the book with a shocking contrast between the inefficiencies of human beings and the efficient way things are done in nature (Emerson, 1976). The example of "nature's pump" illustrated his point. Water is drawn from the ocean to tremendous heights, carried thousands of miles, and deposited on mountains and plains with no pipes, no friction loss, no mechanical parts. If humans could be so efficient, according to Emerson, there would be no bread lines, no poverty. In fact, all people everywhere would be wealthy. Our inefficiency, according to Emerson, causes our poverty. Efficiency in the natural world is a recurring theme in Emerson's writing.

The problem of human inefficiency, Emerson believed, could be traced to two factors. To be efficient we must first devise ways of enabling people to accomplish the most they possibly can relative to the task or goals that are established. This requires careful analysis of the elements of work and teaching workers the best way to do each job. These ideas were shared particularly by the Gilbreths and probably by Taylor as well. Emerson believed that most people are only about 60 percent efficient in accomplishing their work goals.

Second, he argued, we must develop ways of setting goals that require the best performance for which we are capable. In this regard, Emerson believed that our present efficiencies were so far below 1 percent of what we are capable that they did not warrant an estimate (Emerson, 1976, p. 27).

Emerson's travels made it possible for him to draw lessons from other nations in much the same way we seek to learn the secrets of the Japanese. Although he was quick to point out that all nations shared the curse of inefficiency, each country seemed to develop its own unique strengths. He was particularly eager to recognize the successes of England, Germany, and France. At the time of Emerson's writing, Great Britain was the industrial leader of the world. He attributed this leadership to the British discovery of the importance of the oceans. England was always one step ahead of the rest of the world. When most other nations were building fast wooden ships, England was developing steamers.

The Germans' national treasure was their ability to use their brains. The intelligence of the German people remains a resource of economic development. A mere 25 years after studying the American and British systems of shipbuilding, the Germans were building the finest and fastest vessels afloat (p. 41). The French emerged as logical innovators. They developed the fastest trains, the first submarine, the machine gun, and the art of photography. Americans, Emerson contended, excel because of the great accomplishments of individuals—Edison, Ford, Westinghouse, and so on. Whether or not this individuality could provide industrial leadership remained to be seen, and some believe it came to be a unique curse. Emerson's appreciation of the unique virtues of many cultures made it possible for him to think in broader terms about management and productivity and to accept freely the advantages and reject the disadvantages of many national cultures.

▲ Box 3-3

CONTINUOUS IMPROVEMENT AND GERMAN INGENUITY

Emerson appreciated the German intellect and looked at it as their national treasure. The application of German ingenuity in industry is best illustrated by the cases of Daimler-Benz, BMW, Siemens, Bosch, and Krupp. These companies have excelled on three dimensions of efficiency—cost, time, and quality. In all things these companies have insisted on simplicity and the rigorous implementation of strategic and operational plans.

Studies of high-performing German organizations confirmed that they have several things in common: (1) concentration on core competences and customer value; (2) vertical integration with suppliers; (3) integrated operations; (4) clear control priorities; (5) selective technological investment; and (6) market-oriented, self-regulating units, investment in human capital, and flexibility.

Source: Rommel, Kluge, Kempis, Diederichs, and Burck (1995).

Efficiency and Organization

One of the most important differences between the writings of Emerson and others of the scientific management school was the insights the former had into the relationship between efficiency and organization design. There is little doubt from his writings that the years spent in Germany impressed Emerson with the importance of the structure of organizations.

How is it possible, he asked, for small plants all around the country producing everything from ink pens to train locomotives to compete successfully with large corporations? Theoretically, the economies of scale should make the large firms much more efficient. They could purchase in larger quantities and receive discounts; processes could be automated and cost per unit reduced. Dozens of other reasons can be found in elementary manufacturing textbooks for the increased efficiency of larger firms. However, as Emerson noted, this was not always the case, and the reason why it is not can be explained in one phrase—lack of organization (p. 54).

The inefficiencies have become excessive in some industries where terms like "diseconomies of scale" are used to describe the conditions resulting from extremely large organizations. In recent years, companies like General Electric have shifted manufacturing in its Aircraft Engine Division to smaller "satellite" plants, and its Major Appliance Business Group has reduced employment in some of its mammoth factories. Although this seems at odds with the point made in other places about economies

---

▲ Box 3-4
THE CASE FOR FOCUSED FACTORIES—EVEN IN HEALTH CARE!

Some pessimists suggest that if current trends continue, Americans could be spending one out of every five dollars they earn on health care. Such a level of expenditure is neither practical nor is it sustainable. Something has to be done to change our "expensive, confusing, inconvenient, bureaucratic, and all too often inaccessible" system of health care. The solution, according to some experts, is the "focused factory." This recommendation comes as a surprise in light of the fact that most of the recommendations to date for improving the health care system involve large, vertically integrated networks of patient care that carefully control patients from the time they enter the system until they are discharged.

The focused factory in health care does just the opposite. If the system provided customers with the freedom to select their own health care, the market would respond with convenience and service. As in other industries, providers of health care would focus on what they do best, develop a competitive advantage in these areas, and demand efficiency of operations—the focused factory.

Source: Herzlinger (1997).

of scale, it is important to note that in many cases downsizing has taken place in terms of employees but not in the actual scale of operations.

Increased automation has allowed GE, among other things, to reduce its rejection rate by 80 percent. In other words, quality has been increased and allowed significant cost savings. In doing so, the "bureaucracy" of the large factory is discarded in favor of more decentralized operations. Emerson Electric has always maintained a reputation as a company that succeeds by "keeping things relatively small." Reducing layers in the plant organization has allowed Emerson and other firms to improve communication and develop team approaches that have a potential of eliminating many of the diseconomies of scale. Equally important is that fact that smaller operations in service delivery as well as manufacturing demand less specialization and the concurrent "dumbing down" of work as it becomes more repetitive and routine. In the knowledge industry, for example, workers become about 3 times more productive after 10 years with the same employer because of the understanding they acquire through experience and apply directly to the improvement of customer service (Schoenberger, 1996).

These diseconomies are examples of "too much of a good thing" where plants get so large and complex that they can no longer be effectively managed. This leads to decentralizing and downsizing for the sake of efficiency until the new optimum-size plant is found. Size of the organization is not the only factor influencing efficiency. The way work is structured and who performs it also influence cost and productivity. For this reason, few more enthusiastic discussions can be found of the virtues of the line-and-staff form of organization than those presented by Emerson.

Line and Staff

Nature, the human body, and other well functioning organizations are all organized around line-and-staff concepts. Emerson, as well as other early writers, was impressed with the organizational precision of the Prussian army. Von Moltke, the army's great organizer, was one of Emerson's heroes because he recognized the genius of the army's organization. In the organization developed by Von Moltke, line and staff were skillfully combined with functional specialization. No army fought at its best if it went into battle carrying its own supplies. In the Prussian army each important function, line and staff, was performed by a specialist. There were quartermasters, map readers, and gunnery experts so that in time of war there was no doubt about how something should be done—there was an expert present. The limitation, of course, involved coordinating all these specialists, and this, according to Emerson, was the responsibility of a strong executive—to control, adjust, and harmonize the line and staff toward the accomplishment of organizational goals (p. 66).

If line-and-staff units are to work properly, their relationship must be clearly understood. The line has the authority to authorize action, but this should not be done independently of staff officers. There are a number of ways a well functioning staff can assist in the accomplishment of organizational goals.

The staff, for example, is critical in a number of areas. Relative to human resources, staff specialists can assist line workers in the selection and training of employees. Using the example of brick layers, Emerson discussed Frank Gilbreth's example of how, when staff assisted in planning, redesigning, and directing the work more carefully, efficiency was tripled and the masons were less bored with their jobs. When equipment is properly installed and maintained, it can greatly increase the efficiency of ordinary workers. Staff can offer valuable assistance in this area. Finally, staff can provide assistance relative to materials and methods by having the right materials at the right place at the right time for the use of line employees. Line employees also rely on assistance from the staff to ensure that the best methods are used.

Standards and Efficiency

Standards, as discussed by Emerson, were more than goals to be used in evaluating performance. Instead, the term was used in the sense of "professional standards." Standards, in other words, are predetermined sets of rules that are "generally accepted by the majority in a given field." Standards relative to line workers are usually less complex and more stable than those with the staff. Often staff experts have complex and divided loyalties between the organization and an external professional group.

Emerson gave particular attention to the role of standards in cost accounting. The cost accountant, when developing cost standards, must work closely with the efficiency engineer, whose function is to: (1) provide the "industrial and operating world" standards as definite as dollar measurements for all services, materials, and equipment operations; (2) make assays as definite and precise as the assayer's determination of bullion values of all current operations so as to establish the current rate of efficiency; and (3) provide remedies that will bring current efficiency up to 100 percent (p. 160).

Emerson used a personal example to show how, in one of his railroad projects, when he went on the job, the unit costs were $9.55. Working closely with the auditor, standard costs were established along with an efficient staff organization. At first the unit costs increased to $10.31 followed by a slight decrease from this high to $10.16. However, within 6 years, the unit costs were down to an "amazing $3.73" (p. 186).

The final point discussed by Emerson was the idea of standard times and bonuses. For any job, Emerson and Taylor believed that there must be a standard time to accomplish it. The example of an auto mechanic was used to illustrate the point. If the mechanic completed a 4-hour task (standard) in less than the standard time, he was paid the price of the 4-hour task and considered efficient. If it took longer than 4 hours, his company lost money on the 4-hour charge and the mechanic received a poor efficiency rating. There was clearly an incentive for the mechanic to work at 100 percent or above.

It is interesting to note that this very concept of standard cost provided the theoretical basis for the complete change in the way health care costs are reimbursed in the United States. Prior to 1983 health care was a "cost plus" industry. Prices and fees reflected costs plus a markup for profit. In 1983, Medicare implemented a prospective payment system whereby various related groups of procedures were reimbursed according to a standard fee schedule. Other health insurers followed Medicare's lead.

Today, health providers are paid for most services delivered to patients on the basis of standard charges for "diagnostic related groups" (DRGs) of medical problems.

Medicare has established standard charges for a broad array of medical conditions and pays providers according to these standards. If a patient receives a specific type of treatment, Medicare pays the provider, say $3,000. If the provider can deliver the service for less than $3,000, a profit results. If it costs more than $3,000 to deliver the service, a loss is incurred. The incentive for improving efficiency in health care delivery is clear. This system is fundamentally different from the "cost-based" system of reimbursement (retrospective payment) wherein summed costs were added onto a reasonable return to determine health care charges. Cost plus operations clearly provides little incentive to control costs.

The important point, from our perspective, is that an established, fair, and communicated standard cost is an effective way of improving efficiency. Most people respond to incentives, and when the incentive is to be more efficient and share in the benefits, employees are more likely to be productive. Emerson concluded *Efficiency as a Basis for Operations and Wages* by stating that "efficiency is unattainable from overworked, underpaid, and brutalized men." Efficiency is attained when "the right thing is done in the right manner by the right employees at the right place in the right time" (p. 254). There may have never been a more adequate statement of the concept of efficiency (Crosby, 1996).

Emerson's Twelve Principles of Efficiency

Emerson's most influential book was written in 1913 and published under the title *The Twelve Principles of Efficiency*. The principles, Emerson argued, are simple, plain, and elementary. In fact, they have been practiced and accepted for millions of years by plants and other forms of life found in nature. An important point is made that is worthy for us to commit to memory: "efficiency brings about greater results with lessened effort; strenuousness brings about greater results with abnormally greater effort." In other words, efficiency results in improvements because people work smarter not harder! Who would not buy such an appealing idea?

Eastman Kodak became more efficient by working smarter. In Rochester, New York, it was not uncommon for 3 generations of workers to be employed by George Eastman's entrepreneurial legend—Eastman Kodak. The number of employees at Kodak Park peaked at 35,000. However, a century of success can lead to complacency and inefficiency. When Fuji began producing innovative high-quality film products in the 1980s, "Mother Kodak" found itself in trouble.

When the manager of the Black and White Film Manufacturing Division was told to improve productivity, he did not "slash and burn, cut costs, and drop product lines." Instead, with no major infusions of capital or airplane loads of consultants, "we became more efficient" (Frangos and Bennett, 1993).

Integrating grassroots thinking about the business and formal systems such as cycle-time reduction programs and manufacturing resource planning (MRP II) to orchestrate 7,000 products, and systematically preparing for ISO (International Standardization Organization) certification resulted in astounding improvements. The

▲ **Box 3-5**

EASTMAN KODAK AND TEAM ZEBRA

In many ways the Black and White Manufacturing Division at Eastman Kodak resembled a zebra: (1) its products all related to black and white; (2) it was an *endangered species;* (3) it could survive only by sticking together; (4) every person was different just like zebra stripes (5) it had to be smart to survive.

The division created its "smarter vision" and developed many individual visions, such as the Sensi-X (sensitizing excellence) designed to cut cycle time from 42 days to 21 days in year one, 10 days in year two, 5 days in year three, and eventually to 1 day. The team's slogan was simple "One Day!" The film testers developed their own program called RASP (rapid access sensitometric processing), designed to reduce film testing time from one week to "real time." With projects such as this, teams and individuals were genuinely motivated to accomplish the shared "smarter vision."

Source: Frangos and Bennett (1993).

Black and White Film Division became an exciting place to work rather than being simply "what my grandfather did." Manufacturing costs were reduced by $40 million and inventory was cut by $50 million. Finishing time was reduced from 6 weeks to 2 days, sensitizing time was reduced from 42 to 20 days, and the time needed to bring products to market was cut by half. On-time delivery was increased to 95 percent, and productivity and morale were at an all-time high.

Emerson's first principle called for the establishment of "clearly defined ideals." The importance of goals and ideals cannot be overemphasized. It is one of the most basic principles of management. The ideals of a manager should be promulgated throughout the organization, posted everywhere, and inculcated in every other manager and employee. Then, and only then, can industrial organizations obtain a high degree of individual and aggregate excellence (Emerson, 1913, p. 112). "Common sense" was Emerson's second principle. He believed that when a business lacked ideals, organization, and common sense, it tended to become overcapitalized. Machines are purchased and installed that are not needed and are employed less than full time. This adds excessive overhead and becomes destructive to the success of the organization.

In his third principle, Emerson returned to the theme developed in his previous book and recommended the use of "competent counsel." Early business leaders in America relied on personal skill and knowledge even to the extent of scorning the need for expert advice from lawyers, accountants, consultants, and engineers. The increasing complexity of business in Emerson's day, and to a greater extent today, requires the frequent use of technical experts. No single manager can become compe-

---

▲ **Box 3-6**

BENCHMARKING IN AN ELECTRONIC AGE

Benchmarking on the basis of best practices is a great idea. It makes sense to learn from others who have faced and solved similar problems. It sure beats "reinventing the wheel" every time something new presents itself. The problem, however, is the difference between the logic and theory of benchmarking and its practice. Best practices are hard to discover, difficult to document, and the sharing of information can range from guarded to nonexistent. Why should competitors share best practices? What are the advantages to noncompetitors? Even within the same companies, best practices may not be shared.

Tandem Computer has 11,000 employees worldwide and an e-mail system organized around three classes of mail. The second category of mail is for employees seeking information. Employees can broadcast the need for help on a problem to all other employees and colleagues can respond to the requests. One important feature of the system is that solutions are stored in a public file. The existence of e-mail and public files overcomes many of the barriers to communicating real time to problems in a global organization.

Source: Goodman and Darr (1996).

---

tent in all the areas necessary to run a successful business. Therefore, in order to ensure that the "best practices" are used in all areas, competent counsel must be employed and the best managers must be receptive to the advice offered by these advisors.

Emerson's fourth principle was "discipline." Common ideals that are worked for in a disciplined organization result in cooperation. At this point, Emerson provided another of his useful examples from nature. He contended that the fundamentals of discipline are better learned from the "governance of a bee hive than a college textbook." No bee appears to obey any other bee, yet the *spirit of the hive* is so great that every bee works hard at his or her special task and fatalistically assumes that every other bee is also conscientiously working as hard as possible for the good of the hive. When the drones fail to be useful, the working bees "make away with them" (p. 150). The spirit of the hive, like other examples from nature, fascinated Emerson and were frequently used illustrations of the most pure form of efficient processes. Emerson's memorable statement is that "cooperation is not a principle but the absence of it is a crime." If more organizations had the "spirit of the hive," the task of management would be much easier and enjoyable.

Emerson was a believer in preventive control when it came to discipline. He believed the *hiring decision* was a critical point to initiate discipline. Before a prospective employee is hired the individual should be instructed about the ideals of the firm, its philosophy of organization, and performance expectations. Emerson maintained that 90 percent of the "harder" discipline should be applied before people are hired. This would ensure that those who are unfit for the organization because of bad character, bad habits, laziness, or destructive tendencies are never hired in a "high class organization." Like Taylor, he believed one of the worst faults managers can commit is to hire people for jobs for which they are unfit. The organization and the individual lose. Just as the bee depends on the spirit of the hive, the worker depends on the spirit of the organization.

Under the best forms of management there are few rules and even fewer punishments. Instead, there are standard practice instructions and every person knows her or his part in the success of the organization. All employees and managers understand their responsibility, and reliable, timely records are kept on all important aspects of the business. There are standardized conditions and operations and efficiency rewards for those who excel.

The fifth principle is "a fair deal." Managers need three important qualities according to Emerson—sympathy, imagination, and, above all, a sense of justice. The greatest problem in ensuring a fair deal is the failure to establish parity between pay and performance. Wage systems should be developed in a way to ensure that today is made bearable without taking away the hope of a better tomorrow. Such reward systems provide excitement and incentive.

Keeping "reliable, immediate, adequate, and permanent records" is the sixth principle of efficiency according to Emerson. Records make us aware of more information than is immediately available through the senses. They provide us warnings, allow us to recall the past, and make projections into the future. The discussion of records illustrates the importance of cost accounting data in Emerson's system of efficiency. His contention was that no manager could know how well things are operating unless there are records that show standards for materials, material prices, standard and actual wage rates, and so on. Then and only then can the manager monitor actual performance and determine the degree of efficiency compared to standards.

The seventh principle was "dispatching." Dispatching was the term adopted to describe that aspect of planning that involves scheduling. The terminology no doubt results from Emerson's extensive involvement with the railroad industry. However, the eighth principle included "standards and schedules." Standards and schedules may be a matter of precise mathematics, or they may defy quantification. Both are important in building and maintaining efficiency. "Standardized conditions" was the ninth principle. Often it is tempting to skip the present and plan strictly for the future while depending on past techniques and rules of thumb. Emerson stated that even in great American industrial firms conditions imposed by an ignorant and inefficient past are accepted, schedules are toned down, and painful effort crowds out intelligent control (Emerson, 1913, p. 291).

The "standardization of operations" is the tenth principle of efficiency. Good results are never achieved by chance. The standardization of operations makes good outcomes a possibility. High levels of efficiency, according to Emerson, require only proper intelligence, spirit, and organization. The eleventh principle stated that merely having standard practice instructions is not enough. They must be "written." These standard practice instructions are the permanent laws and practices of the plant. They offer the promise of organizational learning, the opportunity to become progressively better in performing the tasks. Unfortunately this is time-consuming, hard work, and the American weakness is to be discouraged by difficulties and retreat instead of overcoming troubles and moving forward.

The twelfth and final principle is "efficiency reward." This is a reward that enables the worker to see and grasp, while the work is being performed, how important

---

▲ Box 3-7
DON'T MESS WITH MY FIFTY

Turner Brothers Trucking barely survived the 1980s. Of Turner's competitors, 75 percent did not survive. For a Houston, Texas, company whose primary business related to oil drilling and refining, pay cuts of 10 percent and layoffs of 70 percent of the workforce was the price of survival. As the economy started to recover, Turner Brothers decided a pay-for-performance system was a *must* and the place to begin was with safety.

Several years ago, a manager held a meeting with 25 employees (truck drivers, crane operators, and field supervisors), put a $1250 check on the table, and said: "If we have less than $300 total losses this month including injuries, cargo damage, driver accidents, etc., the check is yours to divide equally among yourselves. If you go 3 months in a row with less than $300 in losses, we will double the bonus to $100 per person. However, it is all or nothing."

The company estimates that for every dollar it pays in the safety bonus it saves 4 dollars. Most of the work teams have received between 3 and 10 monthly bonus checks, and the company has saved proportionately in workers' compensation and insurance claims.

There are 4 general guidelines to aid in receiving the safety bonus awards:

1. *Personal safety:* Don't have an accident yourself. If you do, it costs everyone $50.

2. *Awareness to others:* If you see an unsafe act—speak up! Tell the other person, "don't mess with my fifty."

3. *Self-control:* Don't get mad if someone says to you, "don't mess with my fifty."

4. *Team work benefits everyone:* Work as a team to earn the $50.

Source: Ritzky (1995).

his or her job is to the corporation. An efficiency reward is paid for individual excellence in the area for which the individual is accountable. The best standard of efficiency is not the maximum muscular effort for a short time but a combination of mental and physical efforts that leave the worker in the best condition possible to make future contributions (Emerson, 1913, p. 363).

When all these principles are practiced together, the outcome is the elimination of wastes. Dreaded inefficiency can exist for only one or two reasons. First, it is possible that in a given plant the principles are simply not known. Second, they may be known but not practiced. In either event efficiency suffers. If the principles are not used, efficiency is not possible. Nor is it possible if the principles are not known. They must be known and applied in real settings.

Emerson believed work should be a blessing rather than a curse. It should be a pleasure, a game, not merely a task. He ended his book with the observation that a person of supreme ability is the one who can create and control an organization founded on and using principles to attain and maintain deals.

Other Contributors

In addition to Emerson there were other engineers interested in efficiency. The theory of efficiency was emerging even if it was doing so at a slower rate than practice. Two of the more important contributors were Morris Cooke and Wallace Clark. The former was responsible for applying concepts of efficiency to organizations outside the industrial sector. The latter was responsible for taking and sending many of the ideas of American scientific management into the international arena.

Morris L. Cooke: Municipal and University Management

Morris L. Cooke was one of only four men Taylor acknowledged as true followers and authorized to teach his system. Cooke was born in 1872 and was trained as an engineer at Lehigh University. Even before he met Taylor he questioned inefficiencies in industry and attempted to apply scientific methods to the elimination of waste.

Taylor was duly impressed with the young engineer when they met and recommended him as being capable of major consulting responsibilities. In fact, he was commissioned, at Taylor's recommendation, to study the American Society of Mechanical Engineers itself. Again, Taylor recommended Cooke as the man to study the efficiency of higher education administration under the sponsorship of the Carnegie Foundation for the Advancement of Teaching (Arnold, 1966). The comprehensive report published in 1910 under the title *Academic and Industrial Efficiency* provided its author with great notoriety.

Predictably the scrutiny of an efficiency engineer was not welcomed by professors and college administrators. It told them what none wanted to hear—their committee decision-making structure was cumbersome, their tenure system protected too many unproductive colleagues, and their departments were uncooperative. His recommendations called for the establishment of "student credit hours" as the unit of efficiency measurement, the rewarding of professors on the basis of efficiency, and a university system that looked at itself more critically rather than believing it was somehow beyond the criticisms of the society that supported it (Trombley, 1954).

Cooke was not through! When he finished with the university, another opportunity presented itself with the help of Taylor. In 1911, the new mayor of Philadelphia invited Taylor to become his director of public works. He refused but recommended Cooke, who was happy to receive a chance to try out his ideas on efficiency in the public sector. In his book *Our Cities Awake* (1918), Cooke presented his case for the improvement of municipal management. In 4 years his management system saved over $1 million on garbage collection alone, and he personally sued the Philadelphia Electric Company in an attempt to force it to reduce rates. The out-of-court settlement resulted in refunds of over $1 million and a retroactive payment of nearly $200,000 to the city. The tradition of productivity in the public sector, while mixed in terms of outcome, has emerged again in recent years.

When World War I erupted, Cooke proposed to Secretary of War Newton Baker that an efficiency organization was needed to ensure that the war was managed scientifically." The secretary adopted the suggestion, and the little known efficiency engineer became a prominent figure in Washington, D.C. At one point President Hoover appointed him to a committee to eliminate waste in industry—another familiar member of the committee, as noted previously, was Harrington Emerson (Drury, 1922).

Cooke's contribution to the efficiency movement was significant. Until Cooke came on the scene, manufacturing industries were the only targets of scientific man-

---

▲ Box 3-8
TOP 5 BY 95

What do you do when you are a century old and are losing protection as a public monopoly? This was the situation facing the Arizona Public Service Company (APS), one of the nation's largest utilities with revenues of almost $2 billion and 7,000 employees. In an environment favoring deregulation, APS found itself in a competitive situation for which it was unprepared. When it completed benchmarking studies relative to competitors, one thing became clear—it required more employees to get the job done than its competitors, and that spelled disaster.

The APS engaged in a series of layoffs to bring its staffing levels in line and invested significant time and energy in retraining and reorienting the survivors. Emphasis was placed on building an efficiency-oriented culture that could compete and even prosper in a new and demanding economic reality. The success of the process was recognized when the APS was awarded the Edison Award, the most prestigious award for achievement in the power industry.

Source: Demarie and Keats (1996).

agement. He applied the same principles to higher education and government at all levels and was convinced that principles of management that were applicable to business were applicable to other fields.

Wallace Clark: Efficiency Goes on Tour

Wallace Clark was born in 1880 and graduated from the University of Cincinnati. He worked in various clerical positions and became the private secretary to the President of Remington Typewriter. He was associated with Henry Gantt's consulting firm before opening his own practice in 1920. Clark traveled extensively in Poland, England, and France applying the principles of scientific management (Smiddy, 1958).

Clark was an admirer of Gantt and his graphical planning or scheduling techniques (Peterson, 1986). Clark believed the Gantt chart would be useful in controlling Russia's "five-year plans" (Clark, 1922). He was associated with people like Walter Polakov, who was instrumental in taking many concepts of scientific management to the U.S.S.R. Clark also reflected many of the ideas about the human being that characterized Gantt. He worked freely with labor unions to improve industrial efficiency, as did Cooke. However, Clark will always be remembered first and foremost for his work in taking the concepts of scientific management and industrial efficiency to many of the nations of Europe.

One of the most distinguished awards given in management today is the Wallace Clark International Management Award for distinguished contributions to scientific management in the international field. Cooke carried scientific management out of the factory and into the university and city hall. Clark took the same message over the sea, and in doing so the circle of groups and people knowing American management systems grew even larger.

Implications and Conclusions

Efficiency is as important today in the sterile production laboratories at Intel as it was a century ago in the smokey steel mills of Gary, Indiana, or the automated factories in Detroit. Granted, efficiency may be realized and developed in different ways, but as long as there are competitive product markets, producers will survive only if they are reasonably efficient. They have to do things right.

If America is to regain and retain its role of world industrial leadership, efficiency must be the top priority of today's managers. There are, of course, other challenges. Some of these may be even greater, such as "doing the right things," as we will see in another chapter. However, global enterprise is a competitive arena, and efficiency is an essential component of competitiveness. Other countries, particularly selected areas, have proven their intention and determination to compete with American firms in their own "ballpark." To date, many nations, such as Japan, Korea, and Hong Kong, have experienced remarkable success. The developing interests in "returning to the basics" of efficient and high-quality manufacturing, however, indicates a renewed determination on the part of the United States and her managers to maintain the hard earned position of number one.

In this chapter several important findings relative to efficiency and its limitations have been discussed. Some of the more important are:

1. Science, not experience, is essential to the development and maintenance of efficiency. Apprenticeships and mentoring are important, but can perpetuate inefficient and customary ways of doing things.
2. Management is ultimately an art, but it can benefit from the application of scientific methods.
3. In order to successfully apply science to management issues an attitude or philosophy is essential. Merely applying techniques to organizational problems will not result in efficiency.
4. Scale economies and specialization are useful concepts for building efficiency, but they can also result in conditions that discourage efficiency.
5. Principles of efficiency such as goal setting, objective standards, and efficiency rewards are consistent among early and contemporary writers and appear to be applicable in a wide range of organizational settings.

Questions for Discussion

1 Is efficiency the "essence" of scientific management? Would the movement have been better served to have been labeled "efficiency management?" Why or why not?

2 Do you think Taylor is unfairly criticized for borrowing excessively from his counterparts? Is there any arguing that he at least popularized the management movement?

3 What role did the rate cases play in assisting the public in understanding the potential contributions scientific management could make to the management of industrial organizations?

4 Do you agree with Emerson that if human institutions were as efficient as nature, poverty and other human ills would be eliminated? Explain.

5 Is it possible to accurately characterize national "gifts" such as German ingenuity, French practicality, and American individuality, or is this simply a form of stereotyping?

6 Is the concept of line and staff meaningful today? Is it possible that in high-technology societies we have lost any real distinction between these groups? Explain.

7 Emerson argued that the role of the strong executive is to control, adjust, and harmonize operations. Compare this with the more contemporary view of the executive as visionary leader. Are they in conflict?

8 Can management really be scientific? Is there any evidence that organizations with natural scientific orientations are better managed than those without such an orientation?

9 Do you think educational institutions and public organizations can ever be made truly efficient? Explain you response.

10 What is meant by scientific management as a "mental revolution?" Why is technique in the absence of philosophy dangerous?

The Challenge of Change: Doing the Right Things

"Efficiency is the product of information, knowledge, and understanding; effectiveness is the product of wisdom . . . By taking long- as well as short-run consequences into account, it prevents the future being sacrificed for the present."

Russell L. Ackoff
The Democratic Corporation (1994)

Early management started with a search for "absolute" principles, and that is as it should be. The legitimacy of a field of research and, ultimately, practice is not built on "what if," "in most cases," and "under certain circumstances." Moreover, the early contributors to the field were engineers trained to look for order in events and the "one best way" of doing everything from laying bricks to building large corporations (Kanigel, 1997). Even more important, legitimacy required the application of respectable science and that precise, normative guidelines be offered to improve management action. When we go to the doctor, we like for her to tell us precisely what is wrong. Hopefully, the information will make us secure in the knowledge that we are in good health. However, even if the news is bad, we can seek a cure for a definite and known ailment.

Corporate executives expect the same from management theory, and employees expect assurance from the boss that things are under control. If the CEO is not confident with the use of the best available knowledge, employees are justifiably nervous about their future and that of the organization. We respect those who know the answers, even if they are wrong on occasion. We want and deserve answers from high-paid consultants, doctors, and lawyers, although we know reality does not always lend itself to precise responses.

Organizational Efficiency and Effectiveness

Efficiency has been discussed in previous chapters. Indeed, we noted that scientific management was, in effect, about efficiency and doing things right. Change certainly occurred, and people living in the late 19th and early 20th centuries probably thought the rate of change was mystifying. It was, as with other generations, unprecedented. Automobiles, airplanes, factories, and telephones were changing their world and ours forever. The management problem, however, was efficiency, and those firms that did things right were the winners. Today, the management problem is more complex.

An Early View of Efficiency and Effectiveness

Being and becoming a manager is hard work. Unfortunately, management is made even more difficult by the paradoxes and inconsistencies (Handy, 1994; Harris, 1996; Mitroff, 1987). One of the most perplexing and recurring paradoxes of management is the delicate balance that must be crafted between efficiency and effectiveness (Worthy, 1994).

The importance of this paradox was recognized by Chester Barnard (1938) but organizations as cooperative systems resolved the inconsistency. To Barnard, efficiency and effectiveness were the essence of cooperative systems. He argued that people voluntarily participate in organizations only as long as they think the benefits gained from participation and the conformance to organizational norms outweigh the loss of personal freedom such participation requires. Barnard called the satisfaction of individual goals *efficiency*.

However, organizational goals also require satisfaction, and the accomplishment of a common purpose in the cooperative system he called *effectiveness*. Efficiency and effectiveness were iterative. The more organizational members were satisfied (efficiency), the more they would contribute to the organization. The more effective the organization, the more it was able to distribute things that satisfied the goals of individuals. Group performance and individual satisfaction were mutually attainable in Barnard's view, and the distribution of additional rewards made a resolution of the paradox possible (Scott, 1992).

The Management Paradox in Our Times

Not everyone defines efficiency and effectiveness in terms that make them complementary elements of cooperative systems. Indeed, a more common view presents these two desirable organizational realities, stability and change, as paradoxical if not conflicting managerial outcomes. These equally desirable outcomes present managers with a most perplexing dilemma, which has been addressed often in management writings.

Perhaps the most useful way to think of the paradox of stability and change is to think of the responsibility of managers over time (Laverty, 1996). Imagine the predicament of managers when they receive their budgets for a new fiscal year. Their responsibility is to use the allocated resources as efficiently as possible. Things must be done right—procedures must be followed, rules must be enforced, and accountability must be maintained. In reality, however, the budget is no sooner approved than things begin to change. Opportunities arise that were not anticipated. A new technology becomes available, or a court case is settled that changes the "rules of the game"

▲ **Box 4-1**

THE BUREAUCRATIC DILEMMA

Former vice president of Sears, Roebuck and Company and advisor to numerous corporations James C. Worthy outlined the nature of the efficiency/effectiveness paradox in a memorandum to the CEO of Control Data Corporation. Worthy referred to this paradox as the *bureaucratic dilemma.* According to him, organizations are inherently conservative because a degree of stability is necessary for survival. The problem is maintaining a balance between the entrepreneurial spirit and stability.

Organizations usually begin with an entrepreneurial spirit; but as they grow, specialize, and become more professional, they acquire more structure and seek stability to deal with operational realities. This evolving bureaucracy takes on a life of its own and can smother the entrepreneurial spirit. Unless controlled, stability mutates by imperceptible degrees into rigidity, which eventually causes inability to change. The larger and older organizations become, the greater the danger of entrenchment and debilitating bureaucracy.

Source: Worthy (1994, chap. 14).

---

in the industry. Managers and organizations cannot compete successfully if they hide behind the budget categories and blindly adhere to policies that put them at a competitive disadvantage.

A similar problem exists at the organizational and top executive levels. If the philosophy of the organization is efficiency at all costs, managers are discouraged from taking the risks and making the investments necessary to ensure organizational survival over the long run. This problem is nowhere more evident than in "growth companies." Wall Street demands that growth companies "make their numbers" relative to quarterly earnings. Even Intel can suffer if quarterly earnings numbers are below estimates. However, the key to survival at Intel and other high-technology organizations is not efficiency and doing things right. To the contrary, it is effectiveness or doing the right things. In order to be effective, these firms must invest large amounts in research and development and product innovation as well as take risks that would be excessive for more traditional firms.

Unfortunately, research and development, product innovation, and experimentation are risky endeavors, and funds diverted for these uses affect the bottom line adversely in the short run. Only the most courageous leader is willing to make the investments necessary for long-run adaptability and change and accept the criticisms that are sure to come from the "Street" (Chamberlain, 1968). In order to understand the extent of the efficiency/effectiveness dilemma, we have to understand its origin, and such an understanding takes us to the very nature of organization theory.

▲ **Box 4-2**

GENUINELY DOING "THE RIGHT THINGS"

In the northern hemisphere the average company survives less than 20 years. Multinational corporations survive, on the average, less than half a century. Very few companies survive for 100 years and virtually none exist for 700 years like Stora, a Swedish company that was founded in the 13th century. Other exceptions include Sumitomo (500 years old) and DuPont (more than 100 years old). In 1983, Royal Dutch Shell commissioned a study of companies that were more than 100 years old. Thirty companies in North America, Europe, and Japan were identified, and 27 had histories with sufficient details for further study.

These *living companies* had 4 key characteristics: (1) sensitivity to their environments; (2) cohesion and identity; (3) tolerance and decentralization; and (4) conservative financing. The authors found that the primary reason for the high mortality rate among most companies is the tendency of management to focus too narrowly on economic efficiency. Specifically, "companies die because their managers focus on the economic activity of producing goods and services, and they forget that their organization's true nature is that of a community of humans." Living companies understand that they cannot control their environment so they learn to adapt to it.

Source: De Geus (1997).

The One Best Way

Efficiency of individual effort, as noted previously, resulted from carefully structured and specialized labor. Specialization of individual work was so successful in creating efficiency that is was inevitable that the logic was extended to organizations. Specialization and structure provided order, and order enabled control. The key to organizational efficiency was to derive the same degree of control over organizational processes as managers had been so successful in doing with regard to the work of individuals. Again, science provided the answer.

Early Concepts of Organizational Design

Many of the concepts of organization practiced in today's modern corporations emerged during the scientific management period. We need not review all the principles to understand what early writers were saying, but we do need to examine a few of the more important ones.

Fayol (1949) popularized a number of organizational concepts but never felt comfortable calling them principles in the scientific sense. Mooney and Reiley were less timid. The revised edition of *Onward Industry* (1931), for example, was entitled *The Principles of Organization* (1947). Most writers agree that Mooney, the President of General Motors Export Corporation, provided the primary ideas on management and organization found in the book and Reiley, a "historian turned executive," according to Wren (1994) provided the descriptions of coordination in historical context. Reiley remains somewhat of a "mystery man" and his contributions appear even less evident in the latter revision.

In *The Principles of Organization*, Mooney and Reiley discussed four basic principles of organization—the coordinative, scalar, functional, and staff phase of functionalism principles. The coordinative principle was the first and "contained all the others." It stated: *Coordination is the orderly arrangement of group effort to provide unity of action in pursuit of a common purpose.* The importance of this principle is underscored by the fact that it virtually encompasses our entire definition of management.

Whereas Fayol thought of coordination as a different function, Mooney and Reiley viewed it as the essence of all the principles. Coordination begins at the top, goes down through the organization, and results in the scalar principle, whereby managerial authority and responsibility are graduated down the entire organization. The scalar principle involves the grading of duties, not according to the work but according to the authority and responsibility of different managers. The effect is a hierarchy, or the vertical specialization of labor. The horizontal division of work (specialization) is referred to as functionalism, where tasks are divided into different duties.

Another important principle was the "staff phase of functionalism." Early organizational design theory devoted significant attention to the idea of staff. Staff units in organizations are created to give advice or counsel to the line. The staff is expected to provide useful creative ideas to line managers (the managers who supervise the actual work of the organization such as manufacturing and marketing). However, staff should exercise only the "authority of good ideas." The line should always command.

Refinement and Integration of Early Ideas

By the mid-20th century, management thought was diverse, often conflicting, and disorganized. It was in need of integration. The ideas of several people were circulating around the best known companies. There seemed to be some logic to what people were saying and doing, but there was also confusion. Two individuals who attempted to make some sense of the confusion were Luther Gulick (1947) and Lyndall Urwick (1944).

Gulick, born in 1892, served as President of the Institute of Public Administration from 1923 to 1961. He was an international consultant to organizations such as the World Health Organization, the United Nations, and UNESCO. Gulick held many important government assignments, including membership on the War Production Board, on the U.S. Reparations staffs in Moscow, Potsdam, Tokyo, and Manila, and on the President's Committee on Administrative Management. His best known work, *Papers on the Science of Administration* (1947), coedited with Lyndall Urwick, is a collection of papers by well-known management writers of the day.

The *Papers* represent, in one volume, some of the most comprehensive statements of the beliefs of the early organization theorists. As with Mooney and Reiley, the overriding principle was coordination, and organization was seen as one important way of achieving it. Since work must be specialized, the organization must provide a mechanism for coordinating different organizational units. Coordination is most effectively attained when specific organizational principles are observed. The "one-master" principle, for example, reinforced the idea of unity of command—no person should have more than one boss at a single time. Also, the span of control, or the number of employees one manager can effectively supervise must be regulated. Urwick (1944) believed the number should be no greater than five or six people whose work is interrelated. The span might, however, be increased through the use of an "assistant to" position.

In Gulick's view, a staff specialist could be used to improve the technical efficiency of a manager's performance even though it should be recognized that specialized staff, by their very nature, tend to be narrow and myopic. Therefore, it is important to recognize the limitations of staff and not allow them to assume inappropriate authority. For example, the role of the legal counsel in the corporation is to provide expert advice on legal matters, not to make decisions. At times, and in an increasingly large number of industries, there is a danger that staff experts will become too powerful since it is the line decision maker who is ultimately responsible for managerial actions.

One of the most interesting discussions presented in *Papers* relates to the vertical and horizontal organization of different departments. It is argued that the vertical division of departments (hierarchy) relates to the purpose of the organization while the horizontal division of departments (specialization) is designed according to the process necessary to accomplish the purpose. The purpose of IBM, for example, is the manufacturing and marketing of products and services relating to information technology. The process of accomplishing this purpose or mission, however, requires a large array of units, such as manufacturing, sales, systems design, and personnel. The managerial challenge is to weave the "tangled fabric" and make the purpose and the process work together for the overall welfare of the organization.

Cornerstone Concepts of Organization

Out of the collective work of individuals such as Taylor, Fayol, Mooney, Reiley, and others there gradually emerged several important "cornerstone" concepts of early design theory. The four most important ones are summarized next.

Division of Work, or Specialization of Labor

The importance of this concept has been discussed in previous chapters, yet it remains one of the most fundamental of the cornerstone concepts. When it is applied vertically in an organization, it relates to hierarchy. If concerns about authority and responsibility are introduced, the scalar principle comes into play. When it is applied horizontally, it involves functions or tasks.

Departmentalization, or the Division of Organizational Function

Organizations can be departmentalized in different ways depending on their purpose and other factors. Functional departments such as production, marketing, and finance are established to allow each unit to concentrate on some aspect of the business and in so doing efficiently accomplish the organizational mission. Departments may be established on the basis of the clients or customers served. Health care organizations frequently organize based on whether the patients require hospitalization (inpatient) or merely a visit to the doctor and a return trip home (outpatient). Departments may also be established according to geographical regions within the United States or they may be global in scope (Gulick, 1947).

Span of Control

A recurring theme in classical design theory was, "how many people can a supervisor properly supervise?" Urwick, as noted before, thought the magic number was five or six. Others argued that it was ten or twelve. Regardless of the exact number, this was an important issue in the development of classical management thought that is not often discussed in the management literature of today.

Unity of Command

Gulick called it "one master" while Fayol preferred unity of command. The idea in both cases was that a person should have only one boss at any given time. To design a system otherwise is to risk reductions in effective coordination. More about this principle and institutional violations of the concept will be discussed later in this chapter. Other principles, such as unity of direction and delegation of authority, were considered important by early writers. Regardless of the exact number of concepts and principles, it is important to note that these writers attempted to provide a view of organization that was precise, rational, and consistent. The goal was admirable, but the effect was confusing.

Principles or Proverbs?

Principles and normative concepts specify guidelines for behavior and in doing so propose relatively universal and inflexible ways of doing things. While such an approach gives us the feeling of certainty, it greatly restricts our ability to reconcile problems of logic and consistency that develop within the framework of normative organization theory.

Herbert Simon (1946) looked critically at the concepts discussed as cornerstone aspects of early theory and concluded that none of them survived his analysis "in very good shape." Instead of unequivocal principles, Simon found "a set of two or more mutually incompatible principles apparently equally applicable to the administrative situation." Anderson and Duncan (1977) provided a similar analysis of paradoxes as-

---

▲ **Box 4-3**

"THE BRIGHTEST STAR IN THE MANAGEMENT FIRMAMENT"

Peter Drucker's description of Mary Parker Follett as the "brightest star" illustrates the significance of her contributions to management. However, Follett was skeptical of the absolute prescriptions of management theory. She lived in the midst of the influence of Taylor, Fayol, Gantt, and others engaged in the search for principles, yet she resisted the domination of these ideas. Her *contra* thinking was more akin to modern theorists than to the management opinion leaders of her day. That alone qualified her as a prophet.

Follett presented a view of organizations where authority was based more on knowledge than position, where cooperation was valued more than competition, where the power of teams was appropriately recognized and the value of the individual was respected. A management discipline searching for absolutes was not receptive to the law of the situation; executives consumed with labor unrest were not interested in "power with" rather than "authority over;" and employees seeking economic security could not imagine participating in decision making. The makings of all these were present, and one cannot help wondering with Henry Mintzberg what management would be like "if we had spent most of this century heeding Follett instead of Fayol?"

Source: Graham (1995).

---

sociated with different "principles" of administration. In many, if not most, cases there was a suggestion that the "situation" operated in a unique way to complicate the application of the principle under review. For this reason, the absolute orientation and the search for the one best way have given way to the more relative or situational view of contemporary organization design theory.

Contingency Theory of Organization

George Lombard (1971) argued that a fundamental change occurred in American society in the 1920s. Prior to this time people seemed content with absolute prescriptions such as the ones providing the foundation for early organization theory and practice. Reality appeared simpler then, and people were more willing to accept traditional explanations. Myths, like science, are designed to help us understand events and make sense out of our surroundings. If the latter could not explain things, the former would suffice. People, after all, make sense of reality retrospectively, and absolutes had worked well for thousands of years (Weick, 1995). Human beings understand events by framing them in terms of the previous events and environments they have experienced. It is no surprise, then, that the first theory of organization would be built on a search for absolute principles.

In more recent times people seem less willing to accept simple, universal, and sometimes authoritarian values. In ethics, questions are more "situational." The fact that something is right or wrong for me in this situation does not imply, to situational proponents, that the same is right or wrong for you in another. Even in medicine, physics, and education, absolute solutions to historical problems are no longer unanimously accepted. It is little wonder, as Lombard noted, that a situational view of the postindustrial society emerged in management. World War I, the Great Depression, and unprecedented technological progress demanded a different view of reality.

Early Doubts

In management, skeptics were present even before Lombard recognized them. One of the most articulate was Henry Sturgis Dennison, a most unusual executive. He was born in 1877 and graduated from Harvard before joining the family business, the Dennison Manufacturing Company. He became its president in 1917 and served in that capacity for 35 years. In *Organization Engineering* (1931), Dennison stated that organizations are composed of 4 interacting forces: (1) members (the strength of any organization); (2) operating measures (policies and procedures); (3) structural relationships; and (4) purposes or goals. Structural relationships are our concern in this chapter.

Dennison, it must be remembered, was the product of the "absolute" view of organizational design theory. He agreed that organizations should have a definite structure. However, he insisted that principles of organization are good only insofar as they assist in building organizations that are better (more efficient and more effective) than would be the case using trial and error. An organization's structure should reflect its purpose and scope of operations, but it must always be adaptable. Adaptability was not a key to understanding in early design theory.

In Dennison's view, departmentalization was a necessary and practical way of dealing with the inability of people to contend with increasingly complex tasks. One way to simplify complexity was to organize activities functionally. Dennison recognized the need for different degrees of centralization. When production is regular and uniform, decision making can be centralized. When it is irregular and highly specialized, it should be decentralized, with decisions being made by those nearest to the changing circumstances. He understood and appreciated the need for staff advice and even advocated the use of committees as a means of coordination. However, it was his insights into situational factors that have been greatly neglected in retrospective evaluations of his work.

We get the first hint of "Dennison the contingency theorist" in his discussion of cross contacts. This is similar to the idea proposed previously as "Fayol's bridge" or the "gang plank principle." It also relates to Follett's idea of cross functioning or the violation of the scalar principle in the interest of faster and better horizontal communication. The way Dennison presented the idea is intriguing. He maintained that

▲ **Box 4-4**

WHERE TRADITION SUCCEEDS

In modern management writers are inclined to depict progressive organizations as experimental enclaves led by radical and somewhat eccentric visionaries. Often this is the case. However, traditional organizations with courageous leaders can change in a more evolutionary and orderly manner. Knight-Ridder, Inc., has demonstrated how an apparently conservative newspaper organization can craft a future by aggressively moving into on-line business information services and creatively experimenting with newspaper formats without becoming strange and excessively experimental. In the process, it has preserved the decision processes, structures, and corporate values that have always accounted for its success.

Organizational change at Knight-Ridder is based on 3 important principles: (1) copious information gathering—due diligence is critical and alternative actions should be evaluated critically by objective information as well as the emotions each action provokes; (2) consensus seeking—share information early, be sure everyone is on board; and (3) nonhierarchical group process—everyone's opinion and input are important. Changes occur through consensus building, generation and sharing of large amounts of information, and continuous examination of underlying assumptions. Knight-Ridder has succeeded by acquiring information, using information, and understanding how to learn.

Source: Wishart, Elam, and Robey (1996).

since all contacts cannot be perfect, communication must be adapted to the physical and psychological difficulties of "each situation." This almost defensive way of justifying cross functioning as a response to imperfect communication revealed his devotion, in principle, to the scalar chain.

The situational theme is developed in greater detail with the introduction of the need for "continuous reorganization." Continuous reorganization demands that the firm constantly rebuild its structure to meet changing environmental realities. The "structure suitable for today may not be suitable for tomorrow." Therefore, reorganization and renewal should be a continuous evolution, and all units should maintain a balance so that one does not become so strong at the expense of others that the purpose of the entire organization is compromised. Dennison believed change or "situations in flux" was not the exception but the rule. Change was not the abnormal but the normal state of affairs. Absolute prescriptions suitable for all situations simply would not do. The stage was set for a more systematic analysis of the relationship between organizations and their environment.

Research at South Essex

It was bound to happen. The growing discontentment with absolute principles forced many managers and researchers to look for other answers to organizational problems. Interestingly, researchers in England were busy working on the solution. The search shifted again to English factories for answers to management's perplexing questions.

We began this book with an Englishman and a Scotsman, Babbage and Ure, examining the factory system created by the Industrial Revolution. In the 1950s the British were again taking the lead by critically examining the way dominant themes in management had progressed for 50 years. They did not like what they saw, so Joan Woodward, an industrial sociologist at the Imperial College of Science and Technology, decided to examine the efficacy of management theory. Specifically, Woodward established a research program to test the usefulness of concepts such as span of control, unity of command, hierarchy, and decentralization. When her research began, she headed a team at the South Essex College of Technology. Thus, the name of the studies. The most comprehensive report of the results is given in *Industrial Organization* (1965).

Initially, the team focused on a narrow range of issues such as the dichotomy between executive and advisory responsibilities and the relationship between line and staff managers at different organizational levels. First, over 200 firms were surveyed. These businesses differed in terms of size and product line. Later a decision was made to drop respondents with fewer than 100 employees, thereby reducing the sample to 110 and eventually to 100.

In order to assess the degree of success of the firms in the sample, Woodward collected information from annual reports and financial statements for 5 years. Using a variety of indicators, she was able to classify participating organizations as: (1) average performers, (2) below average performers, and (3) above average performers. The data were analyzed to see if all these average performers were adhering to the classical principles of management. They were not! The results were disappointing. However, the South Essex researchers were not easily discouraged. They had a large database and a sound hypothesis so, almost automatically, they turned to technology.

It was discovered that the firms in the sample could be grouped according to the technologies they employed. First, there were unit or small-batch production firms, which manufactured products to customer specifications, produced prototypes, or fabricated large equipment in stages. A second technological category consisted of large-batch and mass production firms. Many of these companies used assembly-line technology to produce the large batches. A typical product manufactured by mass production was blocks for internal combustion engines. The third technology was classified process or flow production. Examples were oil refining and chemical production. Some companies used a combination of all three technologies.

When the sample was subdivided according to technologies, meaningful relationships emerged. The median number of levels in the hierarchy, for example, increased as the technologies changed from customized small batches to mass production and eventually to continuous processing. The average span of control, as we would expect, responded in the opposite direction. Whereas the number of levels in the hierarchy varied directly with technological complexity, the size of the span of control varied inversely. This suggested that the "small spans of control and long lines of communication" in process industries made the firms appear peaked and narrow. In unit or small batch production firms the pyramid, by contrast, was short and broadly based (p. 53).

Interestingly, the span of control for the chief executive officers provided an exception. In small batch firms the median span of control for the CEO was 4, in large-batch firms it was 7, and in process production it was 10. According to Woodward, this resulted from a change in the "role and function" of the executives as the technological complexity increased. Management by committees, for example, was more common in process than in less complex systems. The CEO in process firms seemed to function more as a chair of a decision-making group than as an autocratic decision maker (p. 53).

There was also a link between the complexity of a firm's technology and the "relative size" of the management group. As technology became more complex (from unit to process), the ratio of managers and supervisors to nonsupervisory personnel increased. This finding supported the view that as technology becomes more complex, so does the need for management and managers.

Woodward, after examining the relationships between organizational factors and technological complexity, introduced some important factors relating to business success. First, the firms that were successful in each technological category possessed organizational characteristics that "clustered" around the median of the group. Those firms that were below average exhibited extremes relative to these same factors. In other words, companies that were above average in success in the unit or small-batch categories seemed to be average when it came to measures such as the number of levels in the hierarchy, span of control, and administrative ratios. The same was true of successful firms where technological complexity was greater (pp. 68–69).

Second, the findings varied by technological category. In the most successful large-batch firms the duties and responsibilities of managers were defined precisely and written on paper. In process firms, surprisingly, this type of formality was more often associated with lack of success. In fact, the successful firms in mass production industries more often displayed findings that were consistent with the "prescriptions" of classical management. Perhaps the tendency of most people to think of mass production as the "typical system of modern industry" explains the link between success and conformity to traditional management theory in this industrial environment (p.71).

The publication of Woodward's studies did much to encourage and legitimize questions and doubts about the early management literature. Woodward clearly illustrated that there is "no one best way" to organize. Success in different technological categories was obviously not determined by organizational practices or structure. If it were, all successful firms would look the same—at least on the organization chart.

Testing the Theory

Attempts were made in England and the United States to replicate and extend Woodward's studies. One of the most important extensions relates to the study of service as well as manufacturing organizations by what has become known as the Aston Group at the University of Aston in Birmingham, England.

The Aston researchers studied 52 organizations and classified them according to their work-flow integration. This variable related to the extent to which a firm's equipment was automated, the extent to which knowledge, skills, and equipment were rigid rather than adaptable, and the ability of management to objectively and precisely evaluate the quality of the work (Hickson, Pugh, and Pheysey, 1969; Pugh, Hickson, Hinnings, and Turner, 1968). Not surprisingly the researchers found that manufacturing firms generally have higher work-flow integration, and bureaucratic structures are positively associated with the degree of work-flow integration. In other words, manufacturing firms were more bureaucratic than service organizations. The findings of the Aston Group generally reinforced Woodward's findings.

Another study involved 55 firms in Minneapolis in the late 1960s (Zwerman, 1970). In general, the Minneapolis study reinforced many of Woodward's findings. For example, there were no consistent correlates of organizational characteristics and business success. This study also confirmed that the prescriptions of early organization design theory were more applicable to the environment of mass production firms. Finally, and most important, the Minneapolis study reinforced the finding that organizational structures are greatly influenced by the technology of the firm.

There were also findings that were not reinforcing. Span of control in Minneapolis displayed no relationship to technological complexity. This, in fact, was the only finding that directly contradicted Woodward (p. 146). In addition to this study, historical and theoretical analyses have underscored the importance of environmental factors on internal operations.

Alfred Chandler (1962) presented a historical critique of almost 80 corporations while focusing specifically on the organizational evolution of DuPont, General Motors, Standard Oil of New Jersey, and Sears, Roebuck and Company. The historical evolution of these companies illustrated four important stages in the life cycle of organizations and the relationship between these stages and the larger environment.

First, firms expand and accumulate resources. Organization structure follows functional lines and leadership is autocratic. Second, resources are "rationalized" and growth becomes selective as efforts are made to improve the efficiency of operations. The third stage involves expansion into new markets to ensure the effective use of resources. Finally, new structures are developed to optimize operations and ensure effective planning. Firms, at this stage, become more decentralized. Clearly, as the strategies of DuPont, General Motors, Standard Oil, and Sears, Roebuck changed, their organization structure had to respond. The need for strategic change, as Chandler noted, is driven by environmental changes. Thus, when the environment changes, the organization's strategy must change, and this impacts directly on organizational design.

Next, Chandler divided his sample of almost 80 firms into nine industry groups. Some were essentially stable, as was the case with metals and materials, and did not change to the extent of the four focal firms. Other industries such as rubber and petroleum changed in the direction of decentralization, but not as completely as DuPont, General Motors, Standard Oil, and Sears, Roebuck, while firms in industries such as power machinery and chemicals displayed very similar evolutionary patterns. Therefore, Chandler's historical analysis supported the contention that environmental forces influence decision making significantly—organizationally and strategically.

Whereas Chandler (1962) provided historical validation, Thompson (1967) offered a theoretical framework for understanding the relationship between environment and organization. In *Organizations in Action* (1967) Thompson illustrated the difference between closed and open organizational systems. The former seeks certainty and incorporates only those factors that are associated with goal accomplishment. The latter explicitly recognizes the interdependence between the organization and its environment. The open system attempts to establish homeostasis or self-stabilization in its relationship to external, environmental factors.

Thompson skillfully argued the managerial necessity of ensuring the accomplishment of rational, task-related goals in the short run while remaining flexible and adaptive to environmentally induced change over the long run. In accomplishing the first, efficiency and certainty are emphasized while the latter involves "coping with uncertainty." Often in highly dynamic industries special units are needed for purposes of boundary spanning or facilitating the firm's interaction with its environment. Ultimately, Thompson declared, organizations exist as agencies of their environments. This view requires at least a brief exploration of one important contemporary theme that has gained attention in contemporary management literature.

Ecologically Sustainable Organizations

It is probably safe to say that early management writers, if they thought about it at all, viewed the environment as a challenge—something to attack and overcome. They certainly did not entertain Thompson's view that organizations are agents of the environment. Few could imagine a natural environment that would not sustain economic development. The possibility of ozone holes, greenhouse effects, pesticides, and thermal pollution was beyond their comprehension. If the insensitivity of early writers is understandable, many would say ours is not. It is perilous, some say criminal, for management not to extend what we know about organizations and the technological, competitive, and social environments to the more delicate relationships in the ecosystem.

Thompson's recognition of the interrelationship between organizations and their environment was abstract and theoretical. The practicality of his ideas, however, is clearly evident in the *ecocentric* view of management (Shrivastava, 1995). This view conceives of organizations as integral parts of industrial ecosystems, which are ecologically interdependent upon one another and the larger environment. Organizations acquire resources from their environment, sometimes create environmental risks as they produce products and services, and send their outputs as well as their by-products back into the environment, just as Thompson argued (Hart, 1995). Organizations and those who manage them thus become critically interrelated with the welfare of the larger environment.

Well-known companies such as the Body Shop, Proctor and Gamble, Johnson and Johnson, Olin Corporation, IBM, and others have acknowledged this interdependence and provided a degree of environmental leadership. Experiences of these companies and others have resulted in some *best practices* in environmental leadership (Dechant and Altman, 1994). These practices include: (1) development of a mis-

---

▲ **Box 4-5**

ORGANIZATIONS, MANAGEMENT, AND ECOLOGY

Economic development must be sustainable, and sustainability requires that we look at industrial processes in fundamentally different ways than in the past. In nature there are few by-products or wastes, only residues. These residues, the leftovers from one process, are reused in another. Also, industry, like nature, should be appreciated from the perspective of the total system—all things are interrelated.

That environmental concerns, willingly or unwillingly, must become part of the decision-making processes of managers in modern organizations seems inevitable. The problem lies in the manner in which traditional paradigms of decision making have so completely ignored environmental costs. Designing organizations, management processes, and decision-making procedures in ways that incorporate environmental issues will require innovative cost calculations, new budgeting systems, and reward philosophies that are unknown today. However, the challenges of environmentally responsible management create opportunities for new ways of thinking about and doing business. Moreover, environmental responsibility underscores the necessity of thinking in global terms and addressing sustainable economic development for the entire planet.

Source: Graedel and Allenby (1995).

---

sion statement and corporate values that promote environmental advocacy; (2) development of a framework involving all areas of operations in managing environmental initiatives; (3) development of green processes and product designs where pollution is prevented as well as corrected; (4) development of environmentally focused stakeholder partnerships; and (5) development of environmental initiatives internally and externally.

It appears unlikely that anyone today would seriously question the existence of an interrelationship between organizations and their environments. The ecocentric view is one of the latest and certainly one of the most important recognitions of environmental effects on organizations and management. It also makes the connection of the organization's reciprocal influences on the environment. What was needed, however, was a contingency theory of organizations that was general enough to deal with a variety of environmental influences.

Harvard Business School to the Rescue—Again

Paul Lawrence was born in Illinois but received his graduate education at Harvard. Jay Lorsch was born in Missouri and received his doctorate at Harvard. These two colleagues at the Harvard Business School collaborated in writing *Organization and*

Environment (1967), which greatly expanded the findings of Woodward by examining more environmental contingencies than technology and added to the insights provided by both Chandler and Thompson. Their empirical approach was more like that of Woodward and less like the historical analysis of Chandler or the theoretical review of Thompson.

The objective of *Organization and Environment* was to examine the question of how the internal structure of an organization is affected by its environment. The authors argued and presented data to support their contentions that different organizational designs were needed to cope with different environmental realities. An attempt was made to determine how successful organizations in a particular industry differed from their less successful competitors. Lawrence and Lorsch also attempted to determine how effective firms in various industries differed from one another (p. 19).

Information on internal organizational functioning was obtained by distributing 30 to 50 questionnaires to upper and middle level managers in the focal organizations. Personal interviews were also conducted and data regarding industrial environments were obtained through interviews with and questionnaires to top executives in each organization. The sample that was used included six firms in the plastics industry, each of which was a major part of a larger chemical business. The organizations had four functional units—sales, production, applied research, and basic research. Two of the plastics firms were considered high performing, two were low performing, and two exhibited intermediate levels of performance.

Two firms each (one high and one low performing) were also selected in the standardized container and the packaged foods industries. These two industries were included because of the critical differences each demonstrated relative to plastics. The plastics industry is dynamic and changes fast, while changes in standardized containers is, by comparison, slow. The packaged foods industry changes more slowly than plastics but faster than containers. In all, 10 firms in the 3 different industries were included in the study.

Some Findings

Organization charts and manuals were reviewed and interviews regarding the "formality of structure" were conducted in all the various departments of the plastics firms. Production departments were, in general, more formally structured, having fewer levels in their hierarchy and larger ratios of supervisory to nonsupervisory employees than the other departments in this industry. Lawrence and Lorsch also looked at interpersonal relationships, time, and goal orientations in all the different departments. In departments like production, where tasks were more certain, managers tended to be task oriented. Employee orientation tended to increase in departments like sales and research and development with more uncertain tasks. Since research and development personnel was involved in tasks with slower feedback, employees in this department were more tolerant of activities that contributed less to long-term profitability.

In production departments, feedback was faster and employees tended to be more short term in their orientations. When the attitudes of managers in the functional departments such as production, sales, and research were compared and found to be significantly different with regard to time, goal, and interpersonal orientations as well as formality of structure, the organization was said to be "differentiated." High performing groups in plastics displayed differentiation patterns that were consistent with the demands of the various subenvironments like production, sales, and research and development (p. 42).

Integration (not to be confused with Follett's technique of conflict resolution) is the state of collaboration necessary to coordinate the activities of departments. In general, the greater the degree of differentiation, the greater the need for integration. In plastics, for example, the fact that production departments were oriented toward the short run, tended to be task oriented, and were more formal in structure made it inherently more difficult for production employees to work with the long-term and relations oriented employees in fundamental or basic research. The magnitude of the differences made it necessary to devote more attention to ensuring that integration of efforts took place in the pursuit of common goals. In fact, integration was so necessary that all the plastics organizations had formally developed units charged with the responsibility of facilitating integration of the functional units. After a detailed examination of the plastics firms, Lawrence and Lorsch turned their attention to standardized containers and packaged foods. As with plastics, all firms were major product segments of larger corporations.

The firms in the container industry displayed the least amount of differentiation (differences among functional managers' orientations and units' formality of structure) followed by packaged foods. Plastics had the greatest degree of differentiation. The extent of integration, however, did not show such significant differences. As in the case of plastics, firms in the container industry had "achieved states of differentiation that met the demands of their particular environments" (p. 105). Integration was uniformly better in high performing firms than in lower performing ones.

The research reinforced the necessity, in the plastics industry, of developing formal integrative measures between units like marketing and research in order to test newly developed or modified products. It was also necessary to develop close integration between production and research to ensure successful product development.

Lawrence and Lorsch asked the same questions with respect to other industrial settings. In the food industry there was less formal integration than in plastics. Managers in various departments were assigned integrative roles rather than developing integrative units. In the container industry integration was achieved by the managerial hierarchy with some use of direct contact among functional managers. This technique resembled "Fayol's bridge" of direct horizontal contacts.

It was noted that because of different environmental settings and variations in integrative techniques, conflict was resolved in different ways in the plastics, foods, and container industries. In plastics there was a high degree of differentiation among departments, as noted earlier, so that the integrative department was very influential in resolving interdepartmental conflicts. In packaged foods, research and marketing departments had the most influence. In foods, there was no formal integrative unit, so managers in marketing and research became the most influential forces for resolving interdepartmental conflict. In containers, marketing and production managers were the most influential because of the importance of scheduling problems and customer service.

There were also similarities relative to the resolution of interdepartmental conflicts. Of particular significance was the fact that in all three industries, the managers most "centrally involved" in achieving integration and resolving conflict had reputations of being especially competent and knowledgeable. Their influence was based primarily on expertise.

The theories discussed in this chapter represent a radical departure from classical organizational design theory. For lack of a better description, we simply call it the "quest for the one best way." The "holy grail" for Taylor, Gilbreth, and even Mayo was the mystical "best way" of managing. Gilbreth looked for the one best way with motion study, Taylor with time study, and Mayo through experiments and interviews.

The "contingency theorists" discussed in this chapter all agree on one thing—there is no "one best way" to organize or manage. The best way in any particular time or situation is a function of the contingencies presented by the environment. The implications for management of this argument are nothing less than profound. The primary determinant of successful management is no longer finding the best way to do a task. Instead, it is the need for flexibility and the ability to diagnose and adapt to changing circumstances.

Planning Organizational Change

Woodward started the tradition, and Lawrence, Lorsch, and others extended it. Yet, to all it was a contingency view. Woodward's contingency was technology while Lawrence and Lorsch included a broader range of influential environmental factors. Some of the important implications for management of this line of research follow. First, the formal differentiation of organizational units, when based on task and environmental differences, contributes to high performance (Lawrence and Lorsch, 1967, p. 213). This suggests that the principle of specialization remains good economics and management that should be applied as consistently as possible. When distinctly different functional activities are combined such as research and sales or research and production, problems develop. The low performing packaged food company committed this error by combining applied and fundamental research in spite of indications that the two research tasks required different practices to deal successfully with different parts of the environment.

Second, Lawrence and Lorsch suggested that since specialization and the resulting differentiation are organizational realities, attempts should be made to ensure that the "differentiation and integration" approach has as much likelihood of success as possible. Production, sales, and research specialists naturally develop their own ways of looking at things in organizations. It is important to encourage these specialists, however, to tolerate the views of others and not to personalize disagreements that naturally arise. Building this type of tolerance requires conscious management action.

Third, most organizations benefit from using a variety of conflict resolution techniques. When the degree of differentiation is not too great, simply appealing for decisions from the first supervisor with formal authority over the involved departments is often successful. This was the conflict resolution technique visualized most often by classical writers. However, many firms in the Lawrence and Lorsch sample used confrontation or problem solving techniques to resolve conflicts.

The research of Woodward and of Lawrence and Lorsch has significant implications for the design of successful organizations in the future. Almost everyone agrees that technological changes will continue at accelerating rates. Organizations in many industries will face environments not unlike those faced by the plastics firms. Therefore, we can confidently speculate that differentiation will increase, and with this there is a concurrent need for increases in integrative skills. One of the important challenges for management theory and practice will be to provide better ways of achieving integration among highly differentiated functional units. This will require the development of conflict resolution skills on the part of successful managers.

Yet, many behavioral scientists insist that perceptive managers should beware of attempts to entirely resolve conflict because conflict leads, under the proper conditions, to innovation. Thus, it is likely that managers will increasingly confront the dilemma presently felt in high-technology environments. Smooth and efficient operations require coordination of differentiated units, and efforts to achieve integration

---

▲ Box 4-6
MANAGING DISCONTINUITY

Organizational change may be incremental—smooth, predictable, and occurring during periods of environmental stability. Change may also be discontinuous—traumatic, painful, and demanding. Discontinuous change is demanding because it requires that people "unlearn" their ways of thinking, working, and acting. Often these old ways have led directly to success in less complex times.

CEOs are critical to the success of discontinuous change. They must create the case for change and ensure that the pain of not changing is greater than the pain of changing. However, the CEO needs the help of a team to assume the responsibility for change collectively. The support of key external stakeholders is also important. It is important that members of the team understand those aspects of the organization that constitute its strengths and must be preserved and those aspects that need destruction, renewal, and reinvention.

In a word, change is about leadership, and successful managers must assume the role of leaders if they are to be successful in navigating their organizations through periods of discontinuous change. Organizational transformation requires skills different from organizational efficiency, and not all managers will be up to the task of leading discontinuous change.

Source: Nadler, Shaw, Walton, and Associates (1995).

are essential. At the same time, a reasonable amount of conflict is functional in the sense that it stimulates innovation. Managers in organizational environments demanding innovation will find themselves managing rather than eliminating conflict.

Since there is no one best way to manage or organize, it follows that in addition to doing things right, managers must continuously assess whether or not their organizations are doing the right things. Doing the right things relates directly to environmental demands, and these demands change frequently. Therefore, initiating and managing change are key elements in managerial success. Successful managers need to master change and renewal as well as efficiency and order. The first step in this mastery is understanding the change process.

Process of Change

In the literature of management, there are four primary perspectives on how organizations change. The life-cycle view suggests that organizations like individuals age naturally from one state to another and that this progression takes place according to a code that moves the organization like the individual from birth to childhood and eventually to maturity and death. The goal-oriented view of change assumes that organizations move toward the attainment of some purpose. The power view proposes that organizations change as managers attempt to balance the demands of conflicting interests in the organization. Finally, the evolutionary view assumes that the present state of any organization is the cumulative result of competition, selection, and adaptive behaviors (Van de Ven and Poole, 1995).

Leaders and organizational members perform different roles depending on the perspective taken regarding change. Even though major change initiatives are different in every organization and unique to some degree, Kotter (1996, p. 21) suggested that successful change initiatives follow an 8-stage process. The steps in the process are:

1. *Establishing a sense of urgency:* Successful change leaders monitor competitive realities and identify crises, potential crises, and opportunities.
2. *Creating a guiding coalition:* To be successful, change initiatives must have a powerful group in the organization to lead the change, and this guiding coalition must work as a team.
3. *Developing a vision and strategy:* The effective change leader has a vision to direct the change and strategies for accomplishing the vision.
4. *Communicating the change vision:* Successful leaders use every possible means of communicating the new vision and strategies for its achievement.
5. *Empowering broad-based action:* Change efforts involve the removal of barriers, changing processes and structures that inhibit change, and encouraging unconventional means of accomplishing the change.
6. *Generating short-term wins:* It is important to plan for visible improvements, create the improvements, and reward those who make the important contributions.
7. *Consolidating gains and producing more change:* As momentum increases,

the gains are used to create more gains and involve more individuals who can renew and invigorate the process even more.

8. *Anchoring new approaches in the organizational culture:* Successful change leaders carefully point out the association between new behaviors and organizational success and ensure that provisions are made that change initiatives "outlive" any single individual, including the leader.

Following a process such as this will facilitate change because it will provide a logic and enable the change leader to gauge his or her progress toward the accom-

---

▲ Box 4-7
WHY CHANGE FAILS

John Kotter lists eight reasons why changes, and often organizations, fail:

1. *Allowing too much complacency.* Urgency must be created in fellow managers and employees.

2. *Failing to create a sufficiently powerful guiding coalition.* At least a nucleus of senior people must support the proposed change.

3. *Underestimating the power of vision.* Without a vision change efforts degenerate into confusing, time-consuming, and incompatible projects.

4. *Undercommunicating the vision.* Effective communication has to come in the dual form of words and deeds.

5. *Permitting obstacles to block the new vision.* The obstacles may come in the form of organization structures, narrow job descriptions, and so on.

6. *Failing to create short-term wins.* Genuine strategic changes take time, and quick victories allow people to believe in the short term.

7. *Declaring victory too soon.* Celebrating wins is fine, even essential, but be sure the victory is complete before removing the heat.

8. *Neglecting to anchor changes firmly in the corporate culture.* Changes and change agents must be sensitive to "how we do things around here."

Source: Kotter (1996).

plishment of the vision. It will not eliminate resistance or the inherent cynicism for some about organizational changes, but it will increase the likelihood of success (Greenwood and Hining, 1996; Reichers, Wanous, and Austin, 1997).

Every leader will accomplish these stages using a different style. In fact, one useful theory that attempts to describe managerial action and organizational change is based on strategic reference points (Bamberger and Fiegenbaum, 1996; Fiegenbaum, Hart, and Schendel, 1996). This argument, which is based on an extension of the prospect theory, suggests that the same manager is capable of initiating changes that either involve a great deal of risk or cautiously avoid risks, depending on where he or she perceives the organization to be in terms of the "domain of gains or losses." Strategic reference points are the line of demarcation between gains and losses. If the decision maker, for example, foresees a future wherein financial returns will be well below the historical or industry reference point, extremely radical changes such as downsizing or downscoping may be considered and implemented—risky strategic choices may be selected. On the other hand, if the future promises returns above the reference point, the decision maker may choose less risky choices and make changes in a much more incremental manner.

▲ Box 4-8
STRATEGIC CHANGE AND DECISION MAKER CHOICES

The 1980s and 1990s have been characterized by some of the most radical changes ever initiated in corporate America. Firms have downsized and, in the process, destroyed the organizational loyalty of a generation of employees. Downsizing is one of several strategies that could be predicted on the basis of the theory of strategic reference points. For example, an in-depth study of 12 firms (Donaldson) argued that corporate strategies focusing on growth and diversification in the 1960s and 1970s along with the deregulation and tax law changes predicated the financial restructuring of industry that took place in the 1980s. One might infer that decision makers looked at the strategies available in terms of their growth reference points and concluded that only radical restructuring could hope to provide consistently high rates of returns.

Other studies have suggested that prior diversifications have led to such complexity that many organizations are simply no longer manageable. Again, the desire for continued performance in line with historical reference points tempts decision makers to radically downscope and focus the organization. Again, the reference point and the business outlook combine to favor more radical changes than might be attempted in more stable environments.

Sources: Donaldson (1994); Hoskisson and Hitt (1994).

Postmodern Critique

It has been implied, if not argued, throughout this discussion that change is essential to ensuring that leaders and organizations do the right things as well as do things right. In a normative sense, change in management and leadership discussions is thought of as "good" while resistance to change is considered "bad" or at least dysfunctional. The early or what, in this context, is called modern view of organization emphasized order and certainty and achieved these outcomes through hierarchy, specialization, policies, and structure. The resulting organizations were efficient in less chaotic times and provided members with a sense of certainty.

The more contemporary approaches to organization emphasize change, and they achieve these outcomes through less hierarchy, decentralized decision making, empowerment of employees, and similar measures (Parker, 1994). Some refer to the present period of management thought with its focus on adaptive organizations as the postmodern view.

To postmodern writers a major problem of postmodern organizational society and of the organizational forms that have been developed to cope with the new complexity is the absence of structure and ever present change (Bergquist, 1993). The role of the leader becomes one of helping employees make sense out of constant change and offering some sense of direction (vision) in times of chaos. Indeed, leaders must assume new and demanding roles in the postmodern society. So too must organizational members.

The disappearance of the modern organization and the security its structure provided also demands a new concept of leadership. In postmodern organizations leaders emerge at any and all levels of the organization, not just in the executive suite. Leadership in the postmodern organizational world involves the assumption of responsibility. Effective change management and organizational adaptability require initiative and innovative thinking by everyone. Flatter hierarchies work only if employees act without direct orders, and empowerment is effective only when people assume responsibility for doing their jobs. The postmodern world in which we live is different from the modern world, and the organizational forms that ensure that we do the right things (are effective) are different from those that aided us in doing things right.

Summary and Conclusions

"It all depends . . ." is not a good way to begin offering a solution to a management problem. If you are a high, or even low, paid consultant, your clients are likely to doubt they are receiving their money's worth if this is the best you can do. Seasoned executives do not like the uncertainty such an "explanation" entails. However, experience tells us that there is seldom an easy answer or a "quick fix" to complex problems of management and organization. We might like to offer pat answers for all management problems, but such responses would be equally unsatisfactory because they would seldom be correct.

In this chapter a number of important issues have been explored. From this discussion we can conclude several important lessons for managers. These are:

1. Successful organizations must be effective (do the right things) as well as efficient (do things right) in the increasingly competitive business environment of today.
2. Managers need to think about the conflicting demands of efficiency and effectiveness and become comfortable with the conflicting demands of these important managerial challenges.
3. Absolute principles of management and organization are useful tools and should be employed by managers, but environmental variations in the application of these principles must be appreciated and respected.
4. Cornerstone concepts of early organization theory may be violated in the interest of responding to contemporary realities, but the violations result in certain reductions in efficiency.
5. Dealing with organizational change is an increasingly important factor in successful management.

Contingency theory is not likely to be the final answer, although for the present it allows us to understand some of the paradoxes and dilemmas created by "mutually contradictory" principles and prescriptions. If we are smart, and that is the purpose of reading and writing management books, we will not be satisfied with situational explanations for these paradoxes but will use them as they have been used in the physical sciences—as incentives for further study so as to resolve in a more meaningful way the inconsistencies in contemporary management thought. Management has moved quickly from the absolute to the relative and in doing so has achieved a better understanding of organizations, environments, and the relationship between the two. It must continue and offer managers even more assistance in applied decision making. In the process, management and organization theory must become flexible in its application to diverse environmental forces. Sometimes responses require violations of early theories, and such violations, under some circumstances, are appropriate or even advisable. However, caution should be exercised in that the "wholesale violation" of sound principles of organization always involves a cost in loss of coordination and efficiency. Only when the rewards of increased efficiency and effectiveness are great enough to offset the uncertainty created, should alternative organizational approaches be considered and used.

Questions for Discussion

1 Briefly discuss why management writers tend to equate efficiency with doing things right and effectiveness with doing the right things. Is this a meaningful distinction? Which, in your opinion, is most important in contemporary management? Why?

2 Discuss three examples in actual organizations where managers face the dilemma of managing simultaneously in the long run and in the short run. Is there any meaningful way to actually resolve this dilemma, or is it simply the nature of management?

3 Do you agree with many of the early organization theorists that coordination is, in reality, the essence of management? Why or why not?

4 Discuss an example in an organization when the manager might correctly violate a classical principle of organization such as the unity of command, or "one-master" rule. Why is this violation legitimate in the case you discuss?

5 In your experience are management concepts genuine principles or merely contradicting proverbs? Support your answer with an example.

6 Contingency theory has been almost universally accepted in modern management thought. Are there any "traps" to the contingency or situational view? If so, what are they?

7 What lessons does contingency theory provide for managers in the public, health care, and not-for-profit sectors? How does contingency theory assist in resolving the problems of management in nonbusiness sectors?

8 Think of major change efforts you have participated in or observed in organizations. Did the change leaders follow a process such as the one described by Kotter in this chapter? If so, was it successful? If not, how did the change leader alter the process?

9 How do managers deal with resistance to change? Do you think change is inherently resisted by people in organizations? Explain your response with a couple of examples.

10 Do you agree or disagree with the postmodern view of organizations? Do you think organizations have been forever altered through downsizing and downscoping or is this just a temporary stage in the evolution of competitive economic systems? Explain your answer.

The Challenge of Leadership

"Leadership is about addressing questions that others have yet to contemplate."

Gary Hamel and C. K. Prahalad
Strategic Management Journal (1996)

Ralph Stogdill (1974b) observed that "jazz is not the only native American contribution to world culture. Leadership as a body of theory and research is distinctly an American creation." If this claim had been made by anyone other than Stogdill, an early leader in leadership research, we might not take it seriously. Leadership is an important topic to every civilization and, as civilizations go, America is far too young to fancy itself the originator of such an important field. Of course, Stogdill's point is that leadership theory and research, not leadership itself, originated in America.

In addition to its origin, it is also interesting to observe the longevity of the interest in leadership. Management practices and the focus of management research, as we have seen throughout our discussion, are ever changing and evolutionary. Yet, leadership research seems always at or near the top of the list of concerns for managers and researchers alike. Indeed, leadership and leaders remain a human fascination.

Regardless of its origins and longevity, it is little wonder that leadership has received so much attention. Nations have been founded, military victories achieved, powerful corporations created, and mighty labor unions built because of the leadership of one or relatively few people. When we think of Microsoft, we think of Bill Gates. When we think of the Gulf War, we think of Norman Schwarzkopf. Leadership has always occupied a high place in the research priorities of psychologists, sociologists, historians, and management scholars. Although not all leaders are managers, it is difficult to imagine a successful manager who does not demonstrate a degree of leadership. In fact, a brief distinction is needed before we proceed with the discussion of leadership.

▲ **Box 5-1**

DIVERSE ROLES OF LEADERS

Leaders perform different roles in organizations. However, there are 3 things all leaders must do, regardless of the roles they perform. They must: (1) create order; (2) inspire action; and (3) improve performance. In accomplishing these things, leaders perform certain roles:

Leader as sage: The sage has an extraordinary ability to tolerate uncertainty, construct strategic possibilities, and understand complex systems.

Leader as visionary: The visionary infects others with excitement and breaks out of modes of thinking that ensnare others.

Leader as magician: The magician is calm in the face of change and leaps the gap from where the organization is to where it needs to be.

Leader as globalist: The globalist bridges cultural differences by finding common ground where productive work can occur.

Leader as mentor: The mentor helps people gain new perspectives and find meaning in new situations.

Leader as ally: The ally builds alliances and partnerships and takes advantage of every opportunity to improve performance through cooperation.

Leader as sovereign: The sovereign takes risks and deals effectively with uncertainty while empowering others to make decisions.

Leader as guide: The guide is action oriented and enthusiastic. These individuals achieve goals using clearly stated principles based on core values.

Leader as artisan: The artisan is concerned with beauty as well as practicality. These leaders create customer value through simplicity, effectiveness, and efficiency.

Source: Wells (1996).

Leadership in Management

Some researchers take great care to distinguish between management and leadership while others reject any such attempts as useless academic "hair splitting" and of very little practical value. There are arguments to support each view, but it would seem inappropriate in a book of this nature not to at least acknowledge the argument. Moreover, when modern leaders outlined the 6 rules for business success offered by Jack Welch of General Electric, one of the six important rules was, "don't manage, lead." (Tichey and Sherman, 1993) Obviously, Welch believes there is an important distinction between management and leadership.

Leadership versus Management

To some extent we have already engaged in the debate about leadership versus management without knowing it. Our previous discussion of efficiency and doing things right, for example, was about management. Our discussion of effectiveness or doing the right things was about leadership. John Kotter (1990) made a clear distinction between leadership and management. Management, to Kotter, involves planning and budgeting, organizing and staffing, and problem solving and controlling. It is about the traditional management functions and seeks outcomes such as efficiency, order, and certainty. Leadership, on the other hand, involves creating a vision and sharing,

---

▲ Box 5-2
RENEWAL AT GENERAL ELECTRIC

When people think of innovative organizations, they rarely think of the oldest and largest American corporations. Microsoft and Intel make better press than General Electric—or do they? Few corporations have reinvented themselves as often as GE under the leadership of Jack Welch. Welch is not a typical GE executive. He was part of a unit in the Chemical Development Organization that despised the bureaucracy.

During his time at GE Welch has attempted to deliver on his promise to fix or close any business unit that cannot be first or second in its market. He has reduced the GE workforce by over 100,000 (400 of these were strategic planners at headquarters), and insisted on stretch targets and high-quality standards. Today GE is known for its medical systems, financial services, and information technology. "Not bad for a bunch of engineers that make refrigerators."

Source: Tichy and Sherman (1993); "A Conversation," *Fortune*, Dec. 11, 1995; "Jack Welch's Encore," *Business Week* (October 28, 1996).

aligning individuals and building coalitions, motivating, and inspiring. The outcome sought by leaders is change.

Warren Bennis (1989), another well-known writer on leadership, lists some of the important differences between managers and leaders. According to him:

1. The manager administers; the leader innovates.
2. The manager is a copy; the leader is an original.
3. The manager focuses on systems and structure; the leader focuses on people.
4. The manager relies on control; the leader inspires trust.
5. The manager has a short-range view; the leader has a long-range perspective.
6. The manager asks how and when; the leader asks what and why?
7. The manager has an eye always on the bottom line; the leader has an eye on the horizon.
8. The manager initiates; the leader originates.
9. The manager accepts the *status quo*; the leader challenges it.
10. The manager is the classic good soldier; the leader is his or her own person.
11. The manager does things right; the leader does the right thing.

Although the distinction may be of more use to academics than to managers, there does seem to be a fundamental difference in the natures of leadership and management, the outcomes sought, and the processes employed. The unfortunate part is not the fact that a distinction is drawn between leadership and management, but that there seems to be some normative connotation associated with the differences. In fact, as the previous chapters should make very clear, organizations rely on managers for survival and on leaders for change. Managers and leaders are equally important to all organizations. Businesses, universities, hospitals, and religious organizations need vision, but they also need to meet the payroll, adhere to their budgets, and staff appropriately.

Brief Background and Plan

A topic as complex and diverse as leadership provides particular challenges to anyone looking for evolutionary threads and historical triggers. Yet, threads and triggers can be found, or at least imagined, if we look close enough. For example, leadership research began with a focus on the few great people who live in every society, populate every organization, and appear to possess *traits* that are uncommon among the population at large. This is where our search and survey must begin.

By the middle of the present century, leadership researchers faced a dilemma. The trait approach, with all of its intuitive appeal, was not working. There were too many exceptions to every trait identified, and inconsistent theory leads to inadequate practice. A more consistent predictor was needed. In response to failure and skepticism, the focus changed to leader behavior and questions about what is involved in being a leader, the proper way to lead, the influence of the leader's assumptions about followers, and numerous other issues. Ultimately, many believed, the elusive key to understanding leadership lay in a complex interrelationship between the situation faced by individuals and the manner in which they responded to the situation (Blake and Mouton, 1964). This situational or contingency view dominates much of contemporary leadership research.

The plan in this chapter is to steer a course that will allow a view of one, or in some cases two, illustrations of some of the more important phases of leadership theory and research. Our specimens must be selected carefully in terms of how well they illustrate the particular orientation to leadership under review.

The Art of Leadership

Stogdill (1974a) indicated that the earliest systematic research on leadership was directed toward identifying the traits or characteristics of great leaders. This is not surprising. All of us have marveled about the accomplishments of great people. History is rich with examples of personalities who soared to greatness or, as Shakespeare notes, "had greatness thrust upon them." It was only a matter of time until enterprising researchers would look for ways to predict how one might achieve greatness.

An example of this early tradition is advanced by Ordway Tead. Long before he wrote *The Art of Administration* (1951), Tead published a book on leadership. The ti-

---

▲ Box 5-3
LEARNING LEADERSHIP?

A question frequently asked but rarely answered is: "Can leadership be learned?" Ask the question in a group of informed individuals and you are sure to stimulate controversy. No, leaders are born, some will say. Others will maintain, using exciting examples, how the most unlikely people emerge as leaders.

In spite of record enrollments in visionary leadership courses, people remain skeptical about learning leadership. Often we confuse leadership with objectivity and dispassionate decision making. To some, leadership is a matter of character, and they will argue that we have abdicated too much influence to the technocrats. By agreeing to be "led by the judgmentally blind, we have stumbled."

We must be careful not to create the impression that good decision making must always be objective. True leadership is about energy, emotion, imagination, good judgment, and vision. Can these be taught? Perhaps, but it is a serious mistake to reduce "leadership to a task anyone could be taught and management to a kind of paint-by-numbers art."

Source: Pitcher (1997).

tle was, you guessed it, *The Art of Leadership* (1935). In Tead's view, leadership was defined as the "activity of influencing people to cooperate toward some goal which they come to find desirable." He believed people wanted to belong to goal-oriented (purposeful) groups, such as business firms, churches, synagogues, and civic clubs. Since only a few could lead, most people, it could be inferred, desired to be led and were comfortable as followers. A few, however, invariably emerged as leaders, and these individuals were of particular interest.

People can be led in many ways. Suggestions can be used as verbal hints of what people ought to do. Leaders sometimes intimidate, but exhortations and pep talks are usually more successful (p. 37). Tead even gave consideration to the usefulness of persuasive, thorough, logical arguments. However, it was his occasional hint about the situational nature of leadership that was most unusual in his writings. Even though he focused primarily on traits, Tead was aware that leaders use the "logic of events" in arriving at the proper time to exercise their influence. Sometimes leaders even created problem situations to which they could uniquely respond (p. 43). Perhaps that is why we remember the leaders best who set forth worthy and challenging goals and aid us in responding to them.

General Douglas McArthur was known for his pledge "I shall return." Lyndon Johnson was known for the Great Society, John F. Kennedy for his goal of "putting a man on the moon before the end of the decade." The goals that give leaders their influence are definite, appealing, and ones with which followers can enthusiastically identify (p. 60). The "law of the situation," as discussed by Follett in Urwick (1949), implied that the situation was given and the leader merely responded in a unique way. Tead agreed, but added something unique—the situation can be created by the perceptive leader, and history testifies that this often is the case.

Becoming a Leader

It would be a mistake to think of Tead as a true contingency theorist. He, like most early leadership writers, believed successful leaders possessed identifiable traits. The most important were:

1. *Physical and nervous energy:* Leadership is hard work, so the leader must have more than the average amount of energy.
2. *Sense of purpose and direction:* The leader must have goals and inspire others to pursue them.
3. *Enthusiasm:* Good leaders often feel themselves "commanded by power." The enthusiasm they possess is converted into command (p. 98).
4. *Friendliness and affection:* Tead did not believe it was better for a leader to be feared than loved. To the contrary, leaders needed to be liked if they were to exercise influence.
5. *Integrity:* Tead believed leaders had to be trustworthy.

People want leaders who are decisive and create confidence. Followers need to believe things are in good hands. Leaders have to "take the heat" when bad decisions are made and overcome the temptation to blame others. Harry Truman's attitude that the "buck stops here" gained him respect and gave citizens the confidence that someone would address serious problems. Good leaders need to be effective communicators, have a sense of humor, and, perhaps above all, a good leader is always a good teacher. The leader is the only teacher many employees ever have.

How Leaders Lead

Tead was idealistic, but he understood human nature and was a realist concerning it. He admitted that power has a corrupting influence and can lead to vanity. There are genuine hazards along the road to leadership. He recognized that leaders too often insist on having their own way and take it personally when others disagree. Sometimes they identify so closely with their goals that any disagreement is considered disloyalty. It is exciting to read of the accomplishments of the great people in history, but it is disappointing to read of equally, if not greater, weaknesses of these same people who eventually failed in their response to the "logic of other events."

In one of his most profound statements, Tead states: "Good leading depends on good following. The leader points the way but the followers must decide that the way is good" (p. 298). This statement is profound because it hints at an idea in leadership that emerged much later in the development of the field. Indeed, leadership depends on more than the personality of the leader. It depends on the followers, the situation, and numerous other aspects of the situation.

▲ Box 5-4
MAKING HEROES OF FOLLOWERS

Leaders who are strong men and women are followed because they are feared. Leaders who are transactors are followed because they control rewards, and visionary leaders are followed because of the power of their vision and their personal charisma. Superleaders, however, are followed because they make heroes out of followers. Superleaders create a *company of heroes* and themselves become "super" because they possess the expertise and wisdom that has been unleashed by all their followers. In the process, followers develop commitment to and ownership of their own jobs.

The superleader takes a fundamentally different perspective on leadership. The leader is no longer the focus. The follower becomes the center of the superleader's universe. The challenge of leadership is no longer to direct others but to assist others in directing themselves toward the achievement of individual and organizational goals.

Source: Sims and Manz (1996).

Searching for Traits

Much of the early leadership research was sponsored by the military for obvious reasons—the military has always recognized the need for leaders. If the traits of good leaders could be identified, future leaders could be identified. But the list of essential leadership traits became exceedingly long, and the conflicting findings concerning the traits were impossible to reconcile. Frustration led some researchers to simply deny any relationship between personality traits and leadership. Others continued the search, and still others were confident that personality had a relationship to leadership, but the association was more complicated than originally imagined.

This search for the secrets of leadership led researchers through many productive and unproductive mazes of data and information. Along the way the complexity of the problem of leadership began to surface. It became increasingly clear that the leader's personality and style of leadership, as well as the general situation were all important determinants of leadership effectiveness. The trajectory of leadership research as it relates to personality traits is interesting to track. There seems to be an initial enthusiasm about the consistency of traits relative to great leaders, then a cautious rejection of the importance of traits, and then an equally cautious reemergence of interest in trait research.

For example, in a survey of about 125 studies of leadership traits between 1904 and 1947 Stogdill (1948) concluded that leaders appeared to be "different" relative

---

▲ Box 5-5

LANGUAGE AND LEADERSHIP

Winston Churchill, John F. Kennedy, and Martin Luther King, Jr., shared at least one thing—they were all good "framers." Framing is "the skill that enables people to bring others to accept one meaning over another." Leaders are master framers. There are a number of tools that leaders use in effectively framing messages—stories, metaphors, allegories, and spins. However, anyone can use these tools. The uniqueness in leaders is that they are sensitive to the circumstance and know precisely when and where to use these tools.

It is extremely important that leaders communicate effectively by avoiding mixed messages, being mentally ready by becoming sensitive to the situation, and maintaining credibility. Leaders, if they are to be effective framers, must at all times be believable. More than a few leaders have lost their opportunity to lead by losing their credibility and believability. The best leaders seize "every opportunity—from the dramatic to the mundane—to manage meaning, gain support for their vision, and spur action from their constituents."

Source: Fairhurst and Sarr (1996).

to intelligence, alertness, insight, responsibility, initiative, persistence, self-confidence, and sociability. However, he was careful to point out that people do not become leaders merely because they possess these traits. The traits that the individual possesses must be relevant to the situation faced by the leader. In another survey Stogdill (1974a) analyzed almost 165 studies published since his first survey and compared the results. The second survey was, surprisingly, less cautious about the role of traits. In this study, Stogdill identified a number of traits that were positively associated with leadership. One writer argued that Stogdill's "second survey validated the original trait idea that the leader's characteristics are indeed a part of leadership" (Northouse, 1997, p. 15). Kirkpatrick and Locke (1991) are even less timid and state that "it is unequivocally clear that leaders are not like other people" (p. 59).

In fact, one could accurately argue that there has been a return to traits in recent years. The view of traits in some ways is less naïve, but in other ways it is unusually subjective and qualitative. The emergence of charismatic leaders in religion and politics has underscored the view that leaders are not like other people. A substantial number of contemporary researchers have reactivated the search for leadership traits.

Search for a Theory

Tead's ideas on leadership were intuitive and originated primarily from his personal experiences. However, one short decade after the publication of *The Art of Leadership*, some extraordinarily important studies of leadership were conducted in the midwestern United States. Shartle (1979) indicated that even though the multidisciplinary program of leadership research at Ohio State University actually started in 1945, the roots of the studies were established in the occupational research sponsored by the U.S. Department of Labor and the War Manpower Commission that began in 1934. One of the early pioneers of this research was introduced earlier in the chapter—Ralph Stogdill.

Ralph Stogdill was born in 1905 and enjoyed a long and distinguished career as professor of management science and psychology at Ohio State University, where he earned his doctorate. He worked for the Ohio Bureau of Juvenile Research and as an officer in the U. S. Maritime Services. In 1946 he became Associate Director of the Ohio State Leadership Studies (Van Fleet, 1979).

The Ohio State Leadership Studies were significant for several reasons (Schriesheim and Bird, 1979). Many believe they represent an important counterpoint in the way we view leadership. Prior to the 1950s the traitist view was dominant. Stogdill (1974a) to some extent challenged the conventional wisdom by observing that while some traits are found across leaders, leadership is best "considered in terms of the interactions of variables which are in constant flux and change" (p. 64). This caution was enough to alter the view of leadership from that of traits to leadership as an activity. The importance of studying leader behavior rather than leader characteristics became the order of the day.

The most familiar aspect of the Ohio State studies was the identification of two factors or dimensions of leadership—consideration and initiating structure. The former includes the leader's supportiveness of employee behavior, friendliness, and recognition of individual contributions to group goals, while the latter relates to the leader's task-oriented behaviors such as directing followers, evaluating performance, scheduling, and so on. Unlike later theories, the Ohio State researchers did not propose these dimensions as conflicting or mutually exclusive. In fact, effective leaders actually ranked high on both dimensions or some combination of the two. Consideration and initiating structure were thought of more as complementary than conflicting aspects of leader behavior. However, even though "complementary" was stressed, research into leadership behavior and the way in which leadership is exercised began to converge on mutually exclusive, at least by implication, leadership assumptions and styles.

Leader Assumptions

Although consideration and initiating structure were recognized by the Ohio State researchers as complementary, much of the leadership research has compared various mutually exclusive styles of leadership. Perhaps dichotomies such as task-oriented and employee-oriented leaders, autocratic and democratic, and so on are theoretical conveniences that allow researchers freedom in isolating various types of leader behavior. Or, those who proposed the mutually exclusive options perhaps really believed that different styles can be more effective ways of leading. In any event, the dichotomy is real and firmly established in the literature of management.

Consider the dichotomy faced when looking at the assumptions leaders make about followers. This has been conveniently "packaged" for us by Douglas McGregor (1960), who believed the way managers were behaving less than three decades ago placed them in the position of "facing the past while backing into the future." They were basing their actions on assumptions about employees that may have been true in the past but were certainly not descriptive of contemporary reality.

Douglas McGregor was born in Detroit, Michigan, in 1906 and died in 1964. He earned his doctorate from Harvard University in 1935 and served there as an instructor until he became a staff member in the Industrial Relations Section at the Massachusetts Institute of Technology in 1937. Later he directed that section. McGregor served as President of Antioch College from 1948 to 1954, after which he returned to M.I.T. as professor of industrial management until his death.

McGregor's most influential book was *The Human Side of Enterprise* (1960). In this book he proposed the best known dichotomy of management—Theory X and Theory Y. Theory X is the "traditional view of direction and control." When this view is adopted, the leader makes several assumptions about the people under her leadership (p. 35). These assumptions are:

1. The average human being has an inherent dislike for work and will avoid it if possible.
2. Because human beings dislike work, they must be coerced, controlled, directed, and threatened with punishment if they are to put forth adequate effort toward the achievement of organizational goals.

3. The average human being prefers direction, wishes to avoid responsibility, and has relatively little ambition. Most of all security is desired.

The leader who adopts Theory Y, which McGregor refers to as a means of "integrating individual and organizational goals," on the other hand, assumes something quite different about followers. These assumptions are:

1. The expenditure of physical and mental effort in work is as natural as play and rest.
2. The threat of punishment and external control is not the only means available for increasing effort toward the accomplishment of organizational goals. Humans are quite capable of exercising self-direction and self-control in the service of objectives to which they are committed.
3. Commitment to objectives is a function of the rewards associated with their attainment.
4. The average human being learns, under proper conditions, not only to accept but to seek responsibility.
5. The capacity to exercise a high degree of imagination, ingenuity, and creativity in the solution of organizational problems is widely, not narrowly, distributed in the population.
6. Under conditions of modern industrial life the intellectual potential of the average human being is rarely utilized.

According to McGregor, the principle that derived from Theory X was that of direction and control through the exercise of authority. Theory Y, by contrast, was based on the *principle of integration*, or the creation of conditions such that the members of the organization achieve their goals best by aiming their energies toward the success of the enterprise. This principle of integration literally creates the conditions whereby individuals achieve their personal goals in the process of contributing to the objective of the organization—the process of mutual reinforcement.

The assumptions that leaders make about employees are important, according to McGregor, because what you think is true causes you to behave in certain ways. Your behavior, in turn, causes employees to behave exactly as you assumed. Thus, we create the familiar *self-fulfilling prophesy*. If the leader assumes followers are lazy, irresponsible, and must be forced to work, it is likely that a system of incentives and appraisal will be established that guarantees that followers behave in precisely this manner. Precise rules and regulations are developed and leaders supervise closely to ensure that work is not only completed but is accomplished in the precise manner the leader desires. Workers find ways of getting around the system and eventually behave irresponsibly—just as Theory X predicted.

On the other hand, if employees are assumed to be responsible and mature, a system of incentives and appraisal will be set up that encourages them to behave in a mature and responsible way. Opportunities for professional and personal growth are provided, supervision is relaxed, and workers respond with more mature behavior.

Interestingly, McGregor has been criticized for thinking of leadership only in terms of either Theory X or Theory Y when, in reality, followers possess some char-

---

▲ **Box 5-6**

LEADERSHIP AS KNOWLEDGE, TRUST, AND POWER

What was Ross Perot thinking about when he insisted on walking around the General Motors plants after GM bought him out? Perot quickly discovered that management was out of touch with employees, and he made this fact clear at board meetings. GM's response was not to fix the problem but to get rid of the messenger. It was an unfortunate example of "misdirected position power." Ineffective leaders suppress knowledge by attacking those who bring bad news.

Trust is critically important to leaders. Leaders must trust employees (avoid Theory X assumptions) and build trust for the leader among employees. Only when trust is present is the environment conducive to information sharing and knowledge building. Power is also important to leaders. Although leaders as managers maintain the rights of selecting and implementing strategies, it is important to appreciate the importance of consultative behavior. The consultative approach allows leaders to exchange information, overcome authority differences, and build trust in the organization.

Source: Zand (1997).

---

acteristics of both theories. In fact, McGregor clearly recognized the danger of thinking in terms of such extremes and indicated early in his book that leaders should engage in *selective adaptation* with respect to their assumptions. The amount of control exercised by the leader or manager should be selectively adapted to the maturity and dependence of the followers. Immature and dependent employees require a great deal of control. Perhaps they are most accurately described by Theory X. Mature and independent employees, however, require little control and are best described by Theory Y.

Other criticisms of McGregor are more legitimate. His theory of leadership is not a theory and was based more on hopes than on evidence of any substantive nature (Lee, 1980). The *Human Side of Enterprise* is a classic in the field not because of its scientific sophistication but because of its clarity and its focus on a soft although important part of leadership—what the leader assumes about the follower does affect leader behavior. Like the legendary Greek sculptor Pygmalion, managers often create the type of employee behavior they encounter—their assumptions create self-fulfilling prophesies. The importance of managerial assumptions led managers and management writers to consider the relative merits of different styles of leadership and management. Soon, the primary question in leadership research became, "what is the best way to lead?"

Likert and the System 4 Organization

There are many "styles" advocates in leadership research because the focus on leadership behavior highlighted this important issue. We will look at Rensis Likert (1961, 1967) as an illustration of this research direction. Likert's work accurately represents the types of issues managers must consider when thinking about appropriate and inappropriate leadership styles and is based on more and better data than much of the research in this area.

Rensis Likert was born in Cheyenne, Wyoming, and received his doctorate from Columbia University. He worked at New York University and the Life Insurance Sales Research Bureau before he became Director of the Institute for Social Research at the University of Michigan, a post he held for a number of years.

Organizations: Systems 1 to 4

Likert published the foundations of his theory of leadership in 1961. In *New Patterns of Management*, two ideas appear particularly significant for leadership. First, the most effective leaders are those who form a linking function with people above and below them in the organization. In other words, the leader who functions as a *linking pin* keeps employees aware of what higher management is thinking and doing and keeps higher management aware of what is going on among the employees. Second, Likert proposed his *principle of supporting relationships*, which stated that leaders should ensure a maximum probability that all interactions in an organization be viewed as supportive and ones that build and maintain a sense of personal worth and importance (p. 103). In order to achieve these outcomes, Likert contrasted various types of organizations on the basis of what type of leadership style was used. Other factors used to classify different organizational systems included the nature of the motivational forces employed, the character of the communication processed, the interaction–influence process, the character of decision making, how goals are set and prioritized, and the manner in which control is exercised. The resulting 4 types of organizations are (Likert, 1967):

> *System 1 Organizations: Exploitive Authoritative:*   Leaders do not trust followers. Motivation is based on fear, threats, and occasional rewards. Communication flows down from the top and the little that flows up tends to be inaccurate and distorted. Goals are imposed from on high where all important decisions are made. Based on Theory X assumptions.

> *System 2 Organizations: Benevolent Authoritative:*   Leaders and followers exhibit a "master–servant" relationship. There is some involvement of followers, at least more than in System 1. There are also more rewards and better upward communication. The relationship between leaders and followers is best described as paternalistic.

> *System 3 Organizations: Consultative:*   Leaders are clearly in control, but followers are consulted before decisions are made. Upward communication is cautious and unpleasant and information is not freely offered or shared.

System 4 Organizations: Participative: Leaders trust followers and believe individuals seriously work toward accomplishing organizational goals. Communication is accurate and flows vertically and horizontally. Goals are formulated in
a participative manner by people who will be directly involved in decision making and accomplishing the objectives.

Most leaders develop System 2 or System 3 organizations. The move to System
4, which Likert recommends as most preferred, requires significant changes in leadership assumptions, philosophies, and behavior. Moreover, one should not expect
changes to take place immediately. When new programs are established in large, complex organizations, Likert cautions that the manager should expect as much as a year
before employees will recognize changes are actually taking place, and even more
time is required before tangible results can be expected (Likert, 1967, pp. 92–93).
Perhaps this is why attempts to build a System 4 organization sometimes fail—it takes
time. It is difficult to keep the confidence and enthusiasm of top management long
enough to effect the type of changes required by the participative system. However,
research results presented by Likert indicate that it is worth the time and energy spent
in moving from System 1 and 2 organizations to System 4.

Leadership and Organizational Effectiveness

Employees operating in System 1 and 2 organizations generate less group loyalty, develop lower performance goals, have greater conflict, exhibit less cooperation, demonstrate less favorable attitudes toward management, and are less motivated employees.
The end result is lower sales, higher costs, and fewer rewards for everyone. The System 4 organization, with its focus on supportive relationships, group decision making and supervision, and high-performance goals, attains higher sales and earnings
with less costs.

The human relations orientation of Likert is evident throughout *New Patterns of
Management* and *The Human Organization*. The linking pin concept is a fundamental aspect of Likert's theory because of its importance in ensuring the successful overlapping of different groups in the organization. While it is crucial that the successful
leader function as a conduit for vertical communication, the linking pin also facilitates horizontal relationships. When communication is designed according to the linking pin, the production superintendent actually becomes a member, for purposes of
communication, of two or more groups on the same organizational level. Membership in these overlapping groups creates more team spirit and encourages open, free,
and direct communication. This results in higher levels of mutual trust, shared responsibility, and intergroup commitment to organizational goals.

In summary, Likert's ideas are consistent with those of McGregor. Both argue
that the type of climate management established in an organization influences the performance of employees. While both writers recognized that situational variables can
affect leader behavior radically, the theme is clear—more focus on the human factor
will lead to higher levels of individual and organization performance. Moreover, even
though Likert and McGregor would not deny the importance of situational factors,
there is little doubt from their writings that both believed that the human relations

orientation of Theory Y and the System 4 organization was preferred to other styles of leadership. This, however, is less than a universally accepted proposition in contemporary leadership research. In recent times the logic of events and the law of the situation have assumed much greater importance as factors in leadership effectiveness.

Leader–Member Exchange—Extending the Linking Pin

Likert's notion of the linking pin highlighted the importance of the leader–follower relationship. Other leadership theories have placed even more emphasis on the exchanges that take place between leaders and followers. The best known of these is the leader–member exchange (LMX) theory developed by George Graen.

Before the emergence of LMX it was assumed that leaders behaved the same way toward all followers. If the style of the leader was participative, she or he allowed everyone to participate. If the leader was autocratic, no one was allowed to participate. LMX theory, however, focuses on the diversity of the relationships among leaders and followers. For example, initially attention was given to vertical dyad linkages or the relationship the leader formed with each follower in the work unit. Some followers were members of the out-group and relationships with the leader were limited to those required by the formal job description. Other members of the work group achieved in-group status, and the relationships with the leader were expanded far beyond those formally required by the job (Dansereau, Graen, and Haga, 1975). Followers who are members of the in-group receive more information, have more influence, and are more involved than members of the out-group.

Additional studies revealed more about the outcomes associated with leader–member exchanges. For example, high-quality leader–member exchanges were associated with a number of favorable outcomes, such as lower employee turnover, more frequent promotions, greater commitment to the organization, and better job attitudes (Graen and Uhl-Bien, 1995). Moreover, it has been suggested that exchanges between leaders and followers can be useful in the process known as "leadership making." Leadership making is the intentional process whereby leaders go about proactively developing high-quality exchanges with all followers. In other words, leaders take the initiative and attempt to ensure that every work unit member is affiliated with the in-group.

LMX theory is important for several reasons. First, it is simple. It provides leaders with a relatively straightforward way of leadership making. Second, LMX underscores the importance of focusing on the leader–follower relationship. In this sense, it adds an important element to McGregor's Theory X and Theory Y. Not only are the leader's assumptions about followers important, but the entire complex of relationships must be considered. Finally, LMX is consistent with modern motivation theory, as we will see in a forthcoming chapter, in that it emphasizes the uniqueness of every individual and work unit member. Admittedly, dealing with every follower on the basis of his or her uniqueness entails the danger of appearing unfair. However, every work unit member is unique and likely requires special attention in the process of leadership making.

▲ **Box 5-7**

INSIDE INTEL

Has anyone ever heard of Gordon Moore or Robert Noyce? Observers of the high-technology industry probably recognize Moore and Noyce as the founders of Intel. Most people, however, when they think of Intel think of Andrew S. Grove. Some argue that this remarkable company, which enjoys a virtual monopoly in the microprocessor industry, was largely shaped by a single person—Andrew Grove.

    Careful examination of the evolution of Intel and the leadership of Grove provides numerous examples of how leaders can transform individuals and organizations. It also provides examples of the weaknesses of human nature and the weaknesses of even the strongest leaders. Competitive environments require leaders who are driven to achieve and followers who trust the vision of those who lead. Intel may have its ups and downs on Wall Street, but its history under the leadership of Grove has been phenomenal.

Source: Jackson (1997).

A Theory of Leadership Effectiveness

Not everyone agrees that a particular style of leadership will result in the most effective form of organizational behavior. Although there are many dissenters, it was Fred Fiedler who put the argument together and supported it with research data.

    Fiedler was born in Vienna, Austria, in 1922 and received his doctorate in psychology from the University of Chicago in 1949 (Bedeian, 1991). Although he began his distinguished service as professor of psychology and adjunct professor of management and organization at the University of Washington in 1969, he was at the University of Illinois when he published his book, *A Theory of Leadership Effectiveness* (1967). This book reported the results of extensive research and eventually made a significant impact on the way managers think about leadership (Fiedler, 1992).

Leadership under Different Conditions

In developing his view of leadership effectiveness, Fiedler studied a number of different types of groups (pp. 18–20). In characterizing different group situations three criteria were used. These are briefly discussed next.

    1. *Leader's position power:* The relationship of the leader to the group members is determined to a large extent by the power she exercises over the followers. Some positions (army general) have high position power because the position itself enables the general to require group members to comply with orders or directions. Who would dare ignore an order from a highway patrolman with a badge on his chest and a pistol on his side? Power position alone, however, does not directly affect performance, even though a stronger position power does make the leader's job easier to accomplish (p. 2).

2. *Nature of the task:* Tasks in organizations may be structured or unstructured. The structured task is laid out step by step. The steps are predicted easily and can be programmed in advance. The press operator on an assembly line has a highly structured task. The heart surgeon's task, by contrast, is unstructured and cannot be programmed. Leaders of groups with structured tasks have an easier job and require less position power because the leader's power can be inferred to a great extent by the instructions for the job.

3. *Leader–follower relations:* The relationship between leaders and followers "appears to be the most important single element in determining the leader's influence in the small group" (p. 29). When leaders are highly regarded by followers, no signs of rank are needed to get followers to work hard.

Using these three aspects of the task, Fiedler classified leadership situations in terms of their favorableness or unfavorableness for leaders. To illustrate, by arranging the three dimensions of the task (i.e. power position, task structure, and leader–follower relations) into all possible combinations, eight unique combinations or octants were developed (p. 33).

Octant I is the most favorable situation facing a leader where position power is strong, the task is highly structured, and there are good leader–follower relations. An example of this is a well-liked squad leader in the army. Octant VIII is the least favorable, where leader–follower relations are poor, the task is unstructured, and the leader's power position is weak. An example of this is an unpopular project leader working on a complex technical problem. The professional temperament of the engineers makes the temporary leader's power position weak, the task is unstructured, and the leader's lack of popularity makes for bad group relations.

A Matter of Style

In order to determine the most effective leadership style for each of the octants, Fiedler classified the style of each group leader on the basis of how he or she responded to the *least preferred coworker* (LPC). Without going into excessive detail, a leader's LPC score was determined by how she reacted to the person with whom she would least like to work. If a leader scored the least preferred coworker high, she was getting past personalities and still believed the coworker was nice, intelligent, hardworking, and perhaps competent even though there was a preference not to work with him. The leader, in other words, is able to separate the person from his works and is, therefore, regarded as a relationship-motivated leader (p. 44). The leader with a low LPC score, on the other hand, describes the coworker in negative terms, thereby linking an individual's poor performance with undesirable personality traits. The high-

LPC leader derives satisfaction from building and maintaining satisfactory personal relationships. The low-LPC leader derives his major satisfaction from accomplishing the task and, for this reason, is called a task-motivated leader.

In developing his argument, Fiedler used a number of groups ranging from surveying teams composed of civil engineering students to bomber crews. The results of the studies indicated that there is a significant interaction between the personality of the leader and the situation in which leadership takes place. Since the situation varies, different leadership styles will be required in different situations. Fiedler's research has been labeled the *contingency theory of leadership* because of its situational nature.

More specifically, the basic finding of Fiedler's contingency theory is that task-motivated leaders generally perform best in very favorable situations where they have a strong position power, structured tasks, and good leader–follower relations or in very unfavorable situations. Relationship-motivated leaders, by contrast, tend to perform best in intermediate or in moderately favorable or unfavorable situations (Fiedler, 1974). This finding has implications for management that go far beyond those possible with traditional theory.

Implications of the Contingency Theory

Situational theories are realistic. We all know that different things work in different situations. Unfortunately, when we admit to the possibility of situational factors, things become very complicated. Organizations are much simpler when we can have confidence in the "one best way" to lead and manage. Recruitment of new managers and their placement are relatively easy when situations do not have to be considered. You find a person who wants to be a manager, who appears to possess certain desired traits, who is "trainable," and you promote her. The problem is, of course, that sometimes it does not work. Fiedler's theory helps us understand why.

Imagine the frustration of the manager of human resources who finally convinces top management that the company's supervisors would benefit from a course in human relations. The course is presented and paid for, and the performance of some supervisors improves but the performance of at least as many others decreases. Contingency theory has an answer. Perhaps those task-motivated managers who, by accident, had been placed in charge of groups with favorable or unfavorable leadership situations had their styles altered enough to make them more relationship-motivated, just as the seminar proposed. Now their style is not properly matched to the reality of their group situation, so performance drops. The other group whose effectiveness improved was probably mismatched from the beginning. They might have been originally task-motivated and placed in group situations that were moderately favorable, where a relations-motivated leader would have been more effective. The seminar, by helping them focus more on human relations, could be expected to improve their performance.

This illustrates the importance of matching the leader's style with the group situation. Rather than spending a lot of money on human relations seminars, a company might invest its limited funds on recruitment and placement activities to ensure that the styles of prospective managers are properly diagnosed, as are the leadership situations in various groups. The "style and circumstance" can be effectively matched.

Unfortunately, group situations and even leadership styles may change over time. The relationship-motivated leader who is charged with the responsibility of building a new project team might find his natural style effective during the formation of the group, when the situation is only moderately favorable. As the project matures and is functioning smoothly, the work becomes more structured, the power position of the leader more defined, and the leader–follower relations improve to the point where a task-motivated style is more appropriate. Then, as the project begins to wind down, the relationship-motivated style may once again be more effective as the situation evolves again to only moderately favorable.

The relationship between the traits and the situational views of leadership is admittedly complex, and attempts to reconcile them are often inadequate. However, Bavelas (1960) provides a useful summary and partial solution to the apparent conflict. He proposes the following:

1. Similarities between organizations make it possible to say useful things about the type of person who is likely to emerge as a leader.
2. Uniquenesses of any particular organization make it necessary to consider the situational factors that influence who is likely to lead.
3. When situations vary from organization to organization, we cannot say what traits will facilitate the emergence of leadership.

Some Prospects for the Future

The dynamic nature of leadership and the fascination the subject has held for managers and society at large will ensure the continued improvement of our understanding of the field. Today, in addition to the work being done in contingency theory, significant theoretical advances are taking place. Some of these, like Victor Vroom's work in leadership and decision making, represent an extension of the more familiar styles of research to other aspects of leader and management behavior.

Leadership and Decision Making

The Vroom and Yetton (1973) model, as it is called, conceives of the leader's role as controlling the process by which decisions are made in that part of the organization for which the leader is responsible. This model makes a particularly important contribution by illustrating how different leadership and problem-solving styles like autocratic, consultative, and group oriented can be used effectively for different types of problems. Moreover, this approach provides the direct implication that the effective leader may, and should, display different styles of leadership and problem solving depending on the type of problem faced at a particular time. For some problems, like those where time is of the essence and the successful implementation is not de-

pendent on acceptance of the solution by the followers, one might be highly autocratic. Other situations will require more consultative and group-oriented approaches.
The challenge of this theory to the leader is his or her ability to appropriately diagnose the style that is most likely to be successful for the problem at hand.

Vroom and Jago (1974) attempted to take this theory one additional step by developing a leadership training program. According to these authors, the critical skill
of all leaders is the ability to adapt their behavior to the demands of the situation.
An important aspect of this adaptability is the skill to select the appropriate decision-
making process for each decision. In this sense, Vroom's arguments are similar to the
situational view of Fiedler, although it requires considerably more individual adaptability and is applicable to a more limited range of leader behavior (that is, decision
making).

Path, Goals, and Leadership

Another developing trend in leadership research that must be briefly reviewed is
path–goal theory. The primary thrust of path–goal theory is concerned with how the
leader's actions influence followers' perceptions of their work goals, personal goals,
and the paths to achieving them (House and Mitchell, 1974). Many of the details of
path–goal theory will be familiar because it is based on expectancy theory, as discussed in the forthcoming chapter on motivation. Thus, the idea that leadership effectiveness is related to the leader's ability to make rewards available to followers
and to distribute these rewards contingent on the performance of various tasks toward
the accomplishment of specific goals is in line with prior discussions.

In path–goal theory, leader behavior is acceptable to followers if they believe
such behavior will be immediately satisfying or will satisfy some need in the future.
This leader behavior will be motivational to followers if it makes the satisfaction of
followers' needs contingent on effective performance and improves the environment
of the followers by providing the support and rewards necessary for effective performance.

As a practical matter, path–goal theory suggests several ways in which leaders
can provide the types of actions that will motivate higher performance on the part of
followers. A few examples are listed next (House and Mitchell, 1974, p. 4):

1. The leader can increase motivation by recognizing and arousing followers'
   needs for outcomes over which the leader has control. A leader may discuss
   with followers the potential growth opportunities and earnings available to
   those who accomplish specific tasks.
2. Leaders may effectively increase motivation by paying higher incentives to
   those group members who actually attain work goals.
3. The leader may make the "paths" to the attainment of desired goals easier to
   travel by coaching or counseling. The leader who assumes a mentor role, for
   example, can increase follower motivation by assisting them, through sage advice and sharing experiences, in accomplishing personal and organizational
   goals.

4. Leaders can increase motivation by helping followers clarify goals and expectations. Particularly in jobs where ambiguities exist concerning what is expected, the leader can assist in clarifying expectations and by emphasizing the most effective paths for goal attainment.

5. Leaders can improve motivation by removing barriers to goal attainment. Nothing is more helpful to highly motivated followers at times than leaders who make it easier for them to do what is expected.

There are, of course, many other ways in which motivation can be increased by innovative leaders. This brief list, however, is useful in suggesting some practical recommendations from a somewhat abstract theory.

Transformational Leadership

To understand transformational leadership it has to be contrasted to the transactional theories we have already discussed. Most leadership theories are based on a transactional relationship between leader and follower, the most familiar being that of supervisor and employee. The supervisor/leader offers a reward if the employee/follower exceeds minimum performance standards. The teacher/leader offers a good grade if pupils/followers complete their assignments on time.

By contrast, transformational leadership is a process whereby individuals create a connection that raises the level of motivation and morality of both the leader and the followers (Northouse, 1997). A primary goal of transformational leadership is to assist followers in attaining their maximum potential. People who are transformational leaders demonstrate some important characteristics (Bass, 1990).

First, transformational leaders are charismatic. Followers identify with these leaders and want to be like them. Often transformational leaders have high moral standards and are trusted by followers. These leaders offer followers a sense of direction and a vision (hope) of a more appealing future. Second, transformational leaders inspire followers by communicating high expectations. Third, these leaders stimulate followers intellectually by challenging them to "break out of the box" and challenge their own beliefs as well as those of the organization. Transformational leaders encourage risk taking and innovation. Finally, transformational leaders are sensitive to people—they listen carefully, coach, and genuinely care about other people (Bass and Avolio, 1993; Kuhnert, 1994).

Transformational leadership, in some ways, brings us full circle in leadership research. One cannot help but note the individual nature of traits such as charisma. However, the most important point to remember about transformational leadership is its moral as well as its motivational component. When the transformational leader is a person of high character, she or he can bring out the best in followers. However, such a leader can also be disruptive and destructive to organizations and individuals if the leader's vision conflicts with that of the organization or if the leader develops strong emotional ties for selfish and immoral ends (Hughes, Ginnett, and Curphy, 1993).

Managers enjoy talking about leadership and researchers enjoy studying it because so much of the success and survival of an organization depend on the quality of its leaders. Leadership is an art, and one that must develop and evolve. Managers should never deceive themselves by thinking that because they are promoted into an executive position they automatically become leaders. Kotter has dispelled that myth once and for all.

Effective leadership is a unique mixture of placement and style. Great care should be taken to place managers into positions where they have the greatest chance to succeed. All managers should strive to be effective leaders. It is an achievement no organization can bestow. There are no honorary leaders. Leadership effectiveness must be earned through hard work, enthusiasm, and commitment.

Implications and Conclusions

The discussion in this chapter has taken us through the writings of a number of familiar and some less familiar people. One conclusion is clear. Leadership has proven to be a more complex issue than most imagined, and these challenges have occupied the attention of some of the greatest minds in management practice and research for decades. It is safe to say that few, if any, managers today believe the oversimplistic notion that leaders possess specific traits or respond consistently to unique situations. To the contrary, most researchers today are engaged in a continued search for consistent predictors of leadership ability. In the meantime managers of organizations continue to wonder and worry about their ability to attract and retain the supply of leaders needed for effective operations. At the same time we must witness again the mysteries of how leadership emerges. Television evangelists attract millions of viewers and raise incredible amounts of money—transformational leadership in practice. Sports heroes and rock stars have followers that are no less fanatical. How do we explain leadership? Not very well, but we keep trying. We learn what we can from those before us and we add as best we can from our own experiences. The world demands a supply of leaders, and for that reason, leadership research will thrive.

Although much has been accomplished in a relatively short period of time, leadership will continue to occupy the attention of management researchers and practicing managers. Leadership is too important and too fundamental to the success of organizations of all types to be left to chance. In fact, the following list will attempt to summarize some of the important things we know about leadership.

1. Traits of individuals are not unimportant, but they are not the sole determinant of leadership. Traits must bear some relevant relationship to the situation faced by the leader.
2. Leadership research did not emerge unprecedented in the 1950s. To the contrary it was the focus of many early management writers, in particular Ordway Tead.
3. Leadership can be viewed from the transformational as well as the more customary transactional perspective. In the former, the emphasis is on the nature of the exchange between leader and follower, whereas in the latter the emphasis is on the emotional connection.
4. Leadership and management should be equally valued in an organization, but they are fundamentally different. Management is about order and efficiency while leadership is about change and effectiveness.

5. Leadership effectiveness is ultimately determined by a complex interaction of leaders, followers, and situational factors.

Questions for Discussion

1 Is there any genuine distinction that can be drawn between leadership and management? If so, what is it?

2 How can Tead's concept of the "logic of the situation" be related to situational management? Are they identical concepts?

3 Are traits important to the emergence of leadership? Defend your answer with some specific examples.

4 Think about the assumptions you make about employees or the teacher makes about you in a classroom. Do they result in a self-fulfilling prophesy?

5 Attempt to classify the organization in which you work or have worked in the past in terms of Likert's Systems 1 to 4. Based on this classification, how would you suggest improving performance in the organization?

6 Does leader–member exchange (LMX) theory add anything of real value to Likert's idea of the linking pin? Explain.

7 How does Fiedler's theory of leadership effectiveness extend or expand previous leadership theories?

8 Can the traits and the situational views of leadership be reconciled? How or why not?

COORDINATING RESOURCES

PART

III

In Part I we indicated that management emerged because of a need to coordinate specialized individuals and operations. Coordination has been one of the continually recurring themes in early and contemporary management thought. Part III looks at coordination and the tools managers have to aid them in effective coordination.

Chapter 6 begins this part with a discussion of the essential ingredient of effective coordination—goal setting. Clear and concise goals provide managers with a target and individuals with something to accomplish and the basis upon which to direct their limited energy. This chapter illustrates that some of the most basic discussions in strategic management are really discussions of coordination. The cry for businesses today to develop a sense of mission and vision is really a cry for goals and objectives. Some writers have referred to mission and vision statements as directional strategies because they provide the organization with a sense of direction. They also provide employees with a sense of what is important today and what will be important in the future.

Chapter 6 also illustrates another reason why goals are important—they provide the basis for effective decision making. Selecting among alternative courses of action requires that some goal or standard exist to facilitate the choice. Goal setting and decision making are, therefore, closely related concepts.

Chapter 7 examines the issue of coordination and authority. Authority or the rights available to managers to require and prohibit actions is a primary means of coordinating resources. Managers frequently call upon legitimate authority to ensure that individuals and units behave in ways that contribute to the accomplishment of the mission and vision of the organization.

Much of the basis of traditional organization theory and contemporary practice is the result of authority relationships. Hierarchies are defined, managers are designated, and relationships are structured in terms of authority relationships. Power, on the other hand, is more closely related to an individual's ability to get things done. Authority is formally defined and flows down in an organization, whereas power is informal and, as Barnard's acceptance theory best illustrates, flows upward.

Chapter 7 also discusses the necessity to delegate authority. When authority is properly delegated it enables the manager to extend his or her abilities and develops the abilities of employees. Delegation of authority is one of the most effective ways to ensure orderly management succession.

The final chapter in this part, Chapter 8, deals with motivation and the coordination of human resources. The human resources available to any organization are among its most important assets. Chapter 8 provides some discussion of how to manage this critical resource most effectively.

Goal Setting and
Decision Making

"By force of circumstance, then, it is suggested that the most that can be controlled by the total membership of an organization is the determination of ends."

John M. Pfiffner and Frank P. Sherwood
Administrative Organization 1960

The starting point of formal organization and of the coordination of operations that organizations are designed to accomplish is a goal—the organization's *raison d'être*. Krupp (1961) said it well by stating that the attainment of the goal(s) is possible only within the constraints imposed by the environment, and the process of management involves decision making, the selection of alternative strategies, and the evaluation of outcomes in terms of preconceived goals (p. 93). The most fundamental precept of early and modern management thinking is that *it* [management] *begins and ends with goals*. Without clear, concise, and communicated goals, management is not possible. Without understood goals, decision making is merely a response to changing conditions. Without goals there can be no leadership, only confused managers directing even more confused employees. How can managers provide direction and offset uncertainty if they do not have goals as guides to the future? How can managers make decisions (choices) among alternatives and evaluate performance if there are not standards of performance? This chapter is about goal setting and decision making—two of the most important functions of managers.

Goals and Goal Setting

Goals are defined as "conceptions of desired end states." Managers think of them primarily as projections of what they hope to accomplish (Bolman and Deal, 1984). However, if goals are to be useful, they must be more than good intentions. They must "degenerate into work" (Drucker, 1973). There are many kinds of goals, and the terms used to describe them are numerous—objectives, ends, and outcomes are the most frequently used. In this chapter no precise distinction will be made among ob-

▲ **Box 6-1**

ORIGINS OF MODERN GOAL SETTING RESEARCH

Edward A. Locke, one of today's leading researchers in goal setting, traces his interest in the subject to the work of the British psychologist C. A. Mace. Even in the 1930s Mace was discovering things that were later confirmed by contemporary researchers. Some of his more important findings were:

1. For goals to be effective motivators, individuals must know their level of performance and its variance from the expectation or goal.

2. Performance is influenced by ability as well as motivation. Goal setting must consider individual abilities. Impossible goals are rejected.

3. Goals must be accepted to be motivational.

4. Goal achievement should consider the quality as well as the quantity of work.

5. The development of task strategies is important to goal attainment.

Source: Carson, Carson, and Heady (1994).

jectives, ends, and goals. In fact, the terms will be used synonymously to describe an organization's targets, performance standards, or desired future states.

Although objections have been raised (Georgiou, 1973) to the "classical goal paradigm" or the view that organizations are essentially instruments of goal accomplishment, the logic of this view is compelling as we saw in Chapter 4 on organizational effectiveness and the challenge of change. Dissenters say that because decision makers are not always sure of their goals or have so many goals they cannot pursue one to the exclusion of others, the classical goal paradigm is too restrictive. A lack of understanding on the part of decision makers, however, does not alter the fact that organizations have a purpose and are goal directed. People create organizations specifically because they cannot accomplish their goals acting alone (Barnard, 1938).

From Task to Grand Purpose

Most of the interest in goal setting centers on planning and the development of grand strategies for organizations. Strategic management is often thought of as more exciting than the day-to-day battles managers fight in the "trenches." This has not always been the case. In the earliest days of scientific management the idea of the "task" related to the most basic elements of work, and it was a fundamental part of the systems proposed by Taylor, the Gilbreths, and others.

Task Management

Taylor (1914) stated that the "most prominent single element in modern scientific management is the task idea" (p. 39). This idea involved fully planning the work of every employee at least a day in advance and issuing complete written instructions describing in detail the task to be accomplished and the means for accomplishing it. Among other things, the task was used as the standard for determining the bonus that would be earned when work was judged meritorious. Some writers, specifically Locke (1982), Locke and Latham (1990), and Wren (1980), believe that the task idea provided much of the practical foundation for widely used techniques such as management by objectives. There is no doubt that early discussions of the "task" revealed the supreme importance placed on goal setting for purposes of coordination and control.

Taylor's idea of the task was endorsed and expanded by Lillian Gilbreth (1973a). While Taylor presented the importance of the task, Lillian Gilbreth described the nature of the concept. Unlike most scientific management writers, Lillian Gilbreth was trained as a psychologist, and it is impossible to say whether her interest in task management resulted from her knowledge of engineering, psychology, or the fact that she was the mother of twelve children. For those who have read *Cheaper by the Dozen* (Gilbreth & Carey, 1948), written by her son and daughter, the importance of goal setting, organization, and control to the efficient management of such a large household becomes quite clear.

The task, to Gilbreth, was a goal to be sure, but it was not one that was casually or theoretically determined. It resulted from an elaborate process of measurement and synthesis. Gilbreth (1973a) believed that tasks should be determined through a complex process of analysis and synthesis. Analysis involved the separation of anything that is "complex into its constituent elements . . . and the explanation of the principles upon which the division is made" (p. 123). Synthesis, by contrast, was the process of putting things back together, or the combination of separate elements into a whole system. The result of synthesis, which presupposed analysis, involved putting the various elements of a job together into a task. However, when we view the task in this manner, the standard for work is not some abstract objective that is determined theoretically. It is the standard for a particular kind of work based on "what has actually been done and what can be expected to be repeated" (p. 130). The task is not an imaginary ideal or an impossible dream of what we hope can be expected. It is the "sum of observed and timed operations, plus a definite and sufficient percentage . . . for overcoming fatigue" (p. 131).

Resistance to the task idea by managers and workers was impossible for Lillian Gilbreth to understand (Spriegel and Meyers, 1953). This resistance was caused primarily, she believed, by an ignorance of the idea of task. Although she did not like the term "task" because of its inherently objectionable connotation, she could not think of a better label. Gilbreth recognized that the accomplishment of goals involved

---

▲ **Box 6-2**

A LONG LIST OF "FIRSTS"

Lillian M. Gilbreth was a partner in the most famous marriage in management. Lillian and Frank Gilbreth were famous for their contributions to scientific management. In spite of the difficulty Lillian experienced in entering the stereotypical male world of management, she was associated with more "firsts" than any other person in management. Samples of some of her more important achievements are: (1) first female member of the Society of Industrial Engineering; (2) first female member of the American Society of Mechanical Engineers; (3) first woman to receive an honorary master of engineering degree (from the University of Michigan); (4) first female professor of management at an engineering school (Purdue University); (5) first female professor of management at the Newark College of Engineering; and (6) only woman, to date, to receive the Gilbreth Medal, the Gantt Gold Medal, and the CIOS Gold Medal.

Source: Wren (1994).

---

a *means–ends relationship.* She stated that everyone in the organization should have a defined task to perform and that organizations should also have tasks. Individual and organizational tasks should be related in such a manner that the accomplishment of the former led to the achievement of the goals of the latter. This was an advanced and sophisticated recognition of a very complex process that started with an understanding of organizational purpose.

From Task Management to Organizational Purpose

The case for a well conceived and communicated organizational mission is as strong, or stronger than the argument favoring well defined and understood task instructions. The purpose of the business is the fundamental question that must be addressed by all managers and employees. It is not enough to simply and jokingly "cop out" by stating: "everyone knows what we are all about—if we do not make profits we all lose our jobs." Of course, every informed manager and employee knows a business must make money if it is to continue operations.

But that is not really addressing the organization's purpose. This issue is much more complicated. Barnard (1938) stated that organizations require only three things: (1) communication; 2) willingness to serve; and (3) a common purpose (p. 82). All cooperative systems require a purpose that is accepted and understood by the members of the organization. According to him, "the inculcation of the belief in the real existence of a common purpose is an essential executive function" (p. 87). To Barnard, the organizational purpose was distinct from individual motives, but the two were closely linked and necessarily reinforcing (Grundstein, 1981). However, Barnard added another insight into organizational purpose. He believed the purpose was essential to add meaning to the environment. "A mere mass of things" outside the organization does not have meaning to the manager. The mass must be reduced, organized, and structured according to some basis of discrimination (that is, purpose). The purpose transforms the "mere mass of things" into something significant, relevant, interesting (pp. 195–196). This recognition is a fundamental aspect of modern strategic thinking.

Consider, for example, the differences in the way environment is perceived by large, private corporations in the United States and state-owned enterprises in countries such as Brazil, Germany, and Canada. The private American corporation has as its purpose a reasonable return on the capital invested by stockholders. Management's job is to scan the environment and focus on opportunities for investment and gain. The state-owned enterprise may scan the same environment and ignore opportunities for profit because of the excessive risk that must be assumed in a time when the national economic plan calls for a reduction in risky investments (Aharoni, 1986). The environment is thus interpreted in different ways by organizations with different purposes.

In more recent times, the discussion of mission statements is an indication of the continued concern for the purpose of organizations. Drucker (1954) placed a great

---

▲ Box 6-3
GOAL SETTING AS A MEANS–ENDS RELATIONSHIP

Asea Brown Boveri (ABB) coordinates thousands of employees worldwide through systematic goal setting. This global corporation is divided into more than 1,000 operating companies, which are further divided into more than 3,500 profit centers. The executive committee sets "macro-level" targets for the corporation in terms of general performance measures such as growth, profit, and return on capital. Goals are then set by each operating company, which are designed to achieve the macro-level targets with more specific performance measures relative to new orders, revenue, operating company profits, and working capital.

The philosophy of one organizational level's goals being the means by which the next higher organization level achieves its goals is carried to the profit centers. The benefits of such a process of goal setting are numerous. For example, targets throughout the corporation are reinforcing and action is coordinated. Individuals are encouraged to see how their actions at their level ultimately contribute in a tangible way to the success of the corporation.

Source: Bartlett and Ghoshal (1995).

deal of attention on the development and communication of organizational purpose. He contended that many businesses fail simply because they do not ask themselves the elementary question: "What is our business?" The mission statement of an organization precisely answers this critical question. It defines the unique purpose that sets an organization apart from all others and identifies the scope of the firm's operations in terms of products and markets (Cochran, David, and Gibson, 1986). When properly developed, the mission statement of an organization is a comprehensive planning tool that enables managers to focus on the present and future opportunities facing the firm. Studies have shown that samples of firms with more comprehensive mission statements are higher performers in financial terms and that of all the elements that could be included in mission statements components relating to corporate philosophy, self-concept, and public image are the most important (Duncan, Ginter, and Kreidel, 1994; Pearce and David, 1987).

This overview illustrates how the emphasis on goal setting has evolved from the scientific management writers' concern for the task to the modern emphasis on strategic management, organizational missions, and goals. The role of planning as a management function and the specific nature and purpose of goal setting have changed, but each period of management thought has included goals as an important element in the theory of organization.

Goal Setting and Administrative Organization

Henri Fayol, Lyndall Urwick, and James Mooney and Alan Reiley were interested in practical matters, and no problem of management is more practical than how to keep the entire operation pointed in the same direction. No synergism or cumulative effect can be achieved by the organization if there is no common goal.

Purpose, Objectives, and Teamwork

Urwick (1952) discussed many principles of organization and drew freely from the work of Fayol and Follett. When discussing goal setting and purpose he was to the point and left no room for misunderstandings. According to him, "unless we have a purpose, there is no reason why individuals should try to coordinate together at all or why anyone should try to organize them" (pp. 18–19). Urwick presented the *principle of the objective*, which insisted that all parts of an organization should lead to the accomplishment of an objective. The objective provided the basis for coordinating the efforts of the various departments and individuals in the organization.

Objectives flow logically from the purpose, and every organization must be an expression of the purpose it is created to accomplish. Urwick and Drucker noted that even though we may say the purpose of a business is to make a profit or provide a service, in fact, the purpose of all business firms is to make and/or distribute some product or service that customers need.

At a more practical and behavioral level, Henry Dennison (1931) pointed out that teamwork, an essential ingredient in the success of any business, relies on the existence of understood goals. Teamwork did not require leadership as long as the objective or goal to be accomplished did not change. The desire for and the knowledge of the common purpose are sufficient so long as the end remains the same. This approach to examining the importance of goal setting illustrates the concern Dennison had for individual and interpersonal relations and, eventually, how it led him to view all social relationships (Duncan and Gullett, 1974).

Objectives and Coordination

In Chapter 4 the ideas of Mooney and Reiley (1931, 1947) were introduced and considerable attention was given to their ideas about coordination. It is interesting to note, however, that goal setting was an integral part of this discussion. Although much of their writing is devoted to the *coordinative principle*, they concede that organizations begin when two or more people combine their efforts in pursuit of a given purpose. However, they quickly point out that this combination alone does not constitute organization. The first principle of organization is that the efforts of the combining parties must be coordinated—they must act together (Mooney and Reiley, 1931, p. 19). Coordination implies an objective (p. 26).

Even though not every member of the organization carries a "deep consciousness" of the purpose, it is expected that the understanding increases as one moves up the organization and becomes less precise at lower levels. In fact, one of the respon-

---

▲ Box 6-4
DIFFERENT GOALS AND APPROACHES

Americans are fascinated with the Japanese and their organizations. Perhaps the fascination results from the fact that Americans and Japanese are so successful in business, yet so different in the way they approach business decisions. For example, Americans work best when they have clear, concise, and understood goals. Japanese salarymen (middle managers and white-collar workers), on the other hand, do best when goals are vague and ambiguous.

Ambiguous goals frustrate Americans but energize Japanese. Ambiguous goals provide Japanese with more freedom to accomplish things in their own ways. Vague assignments encourage employees to look at all angles of a problem and better understand associated issues. The diverse information, when relayed to the boss, provides both the supervisor and the employee with better preparation to solve problems. Often cultural differences appear to influence basic human processes such as goal setting and decision making.

Source: Yoshimura and Anderson (1997).

sibilities of top management is to ensure that an understanding of purpose sweeps down through the organization since the more the rank and file is permeated with the purpose, the greater will be the coordinated effort. This is identical to the point made by Barnard about the executive's responsibility to inculcate the belief in employees that a common purpose exists. At this point, Mooney and Reiley provide an informative argument which relates organizational objectives to the concept of *doctrine*.

Doctrine in its primary sense means simply the definition of the objective (p. 27). Doctrine captures the idea of credo or philosophy and becomes almost synonymous with the objective. However, the doctrine also deals with the procedure(s) for accomplishing the objective. Mooney and Reiley (p. 28) state that it is essential that the doctrine (objective) be both desirable and legitimate. For example, the objective of the economic organization to obtain profits through service is both desirable to employees and legitimate to society. When the foundation of desirability and legitimacy is established it can be translated into the *unity of spirit*, which ensures that coordinated efficiency takes place. It is this type of coordinated effort that leads us to Dennison's concept of teamwork and illustrates the critical character of common purpose and coordination that is essential for organizational efficiency and effectiveness.

From task management to organizational purposes and mission statements there is a direct route that traces much of management thought for almost a century. However, there are other developments in the area of goal setting that are even more familiar to managers and employees. One of the most familiar is known as management by objectives (MBO).

Management by Objectives

If we accept the classical goal paradigm introduced earlier, we can say with confidence that MBO is nothing new. All management, by definition, is management by objectives. However, not everyone who talks about MBO is talking about the same thing. McConkey (1983) found that 40 percent of the Fortune 500 companies employed some form of MBO, but there was great diversity in the way these programs were implemented.

Most management historians attribute the beginning of MBO to Peter Drucker's book, *The Practice of Management* (1954). That is, while no one argues that elements of MBO have existed from the earliest days of human cooperation—the synthesis, to use Gilbreth's term—Drucker brought all the elements together into a philosophy known as MBO.

The three essential elements of MBO programs are: (1) establishment of clear, concise, and communicated goals; (2) participation in the goal-setting process by those who will be expected to work under the system; and (3) performance evaluation based on results. The purpose of MBO, quite simply, is to provide employees with targets or quantitative milestones to accomplish, allow them an opportunity to offer input into what the targets should be, and evaluation based on the results achieved.

General Electric Company developed a pioneering form of MBO called Work Planning and Review (WPR). The GE program evolved from experiments on goal setting (Meyer, Kay, and French, 1965). The company has continued its focus on goal setting with the practice of *stretch goals.* This process encourages people to set goals for themselves that are virtually impossible to attain, such as doubling sales or increasing speed to market threefold. Steve Kerr, the chief learning officer at GE, points out that when you encourage employees to establish these stretch goals, it is important not to punish people for not attaining them, but to provide people with the training, knowledge, and resources to pursue these goals, and to share the wealth generated when the goals are achieved (Sherman, 1995).

The experience of Purex with a version of MBO known as Goals and Controls was equally favorable. Raia (1974) indicated that improvements resulted in the area of productivity, even though participation was limited. There was evidence that the performance improvements lasted a relatively long time in spite of the fact that managers complained of excessive paperwork and employees felt there was too much emphasis on measurable, quantitative goals to the exclusion of more qualitative aspects of their jobs.

One of the most comprehensive reports of an implementation of MBO was offered by Carroll and Tosi (1973), who described the experience of Black and Decker. These writers reported that more difficult goals resulted in favorable attitudes toward the program and in improved relations between employees and managers. Frequency of feedback was found to be positively related to attitudes, performance, and employee and manager relations. Praise was more valuable than criticism.

When Drucker proposed the concept of MBO, there was great excitement about the success of this emerging philosophy. MBO offered a practical way of managing as it should be done—by investing time in planning so as to reduce the time required for control. Explicit goals improved communication and the opportunity to participate held the promise of increasing the level of employee motivation. Moreover, if the planning was done properly, much of the threat of performance evaluation and control for managers and employees could be eliminated. Everyone was in favor of improving the process of performance evaluation (Lee, Locke, and Phan, 1997).

Unfortunately, many believe that something happened to MBO as it was transferred from theory to practice. Lee (1980) stated that when MBO slipped from a philosophy to a program, it became a fad and just another management fashion. The philosophy could not be "implanted in announcements accompanied by a set of forms and procedures and a few training sessions" (p. 279). Comprehensive evaluations, such as Ivancevich (1972), contained reservations regarding the success of this widely used management technique. Improper use, premature implementations, and related difficulties, however, should not obscure the fact that MBO as a philosophy is logically sound and pragmatically useful. MBO properly places the emphasis on goal setting. Opportunities are offered that allow employees to interact with managers and provide input into the standards against which their performance will be evaluated. It also provides a predictable means of obtaining feedback on how well goals are being accomplished.

In the end, what is it that goal setting is supposed to accomplish? Employees want and need three things from a job. They need to know what is expected. It is impossible to produce at or near one's potential if the task is not understood. In every case the scientific management writers recognized this critical point. Second, employees need to feel they have a part in establishing the standards of performance. Finally, employees need regular feedback on how they are doing. No manager does an employee a favor by not providing feedback on performance. Bad news is not the worst news. At least when the feedback is negative, we can focus our energies on improving performance. The worst news by far is no news. No feedback merely perpetuates unsatisfactory performance and causes bad relations when radical corrective action is initiated (Kerr, 1974).

Goals as Decision Criteria

The primary function of management, says Akio Morita (1986), Chairman of the Board and CEO of Sony Corporation, is decision making. Simon (1960) called decision making the "heart of executive activity." Managers are people who earn their living in high-pressure, uncertain, and unforgiving environments. If they are successful, they must simplify reality and focus their efforts. Clear and understood goals simplify the "heart of executive activity" by providing the key to focusing energy and providing direction.

In Chapter 2 we demonstrated the impossibility of managers acting in a totally logical manner. Interestingly, one of the most influential advocates of the idea of rationality in decision making had little knowledge and even less interest in management (Weiss, 1983). Max Weber was born in Germany in 1864. Weber distinguished himself as a legal scholar and professor of political economy at the universities of Freiburg, Heidelberg, and Berlin.

Weber, like Taylor, was given to episodes of nervous illness. At an early age, the illness became severe and forced him to resign his position at the university and spend years doing little more than traveling. After being drafted and serving time in the army, Weber accepted his first teaching job in 20 years at the University of Munich. At the age of only 56 and at the height of his career he died in 1920. Throughout his brief and difficult life, Weber wrote on a variety of topics, including the sociology of religion, effects of assembly lines on workers, and the theory of social and economic organizations (Kronman, 1983, pp. 191–193). His contributions are so far-reaching that he is claimed by a number of academic disciplines, including sociology, economics, and philosophy. His ideas on the rational nature of human beings and organizations will be our concern here because of the implications they have for decision making.

Rationality and Common Sense

The world observed by Weber was not a pretty place. It was dominated by class consciousness and nepotism. Becoming an officer in the Prussian Army, for example, presupposed an aristocratic birth. Leadership in government and industry was no different. To Weber, this was a ridiculous waste of human resources. Was it impossible for the working class to produce leaders as well as followers? This type of injustice resulted for the most part, in Weber's view, from the imperfection of human judgment. It was an unfortunate characteristic of human nature to hire relatives and preserve the wealth of the rich even if it disadvantaged society in the process. The solution was to free the individual as much as possible from the judgments that were so often clouded by emotion.

This could best be accomplished through the organization of work in ways that followed Weber's "ideal" bureaucracy. The ideal bureaucracy did not exist in reality but provided a basis for theorizing about work and how it was done in large groups. It was, according to Weber, a "selective reconstruction" of the real world.

In the ideal bureaucracy selection and tenure were based on competence not birth—what you know not whom you know! Rules, regulations, and procedures that had been tried and shown to be valid were the basis for decision making, and authority was distributed according to position and rank rather than divine rights and traditions (Weber, 1947). The ideal bureaucracy possessed another compelling characteristic that made it superior to all other known structures. The administrator at the top of the hierarchy could not know everything about the choices he or she was required to make, but help was available. By assembling qualified specialists at lower levels, these "experts" could filter the most appropriate information and send it to the top. Since, in the ideal form of organization, these experts were not motivated to screen information protectively, it was possible, at least theoretically, for top managers to become better informed while dealing with only a portion of the total information.

The result was a form of "rationality" that has become the standard in much of modern decision theory—a rationality not in terms of psychological normality but in terms of information. Thus, the rational manager is the manager who is informed. The nonrational manager merely lacks knowledge. The rational manager or decision maker has a purpose, a goal. The nonrational manager does not. On this basis Weber spoke of rationality as a means of differentiating one type of action from other types. Rational behavior is directed toward unambiguous goals, and the means of achieving the goals are selected on the basis of the best available information (Weber, 1947, p. 16). Rationality, in the Weberian sense, was being informed and goal directed, much like Fayol's reflective calculating manager discussed in Chapter 2.

Operating from the assumption of rationality, even strategic decisions can be structured in a manner that appears very rational. Strategic decisions become defined processes consisting of goal setting, environmental scanning, identifying one's strategic capacity (that is, evaluating strengths and weaknesses), formulating alternative strategies, choosing a strategy, implementing the choice, and following up to ensure that goals are achieved (Ginter, Rucks, and Duncan, 1985). As impressive as the results have been, there has always been a recognition that somehow the assumption of the perfectly rational decision maker was out of touch with reality. Uncertainty was the rule not the exception. Whereas Weber knew his "ideal bureaucracy" was an abstraction, a simplification, a model, there was the suspicion that operations researchers and management scientists had more faith in decision matrices than was warranted. No one is as logical as decision trees made us appear (McKean, 1985).

A Closer Look at Rationality

Weber introduced us to the importance of rationality, but Herbert A. Simon applied it to administrative behavior. Simon's analysis of rationality in decision making initially appears strange. In a time when knowledge is so specialized that we can scarcely master a small part of even a highly specialized field, Simon emerged as one who has excelled in several. He was trained in political science at the University of Chicago, where he received his doctorate in 1943. He worked at the International City Managers Association, the Bureau of Public Administration at the University of California, and taught at the Illinois Institute of Technology before going to Carnegie-Mellon University in 1949, where he has continued to serve as the Richard King Mellon University Professor of Computer Science and Psychology.

Simon has studied decision making, problem solving processes, and artificial intelligence for more than 4 decades. His unusually significant research has been recognized by his election to the National Academy of Science, and with awards from the American Psychological Association, the American Economic Association, and the Institute of Electrical and Electronics Engineers. In 1978 he received the Alfred Nobel Memorial Prize in Economics. Perhaps more than any other person, Simon has increased our understanding of human problem solving and decision making (Neuhaus, 1981).

Simon began developing his ideas on decision making and management in his first book, *Administrative Behavior* (3rd ed., 1976). The book was written for scholars interested in research, managers interested in practical aids for improving their performance, and students interested in learning more about management and decision making. The decision-making orientation of the book is established early, when Simon notes that any practical activity consists of "deciding" and "doing." Management and administration should, therefore, be thought of as decision processes as well as processes involving action.

Simon looked at decisions in terms of hierarchies and means–ends relationships. Each lower level decision is concerned with implementing the goals set forth in the decision just above it. The decisions of the production superintendent in a steel mill, for example, directly involve the implementation of decisions made by the production vice president. Supervisors under the authority of the superintendent will make their decisions and direct them toward implementing the decisions made by the superintendent. Decisions are logical means–ends relationships, whereby the ends (goals) of one level become the means by which the next higher level goals will be accomplished. Decision-making behavior is purposeful when it is goal directed. It is rational to the extent that alternatives are selected that are directed toward the accomplishment of previously established goals. Rationality, as Simon noted, is more complicated.

The rationality envisioned by the operations researchers and classical economists is "objective rationality." It results in decisions that maximize the values of the manager or the organization. This objective rationality never occurs, however, because it requires complete knowledge of all possible choices, their outcomes, and some means of supplying knowledge resulting from a lack of experience (Simon, 1976). If not objective, perhaps we can attain "subjective rationality" whereby we maximize the outcome subject to the limited knowledge we possess about the decision situation. Upon investigation we find that not even this rationality is possible (Wolf, 1995).

To illustrate, Simon defined the general concept of rationality as "concerned with the selection of preferred behavior alternatives in terms of some system of values

▲ **Box 6-5**

USING DECISION THEORY

Decision theory can be put to work in real organizations. The Saab–Valmet plant in Finland used decision theory to improve its competitiveness by improving its inbound logistics. Most of the supplies and materials used in the plant were delivered by truck and ferryboat. If a truck missed a ferry, the delivery could be delayed 12 hours. The decision model used at the plant developed a simulation that demonstrated the relationship between increased delivery frequency, safety stocks, inventory carrying costs, and so on. Using this approach allowed managers to combine human judgment and computer technology for the improvement of decision making.

Health care organizations have used decision theory to improve basic processes such as scheduling operating rooms. Customarily operating room scheduling in hospitals is done either by blocks of time reserved for surgical specialties or by first come, first served. Both methods have advantages and disadvantages. Some hospitals, however, have used advanced manufacturing techniques such as "job shop" scheduling and applied them to the operating room and goal programming methods to improve scheduling. The use of these methods demonstrated how operating room and staff overtime costs could be reduced.

Source: Holmstrom and Aavikko (1994); Ozkarahan (1995).

[goals or ends] whereby the consequences of the behavior can be evaluated" (p. 75). The economic man or woman of classical economics could achieve this state of *objective rationality* but not the administrative man or woman who populates the real world of decision making. This person has limited knowledge, or *bounded rationality*, rather than perfect knowledge. In solving organizational problems these individuals *sequentially search* for randomly generated alternative solutions and achieve satisfactory rather than maximum outcomes. In other words, they make satisfactory decisions because, in Simon's words, they or we do not "have the wits to maximize" (p. xxvii). Even subjective rationality is denied because maximizing choices within the bounds of knowledge are influenced more by the order in which alternatives are generated than by the preexistence of some clear guidelines for ensuring maximizing behavior (Cyert, 1979; March, 1978; Roach, 1979).

The administrative person in Simon's theory of decision making has a sense of what constitutes satisfactory performance through experience. If investors earn, say, 6 percent on their investment, the decision maker notices that employees do not complain that excessive profits are being made at the expense of lower wages, customers do not complain that the profits are being sustained by exorbitant prices, government regulators leave the company alone, and not one investor ever asked whether 6 percent was the absolute maximum that could have been earned. The decision maker thus focuses on this satisfactory return and abandons objective rationality. Second, decision makers search within the bounds of rationality (that is, limits of their information) by randomly selecting alternative solutions in a sequential manner until an option promises a return of 6 percent or more. In the process, subjective rationality is sacrificed. Simon concludes that "what managers know they should do . . . is very often different from what they actually do" (Simon, 1987).

The fame of Simon and others at Carnegie-Mellon University attracted many scholars to Pittsburgh who shared an interest in decision making. Richard Cyert and James March were two of the more famous, and in 1958 Simon and March collaborated in the publication of *Organizations*. The focus of this book is broader than decision making in a technical sense. It is, as the name implies, a book about organizations and management. However, the perceptive reader soon realizes that the ideas developed in *Administrative Behavior* occupy a place of more than passing importance in this book.

Cyert, Simon, March, and others of the Carnegie School of thought likely did not anticipate the importance of their work on management and decision making. With the use of ideas like satisficing, bounded rationality, and sequential search they did much to legitimize the view that managers were not rational problem solvers or reflective calculators. Decision makers do not operate under conditions of perfect knowledge, so uncertainty is the normal state of affairs. So confident did the researchers become in the accuracy of their ideas that they even suggested such things as "garbage can models" of decision making (Cohen and March, 1974; Cohen, March, and Olsen, 1972).

The garbage can model applies to a special type of organization known as the organized anarchy. Organized anarchies such as universities, think tanks, research organizations, and perhaps some health care organizations have preferences that are ill-defined and often inconsistent. Technologies are unclear and participation is fluid, with numerous examples of "going and coming" as well as a high degree of turnover. Objectives or goals are found through action rather than the manager beginning with a set of predetermined goals and pursuing them. The mode of operation of the organized anarchy is best illustrated by the following quotation:

> [These organizations are] *collections of choices looking for problems, issues and feelings looking for decision situations in which they might be aired, solutions looking for issues to which they might be the answer, and decision makers looking for work.*
>
> (Cohen, March, and Olsen, 1972, p. 2.)

Humorous as this may sound, there is much truth to the idea of garbage can models of decision making. For our purposes, it can only be looked upon as one of several nonrational models of decision theory. These theories add an important dimension to be considered by managers as decision makers. Yet the writers of the Carnegie-Mellon tradition of thought always stopped short of actually advocating nonrationality. The credit for legitimizing nonrationality goes to other writers who agree that managers "do not have the wits to maximize," and that, in itself, is a virtue.

Science of Muddling Through

Charles Lindblom (1959) greatly accelerated, at least in terms of public policy, the interest in nonrational models of decision making by introducing the idea of *muddling through*. This idea was formulated with reference to the public sector, but it has implications for all types of strategic decision making.

Lindblom, like March and Simon, begin with the rational view that he calls the *rational-comprehensive* model. This approach progresses logically from goal setting to implementation and follow up or control (Lindblom, 1979). Somewhere between the impossible (rational-comprehensive model) and the unacceptable (grossly incomplete analysis) lie Lindblom's feasible approaches to strategy. All these feasible approaches have one thing in common—they are incremental or proceed step by step from what is unknown to what is known and desirable.

Although Lindblom defines at least three types of incremental analysis, the most important for our purposes is the method of *successive limited comparisons* (SLC), whereby goals are never clearly established and pursued as implied under normative decision theory. Instead, the decision maker chooses simultaneously a policy to attain an objective and the objective itself. Relationships between means and ends in decision making are confused and sometimes impossible to establish. In normative theory, policy decisions are "good" if they accomplish a specified goal. In SLC good policies are those that are agreed on by the key actors in the organization.

In the *rational-comprehensive* method everything important is analyzed only when "important" is so narrowly defined that it becomes meaningless. SLC simplifies this situation in two ways. First, only decision alternatives that differ little from those currently in effect are considered, thereby reducing the number of options that must be considered by the decision maker. Second, potentially important consequences of options are excluded from consideration. Policies arrived at through SLC are not once and for all decisions but products of successive approximations. Theoretically, this method reduces errors because: (1) past outcomes provide the knowledge for constantly defining and refining the organization's direction; (2) as a result of this constant redefinition, there is no need for big jumps toward new and different goals; (3) previous predictions and forecasts can be tested before proceeding; and (4) correcting past misallocations of resources is made easier since small steps in decision making ensure that mistakes are corrected before major errors occur.

Process of Muddling Through

Unlike the decision maker pictured by the operations researchers, the strategist in the process of muddling through does not behave in a totally predictable manner. As with the case of the satisficing manager, the decision maker begins muddling by formulating a few equally simple goals that compromise the values, power, and overall interests of a few groups in and out of the organization (Dror, 1964). Next, an array of alternative options or strategies are formulated that will accomplish the goals. All of these strategies represent small, incremental movements from the present strategy or the status quo. Since only small, incremental strategy options are considered, they are familiar because of the decision maker's past experience.

Finally, the manager selects an option, even though the choice is not necessarily assumed to be the best way of accomplishing predetermined goals. The incrementalist never expects a goal to be fully achieved. Rather, it is expected that decisions will merely bring us closer and closer to the desired outcome. While the details differ slightly, Lindblom's process is not unlike Simon's—at least it is not different in principle. Both picture the decision maker as a nonmaximizing, compromising, and satisficing individual. The thing that distinguishes Lindblom's argument is that he advocates muddling through not as a realistic, *second best* approach to decision making but as the preferred way to make decisions. He makes it clear that muddling through can and should be constantly improving, but in almost all its forms, incrementalism results in better decisions than the most feasible form of the rational complete model (Lindblom, 1979, p. 519).

Systematic Muddling—Logical Incrementalism

James Brian Quinn (1980a) agreed with Lindblom to a point. He finds no argument with the contention that managers are less than perfectly rational. In fact, he states that decisions are an "artful blend of formal analysis, behavioral techniques, and power politics" (p. 3). Decisions, according to Quinn, are "typically fragmented, evolutionary, and largely intuitive" (Quinn, 1978, p. 7). However, he protests the contention that muddling is either nonrational or illogical. Instead of calling the process muddling, Quinn prefers that it be looked on as "a purposeful, effective, proactive management technique that is capable of improving and integrating both the analytical and behavioral aspects of strategy formulation" (p. 8).

Logical incrementalism (LI) begins with the assumption that goal setting is vague. The manager has an idea of where the organization should go, but the objective(s) are not formalized for several reasons. Announcement of a set of formal goals would tend to centralize decision making and give both loyal and disloyal opposition an opportunity to see what you are up to, making it easier for them to rally around defeating your plans. Formal goals also increase the rigidity of thinking and create the impression that goals are carved in stone. Finally, formalized goals can help competitors discover what the manager hopes to accomplish, thereby aiding in the formulation of a defensive strategy. This deference to formal goal setting is one of the truly unique aspects of logical incrementalism.

Rather than beginning as formal goals, strategic concerns arise because the manager confronts some problem in relating the firm and its current way of operating to the larger environment. Often systems for scanning the environment are not present or are ineffective, so the decision maker builds informal networks with people inside and outside the organization (Kotter, 1982; Luthans, Rosenkrantz, and Hennessey,

1985). These networks, however, do more than supplement information from the formal lines of communication. They are built to ensure that people at the top hear what they need to hear rather than having important data filtered or screened out as information flows up the hierarchy (Quinn, 1980b). The emphasis, unlike in the case of muddling through, is not merely to make small, nonthreatening changes, but to actually find and attract effective members of the network who will offer options that go beyond the status quo. Perhaps even radical options will develop if the network is constructed properly.

When problems develop with the organization's interaction with its environment, managers become convinced some type of strategic change is needed and additional information is required before actions can be taken with reasonable confidence. Data are gathered and energy is devoted to building support for the preferred option when it emerges. Unlike March and Simon (1958), logical incrementalism rarely results in the selection of the first, randomly generated alternative. To the contrary, the manager consciously engages in constructing a broad array of options. A case is built to dislodge preconceived notions, even though at this point top executives are careful not to become too identified with a tentative notion that may prove to be a bad idea or to tip off competitors prematurely before a winning plan is developed. During this period of time the decision maker shops freely for ideas among trusted colleagues and employees while carefully testing ideas. Occasionally a task force is commissioned to study the options. After a matter of time, and only after satisfying herself of the likelihood of success, the decision maker acts (Quinn, 1980b).

When the option is selected, implementation begins. At this point Quinn makes one of his greatest contributions to decision making by emphasizing the behavioral and political nature of implementation. The culture of the organization becomes a critical factor in employee acceptance of strategic change, and symbolic acts on the part of the decision maker take on important meanings. The CEO's presence or absence at a meeting, for example, may be interpreted as a signal regarding the importance attached to a new strategic direction.

Initially, the experienced executive is likely to introduce strategic changes as little more than tactical adjustments and to allow the time necessary to build support for the new direction. Particular care is taken not to alienate allies or supporters and to build as much flexibility as possible. Always the decision maker is waiting for just the right time to announce the decision. Key events sometime provide windows that open briefly and offer the opportunity to take the initiative. These windows may be created by the retirement of a strong opponent or a similar event. Even though the decision maker attempts to "lay low, she/he is quite active in the strategic change required by new decisions." As Quinn (1980a, p. 11) notes, these managers frequently use the hidden-hand approach but keep their hands busy even though they cannot be seen. Thus, the case is made for logical incrementalism, not as muddling through but as an attempt to adapt to "the practical psychological and informational problems of getting a constantly changing group of people . . . to move together effectively in a constantly changing environment" (Quinn, 1980a, p. 12).

Quinn offers no apologies for the nonrational process of logical incrementalism. In the case of normative decision theory, making better decisions always implies moving from a second best approach such as incrementalism to the rational, complete, normative model. To incrementalists, better decisions mean practicing incremental-ism more effectively and rarely, if ever, turning away from it to another technique (Lindblom, 1979).

When Necessity Becomes a Virtue

Cyert, March, and Simon talked of nonrational models along with such behavior as satisficing, bounded rationality, sequential search, and so on as things decision mak-ers do in an attempt to deal with the extreme complexity of problems facing man-agers. There seemed always to be the caution that their goal was to describe how de-cisions are made, not how they should be made. That is why their approach is appropriately referred to as behavioral–descriptive theory. It attempted only to un-derstand and describe decision-making behavior. The operations researchers, by con-trast, sought guidelines managers can learn to aid in accomplishing organizational goals. Thus, it is normative because a norm is pursued even though the norm may be revenues, market share, profits, satisfaction, or a number of other outcomes.

In the sense that they are descriptions of how managers make decisions, logical incrementalism and muddling through have much in common with the work of Cy-ert, March, and Simon. However, in the sense that both Lindblom and Quinn believe their processes result in better decisions, they are positioned closer to traditional nor-mative models. However, there is little to suggest that nonrational decision theories result in better decisions than more rational theories (Duncan, 1987). Some of the problems are apparent.

First, neither logical incrementalism nor muddling through insists on statements of clear, concise, and understood goal statements. To measure, monitor, and correct actions there must first exist a standard, goal, or reference point from which devia-tions can be charted. This provides a direct linkage between goal setting and decision making. As Locke and Latham (1984) illustrate, without understood, communicated goals and a timetable for reaching them, planning is reduced to "hollow rhetoric that leads to nothing but inaction" (p. 27).

Effects of Nonrational Models of Decision Making

Adams (1979) presents a convincing argument regarding the kinds of problems that develop when the impossibility of rationality is accepted. Some of the more impor-tant are: Where quality and quantity are difficult to measure and goals are not prop-erly developed, quantity sometimes becomes the substitute measure for organizational effectiveness. The manager may believe he is productive because meetings consume most of the day along with telephone calls and answering mail. Perhaps this explains why Mintzberg (1973) found managerial work to be so fragmentary.

Statistics make it obvious to anyone who reads the facts that managers are busy people who arrive at work early and go home late. They rarely have time to read and stay informed about the important events that could affect their business. Instead, they fight fires, respond to emergencies, and deal with crises most of the day. Even though everyone works hard, unless the effort is directed toward clearly defined goals, productivity is not likely to increase. Symbols replace substance as measures of achievement. Appearances may become particularly important. Where people sit at meetings, where their offices are located, and the kind of car the company furnishes may become the real indicators of performance and success.

When managers are rewarded for taking the course of least resistance, others will follow. Managers especially must know what they are doing if they are going to supervise others in pursuit of organizational goals. The results of all these deviations from the rational, complete method of decision making, even if the latter is recognized as impossible, can be disastrous. An appropriate example might well be the American space shuttle tragedy on January 28, 1986. In just over a minute after it lifted off people all over the nation and the world were stunned to see it explode before their eyes, killing all seven occupants of the Challenger. Tragedy had taken the lives of three other American astronauts in 1967, but it was not witnessed by millions on television and the loss seemed less personal.

While the immediate cause of the explosion was leaking "O-rings," the true cause of the tragedy, many believe, was the faulty decision-making processes at NASA. Since the tragedy numerous theories have been presented to explain how something so horrifying as the explosion could occur. Some blame the temperature on the morning of the launch, some see the fault with a failure to adequately access the risk, but all informed observers of the event and its aftermath were confused at how NASA decision makers could allow such a thing to happen. To understand better, consider the events from the standpoint of decision making.

Perrow (1984) argued that machines and processes have become so complex that even the best scientists, engineers, and managers with the best available equipment cannot anticipate, design for, and allow for all the possible quirks of such complex systems. Serious failures of technology and judgment are capable of leading to disasters like the Challenger, Three Mile Island, and Union Carbide's Bhopal, India, chemical plant. Decision makers, whether scientist, engineer, or manager, cannot deal effectively over long periods of time with the tremendous number of relationships and systems that are necessary to operate high-risk technology. To some extent, these *normal accidents* are even predictable.

Usually disasters begin with small events and trivial failures in the system. At least since 1980, NASA officials had known that there was a problem with the O-rings. In December 1982, after five successful shuttle launches, seal (O-ring) failure was put on the critical list of dangers, and its effects were described as "loss of mission, vehicle, and crew due to metal erosion, burn through, and probable case burst resulting in fire and deflagration" (Biddle, 1986, p. 42). Out of the first 12 shuttle flights investigators found 4 incidents of seal burn through on the primary seal. Seven occurred on the first 4 flights in 1984, and even some secondary O-ring erosion was found. The danger was clearly alarming. However, the rules of NASA were waived in 1983 in the case of the O-rings and were not reinstituted.

Next, Perrow believes that accidents often happen because of production pressures. NASA obviously wanted to prove the commercial value of the shuttle through frequent flights, support for which involved gaining citizen support through the inclusion of government officials, teachers, and journalists in the flight crews. Cost containment efforts frequently encourage compromise of safety standards and controls unless policies are monitored to assure otherwise. Finally, and perhaps most frightening, there is little evidence to suggest that investigations of normal accidents do much to prevent future mishaps. Decision makers, in Simon's words, *do not have the wits* to ensure the perpetual safe operation of the machines they create. We could ask, however, that if we cannot ensure the safety of future flights, can we assess the risk so that everyone knows the chances they take each time a shuttle is launched? The answer here is an emphatic *yes*! NASA certainly had this type of information, but the mere possession of data does not ensure that decision makers will act in accordance with it. McKean (1986) stated that during the days of the Apollo program engineers calculated the risk of successfully sending a person to the moon based on the best technical information. The odds were not very high! The engineers estimated that the chances of an Apollo astronaut returning alive was only 1 in 20. Supposedly, the engineer's manager said the figures were so ridiculously low that he wanted the number buried, the risk analysis group was disbanded, and risk analysis was rarely mentioned again (p. 48).

In spite of NASA's reluctance, the science of risk analysis has continued to develop. Sophisticated techniques like fault tree analysis, event analysis, and failure mode and effects analysis (FMEA) are available to decision makers in all industries. The failure of NASA to fully utilize the available technology in this area hints at a form of decision making that was clearly nonrational. Throughout the modern history of the space agency, the risks have been acknowledged, but it was accepted that test pilots were accustomed to danger and their experience made them aware of the risks. The same was not true of congressmen, teachers, journalists, and payload scientists not trained or experienced as members of flight crews.

There is evidence that Morton Thiokol, the manufacturer of the solid fuel rockets, performed FMEA on the O-rings before 1982 and assessed the probability of a failure at between 1 in 500 and 1 in 5000 launches. The result was the installation of a secondary seal to provide a redundant safety factor. Yet NASA demonstrated an unusual type of certainty in the face of disturbing data. Perhaps it was the macho culture, the *can do* attitude so evident among paratroopers, test pilots, and rocket experts. The space program had been extraordinarily safe. Can anything less than overconfidence be expected after 24 relatively eventless launchings in spite of the fact that one engineer expressed all our fears by saying that every time a "rocket goes up successfully, it's a miracle . . . something always happens that makes you think they will never fly again" (Biddle, 1986, p. 40).

To this point we have examined the relationship between goal setting and decision making. Goals are indeed essential to effective management. The concluding section of this chapter will examine one final aspect of goal setting—the behavioral dimension.

Goal Setting: A Behavioral Perspective

If goal setting is as important as we say and if the tradition that began with task management and continued through MBO to the current emphasis on mission statements and strategic thinking is well established in organization theory and management prac-

tice, we would expect research to focus on the importance of this phenomenon. Fortunately, research has provided us with many insights concerning the manner in which
goals affect behavior.

Goal Setting and Performance Improvement

Management researchers and managers are interested in the influence new management concepts and theories ultimately have on performance. Locke, Shaw, Saari, and
Latham (1981) provided a startling review of the motivational potential of goal setting. They illustrated, for example, that in a survey of more than 100 studies on goal
setting, 90 percent found that goal setting increased performance significantly. No
other motivational technique known to date can come close to duplicating that record.

The research confirms what early writers suspected—goal setting increases productivity. Yet, to the manager, research evidence is not always enough. If the director of human resources or some other executive is to invest thousands of dollars and
hundreds of hours in a comprehensive goal-setting program, it has to make intuitive
as well as scientific sense. Therefore, at the level of intuition, we should ask "what
is there about the existence of goals that makes people more productive?" Three reasons can be offered for such improvements (Locke and Latham, 1984): (1) Goals focus the attention of employees and managers on relevant and important factors. (2)
Goals regulate how hard a person actually works. Energy is spent in proportion to the
difficulty of the goals that are accepted by the managers and the employees. (3) Dif-

---

▲ Box 6-6
DECISION MAKING AS A GAME

Decision making often involves speculating about the behavior of competitors, suppliers, and customers. For example, Toys R Us and Wal-Mart attempted to negoti-
ate quantity discounts with Super Mario Brothers video games at a time when Nintendo could sell more copies than it could supply and there were no major
competitors relative to this product. Nintendo knew that the retail discounters could
sell everything they supplied and demand even more as well as increasingly large
discounts. The result would be significant pressure on profits at a time when price
concessions were not warranted.

In order to counteract this power on the part of retailers, Nintendo decided not
to fill all the orders of the large retailers completely. This created a planned shortage and even greater demand. With the shortage of supply and ever-increasing demand, Nintendo placed itself in a better position to resist the pressure to lower prices
to the retail stores.

Source: Brandenburger and Nalebuff (1995).

ficult goals that are accepted increase an individual's resolve, and persistence is "directed effort that is exerted over time."

This intuitive view of goal setting makes sense to managers and researchers. No one can accomplish all there is to do. Energy and money are scarce. All of us have more to do than energy or time allow. Goals define for us those things that are most relevant and direct our behavior toward the accomplishment of a few important outcomes. It is also clear that we work harder to accomplish those goals that demand our best.

At this point a word of caution is needed. Even though goals should be demanding and difficult, they should not be impossible (DeBono, 1992). When goals are thought to be impossible to obtain, they are not meaningful to employees and the motivational effect is lost. This is where experience is critical for the manager who uses goal setting as a motivational technique. You must know the difference between the demanding and the impossible. Finally, when employees accept the legitimacy of goals, they are more persistent in pursuing them. They not only work harder, they work longer. The key words here are "accept" and "legitimate." Goals, if they are to be motivational, must be accepted, and often an opportunity to participate in goal setting will increase the acceptance of the objectives that are designed to direct behavior. This issue of acceptance and the closely related topic of feedback on performance are perhaps the unique contributions of advocates of goal setting since the introduction of the concept by scientific management writers and the refinement of the process by administrative organization writers. We will conclude this analysis of goal setting by looking in some detail at how managers can encourage the acceptance of goals and what actions they might take to ensure maximum motivational impact.

Participative Goal Setting

One of the key elements of MBO we noted is that goals should be set in a participative manner. This is one way acceptance can be increased. In fact, earlier theories of management, particularly those of Taylor, are often criticized because there was little or no apparent appreciation for participation on the part of workers. Recent research on this issue has provided some interesting results. To the surprise of many, the research of Meyer, Kay, and French (1965) at General Electric suggested that the way goals are set is less important than the fact that they exist to provide direction. More important to the ultimate acceptance of goals are such things as an explanation of why and how goals are assigned, instructions on how to complete the tasks so as to maximize the likelihood of goal attainment, and selection of employees who are capable of performing the work that will be required to attain the goals.

The reason why this is so interesting when we put it in proper perspective is that all of the elements that are really critical in goal acceptance were integral parts of the task management concept of scientific management. To illustrate, the task, as explained by Lillian Gilbreth, was not an abstract, impossible goal that could be achieved only through superhuman or heroic performance. Instead, it was a level of work that was demonstrated to be "achievable" under specific, reasonable conditions. Workers could willingly accept the possibility of the task because they could see it accomplished.

Taylor, in the same way, recognized that tasks could be made demanding only when people were "constitutionally" suited to perform the job. He included as one of the main duties of managers the responsibility to "scientifically select, train, teach, and develop workmen." Hugo Munsterberg, the "father of industrial psychology," agreed that it was critically important to select the right employee for the right job. His pioneering work on the scientific selection of street car drivers and extensions of his research in the selection and training of soldiers in World War I were the beginning of the use of scientific approaches to vocational guidance and selection (Munsterberg, 1913).

No one would suggest that participation reduces the benefits of goal setting, and, all other things being equal, there may be very good reasons for allowing employees input into the goals that will be used to evaluate their performance. The failure of the early writers to focus on participation is not as much of a problem as some critics contend. Acceptance and perceived legitimacy of goals are the key elements in employee acceptance. The scientific management writers accurately focused on demonstrated achievability, instruction, training, and scientific selection of workers as the most critical success factors in the area of goal setting.

Goal Setting and Feedback

One of the fundamental requirements of MBO is evaluation based on results. This implies that managers will, at predictable intervals, provide information to employees on how their performance is measuring up to the standards. Feedback appears to be an essential element in the successful use of goal setting to improve performance. When employees are given information on how their performance is measuring up to the established goal, an opportunity is provided to "stroke" those who are on target and to offer encouragement and assistance to those who are not.

Those who are on target are reassured that their present pace of work is appropriate and that to continue will result in satisfactory or better evaluations. Those who are performing below expectation can take corrective actions by working harder or obtaining assistance and can "salvage" success rather than being "doomed" to failure (Matsui, Okada, and Inoshita, 1983).

When feedback is used, it is important to keep several points in mind. First, feedback should be given on as many aspects of the work as possible. In customer service settings, for example, if only the number of claims is stressed in the evaluation, the quality dimension may be underemphasized. Employees may respond by dealing with as many customers as possible while allowing the quality of each encounter to suffer. Next, feedback should be given at predictable intervals and as fast as possible. One of the reasons the use of computers as "teaching machines" has been so effective is that they give immediate feedback. The recency of the performance information has a significant influence on performance and motivation. Another reason for the success of "teaching machines" is that the feedback goes directly to the employee. Ivancevich and McMahon (1982) demonstrated how information on the performance of engineers generated by the engineers themselves was more effective in improving performance than information that came to the engineer through a supervisor. Finally, it is important to provide feedback only in the quantities that can be dealt with and acted on by employees. If the feedback cannot be managed in a way that allows employees to digest the information in a relatively easy manner, it is not likely to impact positively on performance.

Goal-setting theory and practice have much to say to modern managers. What Taylor and the Gilbreths observed about goals at the turn of the century is equally true today. Goals motivate higher performance. While participation in goal setting is desirable and builds commitment, the existence of goals, regardless of their origin, and regular feedback on performance are more important. Knowledge of goals and performance data consistently improve motivation.

Perhaps, however, there is another reason why goals should be established and feedback regularly provided. It is the right thing for managers to do. This adds an ethical dimension to goal setting. Making sure that employees understand what they are expected to do increases the likelihood that they will do it. Making employees aware of how they are doing provides an opportunity to overcome failures and build a successful future. Managers who provide employees with opportunities to succeed can rest assured knowing they are providing tangible improvements in the quality of life at work.

Implications and Conclusions

Most managers should spend more time setting goals and communicating them to employees. In the hectic day-to-day world of crises only the most courageous managers will have the nerve and the will to take time to develop and communicate goals. In this chapter we have attempted to discuss goal setting and decision making and illustrated the interrelationship of these two management functions. Some important conclusions we have drawn are listed next:

1. An investment of time in serious goal setting can pay large and tangible benefits. Goals provide employees a sense of direction that is necessary for the coordination of diverse functions.
2. Goals offset uncertainty, and they provide a standard or basis for evaluating the results achieved.
3. Effective decision making is goal directed and the determination of the success of a decision is related to the objective it is intended to accomplish. Goals are decision criteria.
4. Understanding decision making requires not only an understanding of rational and theoretical approaches but an appreciation of the psychology of human problem solving as well.
5. Technical precision and expertise can be neutralized in the face of flawed decision-making processes.
6. Participation is good, but the existence of goals is better. Research shows that people are more concerned with the attainability of goals than with participation. They are even more interested in the nature of the feedback that is instrumental in determining the types of rewards employees and managers will receive.

7. Although participation does not improve performance directly, it is a good idea to obtain as much input as possible from those who know about the particular task for which goals are being set. The opportunity to participate can be very helpful in establishing the legitimacy of the goals.

8. Plans must be well conceived, communicated, and implemented.

9. Controls must be established in a manner that focuses on performance rather than on things that are only remotely related to the real mission of the organization.

10. Working hard today is not enough. Successful managers work smart. Part of this "smartness" is anticipating the future, setting goals that are ambitious yet obtainable, communicating expectations, and carefully recognizing and rewarding goal accomplishment.

Questions for Discussion

1 What did the scientific management writers mean by the term "task management?" Why is this concept important to goal setting?

2 Why are goals so important to the effective coordination of organizational behavior?

3 Do you agree with Dennison that teamwork and goal setting are closely interrelated? Why or why not?

4 How do you account for the popularity of management by objectives? What are some of its major implementation problems?

5 How were Simon's and Weber's notions of irrationality similar? How were they different?

6 Do you think public policy makers really muddle through when they arrive at decisions? What about business executives? Is logical incrementalism a genuine improvement over muddling through?

7 What are some of the primary advantages and disadvantages of incrementalism in decision making?

8 Why are muddling through and logical incrementalism similar to Simon's concept of satisficing? Are muddling through and logical incrementalism accurate examples of prescriptive decision making? Why or why not?

9 How important do you think participation really is when it comes to goal setting? Does the quality of goal setting improve when people are encouraged to participate?

10 How was goal setting related to coordination in the discussion presented by Mooney and Reiley?

Coordination and Authority

"Authority is another name for the willingness and capacity of individuals to submit to the necessities of cooperative systems."

Chester I. Barnard
The Functions of the Executive (1938)

Mooney and Reiley (1931) praised coordination as the first principle of organization. Organizations could accomplish their full potential and avoid the inefficiencies of conflict only when each unit was properly coordinated so as to obtain unity of effort. Remember, management is the *coordination* of individual and group actions toward the accomplishment of organizational goals. There must be someone to coordinate diverse specialists and work units. This is the work of managers.

Without coordination, organizations could not exist, and without authority, coordination is unlikely. To Mooney and Reiley "authority was the supreme coordinating power" and an essential ingredient of organizational success—particularly to the extent that success related to efficiency. The relationship of authority, effectiveness, and change is more complex.

One who is interested in authority in management will not have to look far to find others with similar concerns. Beware, however, of the confusing task facing you if you wish to avoid becoming side tracked by semantic controversies. Perhaps the most familiar relates to similarities and differences between the terms *authority* and *power*.

In recent years there has been general agreement that authority is the *rights* someone has by virtue of the position occupied in an organization. Authority, when viewed in this manner, is impersonal and has nothing to do with the particular individual occupying the position. It is the prerogative of managers. By contrast, power is more personal and concerns an individual's *ability* to get things done by influencing others. Power is personal and the direct result of the personality of the individual exercising influence. It is the prerogative of leaders.

This misunderstanding about authority and power is interesting and potentially important because it helps explain reality in organizations. We have all seen cases

▲ **Box 7-1**

HIJACKING ORGANIZATIONS

The Turkish Airlines DC-10 that crashed outside Paris killing more than 300 passengers supposedly went down because a ground mechanic failed to close a luggage compartment. One of the lowest skilled members of the ground crew had the "power" to destroy one of the most complicated and fragile human creations and the lives it contained. Traditional organizations are designed with specialized roles, duties, and procedures. The functioning of the organization depends on individuals performing their assigned roles, and when they fail to do so, the entire organization can cease to operate properly.

How many times have we experienced a problem in an organization only to be told that the person in charge of fixing the problem is off today, out of town, in the hospital? We simply must wait until the person returns before the situation can be corrected. This negative power resulting from role specialization and lack of integration can destroy airliners and cause organizations to "grind to a halt."

Source: Handy (1995).

where high-ranking managers who possess all the rights and privileges that accompany an office appear to have little power or ability to influence others. At the same time, we have seen an equal number of people with no right to influence others who are extremely powerful. We will return to this topic later.

Careful distinctions between authority and power are a relatively recent development and were made necessary by deeper investigations into organizational behavior and the changing nature of organizations. Such distinctions did not occupy much time in the early discussions of authority. The lack of concern about the subject is evident in Mooney and Reiley's definition of authority as the supreme coordinating power.

Understanding Authority

We began our analysis at a time when authority was indeed the supreme coordinating force and the first available option for managers attempting to build and maintain efficient operations. Early writers were not timid about advocating the use of authority as a coordinating tool. Authority, however, fell out of favor as time passed. Today it is less prescribed as an appropriate path to efficiency, and the exercise of authority has slowly, but surely, been regarded as an artifact of early management practice.

Today authority is regarded as something that should be relied on only when other, more preferred methods of influence fail. The image of the manager as a gang boss has given way to the image of the manager as a coach, mentor, facilitator, and change agent. The manager is expected to skillfully use the techniques social science has to offer and is discouraged, if not forbidden, to call on the legitimate authority of the position. The prohibition against authority, however, gets us ahead of the story. Our tale begins long before the days of the behavioral scientists.

Weber on Authority

For one with only passing interests in the practical aspects of business, Max Weber contributed much to our understanding of how organizations operate. Weber was concerned about social order and the ways in which it was best achieved. Social order, however, does not exist in the absence of a coordinating influence. There is much validity in David Ricardo's (Heilbroner, 1967) view of human beings as self-interest-oriented animals. Without social order human beings become "rabble" and without authority social order is only a dream. Even though Mayo (1945) and others found this opinion objectionable, it remained a realistic concern of Weber's.

In discussing authority, Weber did not find it necessary to distinguish between authority and power. He defined power as the probability that one person will be able to carry out his will despite opposition or resistance from others. Domination similarly was the probability that a command with a specific content will be obeyed by others (Weber, 1947). Both of these ideas possessed some properties of authority, and the successful use of either could add order to organizations and society.

Weber appreciated the fact that organizations require order to regulate the behavior of individual members. He observed that members of organizations generally honor rules because they are "legally" required or because it is the convention for them to do so. Employees frequently agree to accept authority because it ensures harmony and aids productivity (p. 124). It is, in other words, in their own self-interest to do so.

In dealing with domination or imperative control, Weber made an important and surprising point that is most often associated with Chester Barnard. He noted that for imperative control to work there must be a certain degree of willingness to submit or acceptance of the domination on the part of the follower (p. 324). This sounds like Barnard's acceptance theory, which will be discussed later. Did Weber propose the acceptance theory that has been attributed to Barnard all these years?

Legitimate Authority

Actually, whether or not Weber proposed the acceptance theory has only vague historical significance since he was most concerned with legitimate authority. The right to influence others gains legitimacy from a variety of sources, the most common of which is the legal system itself. According to Weber, legitimate authority can be one of three types. It can be rational, traditional, or charismatic.

Rational authority is based on a belief in its legality and the ability of people in positions of influence to give orders and require conformity. Admirals in the Navy and provosts in universities all have rational legitimate authority, but few enjoy the authority of the corporate CEO.

Take, for example, the case of Louis V. Gerstner. In 1993, Gerstner became the first outsider to head IBM. Previously he had experienced a meteoric rise at McKinsey and Company and held top positions at American Express and RJR Nabisco. He has worked wonders at IBM. When he arrived, IBM's stock price was at its lowest point in almost two decades. In 4 years it was trading at its highest level since 1985, and more that $40 billion had been added to the company's market value. In doing so, Gerstner had called upon a great deal of legitimate authority (Morris, 1997).

This CEO had exercised his rights to arrive shortly before board meetings and leave immediately after they were concluded. He had little time for chitchat! He sized up people quickly at meetings and rejected attempts to "feed him" bad ideas and pet projects. He freely asked subordinate managers what they thought of their bosses and exercised all the rights of his office. In the process he revitalized IBM in a way that might have been accomplished using a more gentle style, but it would certainly have taken longer.

▲ Box 7-2
AN UNEASY BALANCE OF AUTHORITY AND POWER

Robert Crandall, CEO of American Airlines, and American's pilots represent extremes of the authority–power relationship. Crandall uses his position and combative personality to threaten pilots and enforce a two-tier salary scale. He makes it clear that in the end if the pilots demand too much, he will close down the airline rather than give in to what he considers excessive demands. If he does, pilots can go to other airlines, but they will start over in terms of seniority.

The pilots have virtually no formal authority but tremendous power. They cannot officially close the airline, but by refusing to fly they can bring operations to a halt. Airline pilots, in large numbers, are simply not easy to replace. So the conflicts and occasional standoffs continue.

Crandall, who retired in 1998, attempted to influence the behavior of pilots by exercising his rights as CEO. He had the legitimate authority to do so, and the contract with the pilots represented his legal rights. The pilots, on the other hand, also had rights under the contract. Ultimately, however, their influence resided in their critical skills, the relative scarcity of these skills, and the pilots' ability to act cooperatively.

Source: Adapted from "One Tough [Expletive]," *Newsweek,* June 1, 1998, p. 50.

From Laws to Traditions

Traditional authority, unlike the rational legal variety, is based on the sacredness of customs or established principles and concepts. Parents have authority in the family because it is a tradition that has served society well. The monarchs of Europe, because of their ancestry, and the Pope also enjoy traditional legitimate authority. Finally, charismatic authority is based on the perceived holiness, bravery, or good conduct of a person. Unlike the other types, charismatic authority is extremely personal and relates to the personality of a particular individual.

To understand charismatic authority we will do well to leave the realm of management and study the lives of John F. Kennedy, Martin Luther King, Jr., and Oral Roberts. Although the reality of charisma was recognized, Weber believed it came into play because of a failure of other forms of authority to provide the desired level of order. Charisma was to Weber, in other words, a last-ditch grasp for order. The sociological view of authority provided by Weber is valuable to managers even though it was not meant to have such practical implications. However, the views of Mary Parker Follett, herself a political scientist, often focused on applied aspects of management.

Mary Parker Follett on Giving Orders

Mary Parker Follett was like Weber in many ways. She had much to say about many topics, and for this reason her name appears frequently in management thought. Her most important ideas on authority are recorded in *Freedom and Coordination* (1949), a series of lectures edited by Lyndall Urwick.

Authority as Illusion

Even though Follett was knowledgeable about authority, particularly the formal theory, which states that authority always flows down in the hierarchy, she believed all authority was *functional*. It belonged to the position or job, and when people talked about the limits of authority, they were really talking about the definition of the task. Since Follett believed authority was derived from the function or task, in her view, it had less to do with the vertical dimension or hierarchy of the organization. Bosses, according to her, do not delegate authority. The extent and direction of delegation is instead inherent in the plan of organization. The philosophy of delegation is established when the organization is structured.

Follett was convinced that orders and authority came from the work or the job to be done. Thus, her view was less personal and emphasized the need to be certain commands were not directed toward individuals. The *law of the situation* should operate freely since it is inherently arbitrary to direct orders and authority toward individuals. The important thing was for the manager to consider the total situation before issuing commands. She favored, to the extent possible, the replacement of authority with a careful instruction and education of people to ensure that followers

---

▲ **Box 7-3**

MYTHS AND DELEGATION

There are some common myths associated with the delegation of authority. Three of the most common are:

1. *Superworker myth:*   Do you work longer and harder than everyone else? That is commendable, but one reason superworkers work harder is because they do not work smarter. Superworkers lack focus because they do not use the talents of others effectively.

2. *Perfectionist myth:*   Why delegate when I can do everything better than anyone else? My way is the only way, and other people just do not get it. Remember, it is possible to give guidance and leverage resources without excessive control.

3. *Replacement myth:*   If my employees are good at what I do, my boss will give them my job. Not really. The ability to effectively develop employees through delegation is a rare managerial talent.

Source: Nelson (1994).

---

know and use the best available business practices and understand the reasons why orders and directions are necessary. In this manner, obedience to legitimate orders is active rather than passive. People submit because it is in their best interests to do so, not because they fear the consequences of nonsubmission. This places a perspective of voluntariness on authority and again hints at the acceptance theory of Barnard.

In developing her approach, Follett related delegation of authority and task management and illustrated the interrelationship between authority and organizational design. For example, organizations often face conflicting demands in their need to closely control critical resources while ensuring flexibility with regard to operational matters. In fact, Keidel (1994) suggests that organizations are most effective when they carefully balance formal authority (control), individual autonomy, and cooperation within teams. Highly innovative organizations such as 3M effectively manage their need to meet operational objectives while maintaining the flexibility necessary to stimulate innovation.

Follett, however, was basically skeptical about authority and, like many human relations writers who followed, believed that overall authority should be minimized and people in organizations should have "just enough" authority to accomplish their task—no more and no less.

▲ **Box 7-4**

MARY PARKER FOLLETT

Mary Parker Follett was born in Boston in 1868. She graduated from Harvard and studied at Cambridge University. Although trained in political science, her interest ranged from vocational education to social psychology and organization theory. Follett greatly valued the potential of cooperation and even recognized that conflict, under the appropriate conditions, could be constructive. Wren (1994) accurately describes how important Follett was in linking scientific management and human relations.

Over time, Follett lost interest in political philosophy and even came to regard it as irrelevant to the problems of the day. She turned to business and to business leaders, for it was there that she "found hope for the future." Through her subsequent lectures to business leaders and her writings she was recognized as an important contributor to management thought. Business has benefited greatly from the ideals proposed by Follett. Her insights about authority and governance added an important dimension to our understanding of organizations and provided new ways of looking at the role of the individual within more complex organizational systems.

Source: Wren (1994).

Power With Rather Than Power Over

At no other place do we gain such insight into Follett's views on authority as we do in her opinions on the exercise of power. She saw no need to differentiate between power and authority. To exercise power meant merely to make things happen—to be an agent of change. Control, to her, was simply to exercise the power as a means to a specific end.

Traditionally in management we have thought of power over the various resources of production and little difference was made between human and nonhuman resources. Follett believed that *power with* was a more constructive way of exercising influence. She presumed power could be jointly developed and coactive rather than coercive. Power-with concepts are possible to build through circular behavior, or the process whereby it is possible for you as a manager to influence other managers while the other managers are simultaneously influencing you.

Workers at the same time are given open communication channels and allowed to influence managers, while managers are in the process of influencing workers. This, in the view of Follett, was the iterative–integrative way organizations should operate. She stated that the functional unity of organizations was a high and worthy goal that occurs when all individuals and groups know their function and each function corresponds as closely as possible to the abilities of the individuals and groups who perform the tasks. Moreover, each individual should be given the authority necessary to get their job done and should be held accountable for accomplishing the tasks.

The ultimate outcome of this type of relationship is participation—not merely consent, but genuine participation. Participation meant, in Follett's view, everyone taking part in the success of the organization according to the capacities of each person. True participation resulted in a unified whole made up of many related parts and functions that culminate into the consolidated organization all managers dream of and desire.

True participation is not self-sacrifice but self-contribution. At Ben and Jerry's ice cream company, for example, employees are encouraged to share their ideas for making work easier and more efficient. When hand mixing of nuts into ice cream was recognized as time consuming and potentially harmful to wrists, employees invented a way to automate the process. Another employee designed a mechanical finger to flip boxes and eliminate another potentially harmful and repetitive motion (Deal and Jenkins, 1994). Participation encourages ownership, and ownership leads to the involvement of all employees in improving work and eliminating waste. This represents the true win–win situation visualized by Follett.

Finally, interdependence between individual and organizational goals is essential to the encouragement of Ben and Jerry's type involvement. For our purposes, the important point is that when employees are genuinely involved, formal authority is minimized. This does not mean that accountability is lost nor does it mean that production will fall. In fact, high-level performance expectations are established by the most engaged groups, and individuals are expected to equal or exceed expectations. Participation is encouraged, communication is improved, and trust levels between workers and managers increase.

More Precise Distinctions

To this point, we have minimized the importance of precise semantic distinctions between authority and power. In fact, although not widespread, some precise distinctions did appear in the writings of Urwick (1944) and his summaries of Fayol and other classical writers. Urwick talked of authority as a principle and stated that the supreme authority for making any type of decision had to reside somewhere in the organization. Not only should the supreme authority exist, but a scalar process should provide a clear line from the point of supreme authority to every person in the organization. Authority moves down through the scalar chain assigning and coordinating activities.

Urwick's Interpretations and Views on Authority

In the process of discussing and integrating many of the ideas of other writers, Urwick (1944) arrived at some useful definitions. According to him, *duties* are the activities individuals are required to perform in connection with their jobs. *Authority* is the right to require actions of others. This authority or right, as he saw it, derived from a formal statement of such rights by the organization, because of the technical expertise a person possessed, or personal characteristics such as popularity or seniority. *Power* was the ability to get things done, and *responsibility* was the accountability for the performance of one's duties. The definitions sound precise, but the potential semantic problems are numerous.

Pfeffer (1981), for example, introduced an additional complicating factor by suggesting that authority is merely legitimized power. When power becomes legitimate through custom and/or acceptance, it becomes authority and most people rarely question it. The vines of controversy spread everywhere throughout the management theory jungle when it comes to discussions of authority, power, accountability, and responsibility.

Summary of the Classical Concept of Authority

Regardless of how much time a particular writer devoted to the nature of authority and in spite of the relatively progressive insights each had into the importance of the employee's acceptance, the dominant view of authority in early management thought was consistent. Authority was related to the rights of the manager, and these rights always descended from above.

Ultimately all rights originated with the right of private property. The rights could be delegated from one manager to another, and eventually they could even be delegated to rank-and-file employees. As we noted before, there was a concern for participation, but the strength of the concern was evident in the writings of only a relatively few.

The traditional view of authority required managerial decisions concerning the exercise of influence and the need to share the rights of influence with others. This led directly to the question of delegation. When examined from the perspective of conventional wisdom, delegation expanded into one of the most sacred prescriptions of management. Everyone knows that managers rarely have the time to do the many things required of them. In spite of useful time management techniques, few managers have the time required by their complex and demanding jobs. For decades managers have been taught that the proper response to this work overload was to become an effective delegator of authority.

The logic of effective delegation argues that, if managers are to be successful, they must expand their abilities through the sharing (delegation) of authority. When promising followers are identified and given the opportunity to make decisions, they can frequently accept increasing levels of authority. This provides two valuable outcomes for the organization: (1) higher level managers are freed to "be in more than one place at a time"; and (2) those employees to whom authority is delegated obtain an opportunity to develop and practice their management skills. If the lessons are learned well, delegation will ensure the company a long succession of qualified and promising managers.

Although delegated (shared) authority can always be recalled by the higher level manager, while the delegation is in effect and the subordinate is responsible for completing the delegated task, the original manager must give up the authority necessary for the subordinate to do the job. To do otherwise would result in a violation of the principle of unity of command (in Fayol's terms), or one of the essential principles of organization discussed earlier. If the boss fails to genuinely delegate the necessary amount of authority, employees will have more than one boss. Such a situation is always confusing and dysfunctional for subordinates.

Even though authority should be delegated, to do so is very risky business for a manager. The manager temporarily gives up an amount of authority, but he can never relieve himself of the accountability for getting the job done. The failure of the subordinate is not a valid excuse. The manager is accountable for getting the job done, and if a poorly selected employee fails to see to the delegated duties, accountability can never be removed. There are no excuses accepted when it comes to delegated authority. Watergate, Iran Contra Affair, campaign fund raising, and other familiar scandals provide evidence of this *iron law of accountability*. Chief executive officers in business and government may attempt to blame others for the lack of their personal oversight, but the law is clear—accountability for entrusted authority cannot be delegated!

In the 1930s many of the prescriptions of early management thought were challenged and changed. Others remained intact even though they had experienced major revisions. Writers with more humanistic persuasions not only revised ideas relating to authority in organizations; but more than an influential few actually began to reject traditional concepts of authority and the need for this supreme coordinating power altogether. The result was a seemingly revolutionary new way of conceptual-

---

▲ Box 7-5

CAN'T HAVE IT BOTH WAYS! OR, CAN WE?

If employee involvement is so effective, why do so few companies encourage it? Using the New United Motor Manufacturing Inc. (joint venture between Toyota and General Motors) as a case study, an attempt was made to answer this perplexing riddle. The answer is simple, but the solution is complex.

Few dispute that high-involvement organizations offer long-range potential for organizational improvement. However, *long range* is the problem. Capital markets are short range in outlook and impatient for results. Moreover, the success of high-involvement organizations relies on mutual trust and cooperation. If workers share ideas with managers looking for short-term gains, the workers' only reward will be a punishment—higher performance expectations and lower wages. High-involvement organizations rely on the support of employees, owners, managers, and a capital market that is patient and willing to wait for the benefits of new and improved ways of doing things.

Source: Levine (1995).

izing authority. This radical view also established the conditions necessary to ensure that controversies regarding authority continued in contemporary management thought.

Barnard's Acceptance Theory

Chester Barnard (1938) introduced, under what he called the elements of formal organization, his now famous theory of authority. As was his style, Barnard did not introduce a simple theory, and the way he explained it was more than a little confusing. Yet, his points are important and are worth the trouble involved in understanding them.

Chester Barnard was not a professor but a businessman and philosopher, an admittedly unusual combination. He was born in 1886 in Malden, Massachusetts, and died in 1961. Barnard attended Harvard but did not graduate. He said he got his degree the hard way, "he earned it" in business. In 1909 Barnard went to work for AT&T as a statistician and moved quickly up the hierarchy. His rapid rise in the corporation was not the result of his education, so it probably had something to do with his knowledge of foreign languages. He soon became an expert on international telephone rates, and by 1927 he was President of the New Jersey Bell Telephone Company. His only book, *The Functions of the Executive,* remains widely recognized as one of the true classics of management.

Subjective and Objective Aspects of Authority

Barnard thought authority was closely related to communication. In fact, he defined authority as the "character of the communication (order)" by virtue of which the communication was accepted by members of the organization as governing their actions. Usually authority is accepted when orders are considered legal, legitimate, and necessary. Barnard pens his famous acceptance theory by stating that authority is rested in the people who are willing to be controlled.

Thus, the reality of authority, in Barnard's view, has less to do with managers and more to do with employees. Instead of the manager possessing formal rights granted by the organization and forcing imperative control on employees, the employees were really the holders of authority because it was their decision to accept or not accept orders and thereby determine whether or not influence would take place and, if so, where it would be directed.

The subjective element of authority was the acceptance by employees while the objective aspect related to the character of the order or communication itself. Authority, according to Barnard and contrary to most of the arguments stated previously, flows from the bottom to the top of the organization.

The degree to which this authority is accepted is related to the following conditions. First, it is related to the extent to which the follower understands the communication from the manager. Frequently, the manager needs to interpret the order to assist an employee's understanding. Second, acceptance is influenced by the extent to which the order or communication is considered in line with the purpose of the organization. If it is not consistent with the purpose, it is not legitimate. Third, em-

---

▲ **Box 7-6**

POWER OF UNWRITTEN RULES

An office supply company had serious problems of customer service that resulted from the power structure of their 30 warehouses, which were spread over several hundred square miles. Each warehouse manager ruled his fiefdom—they liked the power this situation created. Workers and managers developed their set of rules for success:

- Warehouse managers have as much freedom as they can create for themselves. Stay out of the clutches of the home office.

- Warehouse managers can do favors for employees in the head office. Don't rub them the wrong way!

- Warehouse managers have strong personalities and can cause you problems if they are not on your side. Divide them and you can conquer them!

Source: Scott-Morgan (1994).

---

ployees are more likely to accept authority to the extent that the order is consistent with the personal needs of followers and in line with their own interests. Finally, orders are accepted to the extent to which the follower is able mentally and physically to comply with the order.

It is true that *zones of indifference* exist, whereby orders are acceptable without conscious thought, and directions are frequently accepted because of the "authority of position" or the "authority of leadership." The former results from position while the latter derives from superior knowledge, ability, or understanding. As with Follett, Barnard found no reason to draw a careful distinction between power and authority. In fact, had he recognized or acknowledged a difference, his theory of authority would have really become a theory of power. This would have made the theory much less novel than it is in its present form.

An Extension of Barnard

Simon (1976) was not concerned with distinctions since he defined authority as the "power to make decisions which guide the actions of another" (p. 125). Unlike Follett, Simon believed that authority created a hierarchical relationship between two or more people—some are the superiors and some are subordinates. The unique distinction provided by Simon is the way in which he explained authority in purely behavioral terms. Authority takes place only when certain behaviors occur regardless of the "paper theory of organization" (p. 125). The superior behaves by issuing a command and develops an expectation that the subordinate will accept the order. The subordinate behaves by following the command and accepting the behavioral option that "is selected for me by the boss."

Interestingly, Simon did distinguish between authority and other forms of influence, such as persuasion. The distinction is that with authority, the subordinate "holds in abeyance his own criteria" for choosing behavioral alternatives and uses the superior's command as the sole basis for choice (pp. 126–127). Simon goes on to accept the notion of zone of indifference discussed in Barnard, even though he refers to it as the *area of acceptance* (p. 133). The most striking aspect of the subordinate role is that it establishes an area of acceptance within which the follower is willing to accept the decisions made by the superior. This zone varies in size, but its existence is determined by the legitimacy attached to the order by the employee.

Authority, according to Simon, is important in organizations for three primary reasons. These are:

1. Authority enforces responsibility on the part of the follower to those who exercise control. This is closely related to Weber's idea of legitimate or legal authority. When authority is used for this reason, sanctions play an important part in the process (p. 136).
2. Authority secures expertise in decision making. The expert on a particular issue may be located in a strategic position in the hierarchy of authority where the expert's problem-solving premises are accepted by others in the organization.
3. Authority permits coordination of activities. Coordination is aimed at getting members of the group to accept the "same" decision whereas expertise involves the adoption of "good" decisions (p. 139). This view of authority from Simon's decision-making perspective highlights the fact that influence is important behaviorally as well as structurally and helps explain why authority and influence have continued to be a recurring theme of management, even after the advent of the human relations orientation.

It is interesting to note, for example, that even in books such as Elliot Jacques' *The Changing Culture of a Factory* (1951), to be discussed in Chapter 10, almost half of the issues discussed related to authority, power, and influence. The regulation of power, elucidation of policy, organization of authority, and the extended chain of command at the Glacier Metal Company were major topics addressed by Jacques and his associates. Throughout the book discussions are presented of how modern organizations attempt to balance the critical need to control operations while providing as much flexibility as possible relative to decision making. This issue remains an important challenge for management today.

Authority and Human Relations

McGregor (1960), as we noted in the chapter on leadership, and even before he introduced Theory X and Theory Y, stated that control in organizations was a process of selective adaptation. It involved the selection of the appropriate means of influence over the people being managed. While all the human relations writers were aware of the fact that authority did exist in organizations and some even admitted to its necessity, most believed the best thing to do with traditionally conceived authority in organizations was to remove it. McGregor argued that less emphasis should be placed on formal authority and the rights of position and that more emphasis should be placed on "integration" or the creation of conditions that allow members of an organization to achieve their own goals while working toward the success of the enterprise.

Using Authority to Improve Performance

It was McGregor's contention that all organizations require some system of influence and control. Historically, in scientific management and early organization theory, control was based on the simple assumption that authority was an indispensable aspect of effective management (Kahn and Kram, 1994).

Managers too often assume that the authority they possess over subordinates is all they need to motivate successfully and ensure high levels of performance. In reality they should freely use other forms of influence as well. Some of the more important are persuasion and professional influence. McGregor believed that through authority managers could force individuals to perform at minimally acceptable levels, but authority could not command maximum performance. Individuals are committed to work toward organizational goals only when their personal needs are simultaneously fulfilled. The key to motivation is to adapt selectively that type of influence process that will build an interdependence between individual and organizational goals.

Authority and the Linking Pin

Rensis Likert (1967) followed up on some of the views of authority and power presented by Barnard and added some insights of his own. Managerial power or authority, in Likert's view, depended on how much influence employees allowed the manager to exercise over them. Because of this, he reasoned, employees would feel more a part of decisions, be more committed to accomplishing organizational goals, and allow themselves to be influenced more by managers if they had an opportunity to participate in their formulation.

However, in developing the idea of the linking pin, as we stated in the last chapter, Likert introduced a novel idea. It was the view that the degree of power managers have upward with their bosses and laterally with their peers will constitute a major influence on the amount of power they have downward on employees. If the manager can build credibility and influence with her boss and gain support for actions that will reinforce employees' goals, it appears reasonable to assume that this would increase the support of lower level members of the organization.

Likert and Likert (1976) illustrated the importance of their view of authority and influence in the practical area of conflict resolution. They began by agreeing in principle with McGregor that most conflicts historically have been settled using win–lose strategies. That is, when one person or party wins the other must lose. This is the case in the authority-oriented solutions to organizational problems advocated by much of classical management theory and practice. Confrontations and ultimatums are frequently thought of as the only way to deal with deep-seated differences that sometimes exist between departments such as production and sales or data processing and marketing. Departments expend their efforts on mustering all the forces they can to compel other departments to do their bidding. Often one or a few powerful individuals emerge to ensure the success of this steamroller technique. The result of this exercise of negative power is all too often strikes, lockouts, work stoppages, and maybe even worker sabotage.

More productive approaches, according to Likert and Likert, are those leading to the exercise of positive power. Sometimes such approaches even result in "win–win" strategies of conflict resolution. Such approaches involve disputing parties that are genuinely trying to understand the perspective and needs of others. Sometimes they are even willing to go more than halfway in reaching solutions that will be to everyone's advantage.

Again, in terms that remind us of McGregor, the point is made that conflicts are resolved on the basis of one party influencing another. When one disputing party begins negotiation through the use of negative power (that is, attempts to compel a resolution), that very party's influence may be reduced by the negative response such approaches receive. On the other hand, efforts to resolve conflict that are based on positive power often increase influence because they do not entail negative attitudes. Even conflict with all its reduction of coordination can be channeled toward constructive results.

Confronting the Controversy

Now that we have discussed authority and influence in detail, we can conclude with an examination of the controversy we have attempted to avoid throughout this chapter. This has to do with the distinction between authority and power. Both of these themes, authority and power, have been debated and examined for years. According to Tolstoy, the question asked in *War and Peace*, "what is power?" is the essential question of history. It may be accurate to say that the more fundamental the question, the less certain we are about the answer.

We noted earlier that the basic controversy relating to the definition of power and authority revolves around two basic theories or views on how influence originates. The traditional, formal theory of authority, often attributed to Weber, views authority as rights and proposes that such rights always flow down an organization. Of course, we pointed out the fact that Weber did assign importance to the acceptance of these rights by followers. In spite of this, the formal theory dominates most discussions of Weber's ideas on the subject. By contrast, the acceptance theory, which supposedly originated with Barnard but clearly predates him, maintains that a manager's authority rests in the willingness of followers to accept the commands of the manager. Clearly, much of these differences could be clarified by simply referring to a formal theory of authority (rights) and an acceptance theory of power (ability). Such agreement, however, is not likely.

To illustrate the magnitude of the controversy, consider one of the most famous papers written on the subject of social power. This paper by French and Raven (1959) illustrates how confusing distinctions can be. French and Raven state that power can originate from one or more of the following sources. Using the criteria cited to distinguish between authority and power, consider in each case whether it is power or authority that is being discussed.

- *Reward power:* A manager can have influence over another person if the other person believes the manager can provide or withhold rewards. If we are talking about the rewards distributed by the manager as a representative of the organization (that is, monetary incentives, promotions, etc.), this would be considered a source of authority rather than power. If we are referring to informal rewards like acceptance into a group, this would refer to a type of power.

- *Coercive power:* A person can influence the actions of others if the former controls the amount and type of punishments that can be administered to the latter. Again, if this is official demotion or the withholding of pay for violations of organizational rules and regulations, it can represent the authority that goes with management positions. If it represents social punishments, it is more accurately described as power.

- *Legitimate power:* This power (actually it is authority) is based on the rights of one person to rule over another because of their respective positions in the organization. This appears to be a relatively clear case of authority.

- *Referent power:* This type of influence, which is more often power than authority, accompanies one person's identification with another. This appears to be more clearly a case of power.

- *Expert power:* When one person is perceived to possess a unique and valuable type of knowledge or information, people may grant her a degree of power. This type of influence, it should be noted, has become increasingly important in high-technology industries and other industries that require large numbers of highly trained professional employees.

A review of this list reveals the confusion associated with the terms "authority" and "power." Such a confusion is unfortunate because it diverts too much attention from the more important issues involved in the nature of influence in organizations. Moreover, arguments over mere words blind us to the changing reality around us. For example, whether by rights or abilities, the growth and development of high technologies has greatly increased expert power as a source of influence in many organizations. In new and innovative industries much of what we think of as traditional and legitimate authority is being replaced by influence based on the possession of knowledge.

Managers must be aware of these changing realities and recognize and appreciate the implications they will have for building effective organizations. Managers influence people in many ways. Sometimes their influence results from the position they occupy and sometimes it results from the manager's personality. Both types of influence are important and are needed to assist in the accomplishment of organizational goals.

Much of this chapter focused on classical views of authority. Authority is called the glue that holds organizations together. Perhaps the most important lesson managers should remember from the early writers is the necessity of delegating authority effectively. Effective delegation is one of the manager's primary aids in time management. Few managers have the time to do all they are expected to accomplish. The only practical way they have to expand their ability is to delegate some of their authority. It expands the manager's time, and it provides valuable training and development opportunities for deserving followers.

Implications and Conclusions

This chapter has looked at the question of authority and influence in organizations. The early emphasis was on the use of legitimate authority as the most efficient way to ensure the coordination of diverse organizational units. This is illustrated best in the terms of Mooney and Reiley when they refer to authority as the "supreme coordinating power."

Although questions of authority, power, and control in management are frequently contentious, they are essential aspects of organizations. For this reason, it is important for managers to consider some of the more important points we have discussed. These are summarized next.

1. Coordination is increasingly important as organizations grow larger and become more specialized. Authority is considered by many to be an important element in assuring coordination.
2. It is generally agreed in modern management thought that authority and power are different but closely related concepts. Authority is recognized as the manager's right to require or prohibit things while power is a manager's ability to get things done in organizations.
3. Weber's concept of legitimate authority provided the foundation for early organizational design theory. Legitimate authority was formal and always flowed down through a chain of command or hierarchy.
4. Follett's view of authority was functional. It was associated with the job rather than the individual.
5. Barnard's acceptance theory of authority visualized the employee as the ultimate source of authority, and the flow of influence was upward. Authority was operative only if employees accepted it.
6. Delegation of authority is essential to managerial success because it allows managers to "be in more than one place at a time" and is important to management succession.
7. Delegation is risky for managers because accountability cannot be delegated.
8. Integration is a recurring term in management and has a variety of meanings. In human relations thought it involves a concept of coordination whereby individuals accomplish their goals while contributing to the success of the firm.

Questions for Discussion

1 Is the distinction between authority and power necessary and meaningful? Can you think of situations when the distinction is important and other situations when it is not important?

2 Why, in your opinion, do terms such as authority and power have such negative connotations to many people? How can terms of this nature be presented in more positive terms?

3 Think back over previous discussions of efficiency and effectiveness. Does efficiency have more to do with authority or power? Explain your response.

4 Do you agree with Weber that charisma is an important type of authority only when legitimate authority fails? Why or why not?

5 What did Follett mean when she stated that authority was essentially functional in character? Do you agree or disagree?

6 Discuss two reasons why delegation is so important to managerial success.

7 What is the iron law of responsibility? What does this law have to do with the delegation of authority?

8 What is meant by Barnard's zones of indifference? How are these zones related to the acceptance theory of authority?

9 What is meant by the term *integration* in the human relations theory of organizational authority?

10 How are McGregor's concept of selective adaptation and Likert's linking pin (two concepts introduced in our previous discussion of leadership) relevant to the analysis of organizational authority?

Motivation and Management

If we choose to despair at the lack of change with regard to the social responsibility of management as we will in the next chapter, our hopes might be elevated with regard to motivation. Even if philosophies remain the same, times change in management as in society. Nowhere are the changes more evident than in the views of management pioneers about human nature and motivation. Some of the earlier views, by today's standards, are shocking. Taylor was concerned with justice and fairness, although his comments may surprise even the most insensitive reader. He once stated, for example, that successful pig iron loaders are "so stupid and so phlegmatic" they more closely resemble in their "mental make-up the ox than any other type" of animal (Taylor, 1914, p. 59). Skinner (1953), in a similar manner, teases us into believing that human behavior is no more complicated than that of his experimental pigeons. Obviously, our understanding of human nature and the realities of the work place have evolved significantly since the scientific management era (Mirvis, 1997). The majority of contemporary management writers are emphatic in their belief that human beings are unique with regard to matters of motivation.

Notwithstanding the counterinfluence of Skinner, the predominant view of the worker has changed from that of a simple, economic creature to a more complex psychosociological human being who is an individual, yet greatly influenced by fellow workers and the environment within which work is performed. In fact, the image of human beings at work changed so drastically from the time of Taylor to Maslow that one cannot help but wonder if humans are the objects of both theories. The *ox* in Taylor's steel mill becomes the social creature at Hawthorne and perhaps even an angel or some similar almost divine being in the view of Maslow's humanism. Our task in this chapter is to reconcile the views and make some sense of motivation theory and practice as presented in selected theories from human relations and behavioral science applied to management.

Counterpoint at Hawthorne

What can one say about the Hawthorne Studies that has not been said many times before? Perhaps nothing; certainly very little. Yet, beginning in the late 1920s something was going on at the Hawthorne, Illinois, works of Western Electric that would radically alter management thought regarding human motivation. The most comprehensive report of these events is provided by Roethlisberger and Dickson (1939). However, the "roots" of the events can be traced as far back as 1910 and involved seemingly unrelated firms such as General Electric, Commonwealth Edison, trade associations, the National Electric Light Association, the Harvard Business School, and the National Research Council.

Apparently it all began with General Electric's desire to sell more lightbulbs. Of course, more lightbulbs meant more electricity, and that interested Commonwealth Edison. Since the National Research Council relied on influential executives from firms such as Commonwealth Edison and General Electric for advice and assistance, it suddenly became interested in lightbulbs and electricity.

Some small-scale studies suggested that a relationship existed between worker productivity and illumination, but a careful scientific inquiry was needed to prove the association, and true science demanded the noncommercial image that could be provided by the National Research Council. The council was persuaded to form a committee on industrial lighting by its honorary chair, Thomas Edison. One of the council's members who worked for AT&T quickly volunteered the Hawthorne Works as

---

▲ Box 8-1
THE COMPLICATED HUMAN BEING

Motivating human performance is a complicated challenge. Individuals must perform individually but must work in teams. North American Tool and Die has bet its future on its ability to motivate individual and team performance at higher levels than its competitors. Managers are expected to demonstrate continually that they care about employees and their well-being.

Some of the most successful ways of demonstrating that managers really care are: (1) recognizing employees when they excel; (2) providing the information necessary to do the job and providing feedback on performance; (3) giving employees a sense of and opportunity for ownership; (4) ensuring pay for performance; (5) always demonstrating trust and respect for individuals; (6) complimenting employees daily; (7) performing acts of caring and kindness; (8) delegating authority and maintaining responsibility for results achieved; (9) encouraging partnerships with customers.

Source: Melohn (1995).

a test site (Greenwood and Wrege, 1986). The components of a noncommercial scientific study suddenly fell together. For some interesting and generally unknown details about the Hawthorne Studies one should refer to Bolton, Toftoy, and Chipman (1987) and Greenwood, Bolton, and Greenwood (1983).

Brief Details of the Studies

The studies at Hawthorne progressed through four stages and involved more than 20,000 workers (Cass and Zimmer, 1975). The Relay Assembly experiments were conducted controlling for shorter working hours and the addition of rest periods. Even a wage incentive program was introduced. Other studies, including the mica splitting experiment, were conducted along with a large-scale interviewing program.

While the details of all the experiments are important and interesting, it is with regard to the Bank Wiring Observation Room that the radical changes in motivational philosophy began to emerge. The researchers gradually came to recognize that work was more than earning a living, even in hard times. Employees received important social benefits from work. In fact, the work group was a social unit that could restrict the output of the individual, develop its own standard of a good day's work, and even use its influence to ensure that rewards did not go to people in direct proportion to the quantity and quality of work they performed.

People behind the Studies

A retrospective view of the Hawthorne Studies immediately brings two names to mind: Elton Mayo and Fritz Roethlisberger. George Elton Mayo was born in Australia in 1880 and educated in ethics, logic, and philosophy. He even went to medical school but did not graduate. Mayo came to the United States in the early 1920s to conduct research for the Rockerfeller Foundation before joining the Department of Industrial Research at Harvard in 1926. His two most important books for our purposes are *The Human Problems of an Industrial Society* (1933) and *The Social Problems of an Industrial Society* (1945).

Fritz J. Roethlisberger was born in New York in 1898 and was a gifted child fascinated with geometry, chemistry, and physics. He attended Columbia University and M.I.T. and received degrees from both, even though he became disillusioned with schools and retired to Greenwich Village with dreams of becoming a writer (Roethlisberger, 1977). Fortunately, he decided to give education one last try and enrolled at Harvard, where he was "taken in" by an Australian professor—Elton Mayo. This chance meeting changed the course of management history.

How Hawthorne Influenced Motivation Concepts

The introductory statement by Taylor about pig iron loaders illustrates the direction of motivation theory and practice during the scientific management era. All this changed with Mayo and Roethlisberger. In *Management and the Worker* (1939) Roethlisberger and Dickson (an executive at Western Electric) promised not just to report the research but to provide accounts of the "trials and tribulations" they encountered along the way. Because of the social nature of work, the authors recommended that organizations introduce the explicit skill of diagnosing human situations. This should be a philosophy of the organization and extend to all people in management and supervisory positions. To have simply a few highly trained individuals capable of counseling was not enough.

It was, in their judgment, important to involve many people and create an organizational climate that emphasized interpersonal relations. Managers should commit themselves and their organizations to the conscious process of studying human situations and conduct affairs on the basis of what they learned (pp. 604–605). The insights into human nature gained by Roethlisberger at Hawthorne developed quickly in his writings. In *Management and Morale* (1941) he stated boldly that people are motivated more by sentiments than by money and that groups influence the behavior of individuals in such significant ways as to make it essential that managers recognize that business firms are more than mere economic institutions. They are social organizations composed of human beings and should be managed accordingly. In *Man-In-Organizations* (1968) insights were provided into the breath of Roethlisberger's thinking.

▲ Box 8-2
MOTIVATING THROUGH CHOICES

Creative Staffing, a well-known employment service, recognizes people for doing a good job. Employees decide what rewards they want and what they will do to receive things such as parties in their honor, expensive dinners, flowers, sessions at spas, and shopping sprees. In order to build team spirit the competition for rewards is relative to prior performance not other employees.

Mary Kay Cosmetics has demonstrated the willingness of people to work harder when they have a reward to anticipate. Often the gifts are small recognitions such as birthday cards, a voucher for an inexpensive lunch, or a holiday bonus. Tiffany & Company has a long history of honoring the achievements of employees through well-intended rewards.

The motivational power of receiving recognition for a job well done and the anticipation of a reward have been used successfully by a number of companies. Often rewards are thought to have appeal only to sales personnel. It has become increasingly evident, however, that rewards carefully tied to desired accomplishments can be highly motivational.

Sources: Keenan (1995); Sunoo (1995).

The relationship between the worker and the efficiency expert or engineer (that is, the technologist) is an illustration of the types of insights of which Roethlisberger was capable. The technologist, according to him, operates on the basis of the logic of efficiency and views technology, specialization, and automation as ways of reducing fatigue. Remember how all the engineers in scientific management argued that specialization and automation would free workers from heavy toil. Workers, however, viewed the same factors in terms of the reductions in skills required for the job and a consequent reduction in the perceived importance of the individual. What began as a source of help in the language of efficiency became a source of grievance in the language of sentiments (p. 29).

Roethlisberger recognized the unique position of the first-line supervisor as the "go-between" or "person in the middle." He was an advocate of supervisory training but believed that only those people with the appropriate attitudes should be placed in such training programs; that supervisors should be prepared for lifetime learning; and that supervisory training should aid prospective managers in asking better questions, becoming better observers, and making better decisions.

Mayo's View of Human Nature and Motivation

One might expect that students of Roethlisberger's ideas would mirror those of his mentor (Mayo). To some extent they did. To a greater extent they did not. There is a distinctiveness to Mayo. He begins *The Human Problems of an Industrial Society* with the caution that "in industry, as in medicine, the inquirer who seeks a single remedy for all ailments is doomed to failure" (p. vi). In management there are never simple answers or a "quick fix," and woe to the manager who looks for them. If one is found, it is probably wrong!

The writings of Mayo address a number of industrial problems such as fatigue, monotony, and motivation. In his study of a mule-spinning department of a textile mill near Philadelphia he notes how the job fit all criteria of the "monotony model." The semiautomatic process required enough of the worker's attention to be irritating but not enough to absorb his mental abilities totally. The department never produced up to standard, and workers were pessimistic about all aspects of life. The turnover rate was 250 percent.

Mayo's interventions included rest pauses, and pay for output resulted in a stabilization of the turnover at 5 or 6 percent. The department became the standard for all other units in the mill. In this discussion, Mayo presented one of the fundamental principles of all human relations theory—the maxim of "individual differences," which states that "all individuals are different. What bores one may stimulate another." Workers are individuals, and any theory of work that tempts managers to treat everyone the same will fail. The successful manager and the effective organization always recognize the uniqueness of each person. This maxim sounds simple, but it is complex. It sounds trite, yet it is profound. A worker may not like a particular incentive program and may even resist all types of change, but everyone likes to be recognized and treated as a unique person (Bartlett and Ghoshal, 1995).

Mayo defended the sociopsychological explanation of productivity improvements at Hawthorne. Production increased, he believed, because working conditions were made more pleasant and greater freedom was provided to workers. In fact, his interests became progressively social and political. The third book in his trilogy was *The Political Problems of an Industrial Society* (1947). This book, however, never attained the recognition of the first two publications.

Mayo pointed out that all societies have two primary goals. The first is to ensure the material and economic survival of their members. The second is to maintain "spontaneous cooperation" throughout the entire structure. The challenge to management was to develop ways of accomplishing these objectives. The *rabble hypothesis*, or invisible hand, of classical economic theory seemed no longer capable of achieving voluntary cooperation. Management had to be proactive if coordination was to be achieved. Chandler's (1977) visible hand was not only a reality to Mayo, it was a necessity if economic survival and cooperation were to be achieved. In summary, we can say that Mayo, and to some extent Roethlisberger, provided managers several guidelines that are as useful as they are practical. These are:

1. Individuals are different with unique wants, needs, goals, and motives. Successful motivation demands that workers be treated as individuals.
2. Human problems are never simple.
3. Workers' personal or family problems may adversely influence performance at work.
4. Communication is important, and effective communication is critical. Few managers, in Mayo's opinion, were prepared educationally or practically for the human, social, and political problems of an industrial society.

Need Theories and the Humanization of Work

Mayo and Roethlisberger moved motivation theory away from the economic view of scientific management. They introduced ideas that were influential in their time and set the stage for new contributions by others. Discussions of sentiments, motives, and individual differences made the movement to theories of human needs less difficult.

Abraham Maslow and the Theory of Human Needs

Ask any junior business, education, or arts and sciences student what he or she remembers about introductory psychology, and more likely than not Maslow's need hierarchy will be mentioned. This is not surprising since it is likely that the hierarchy has been discussed in at least a fourth of all the courses they have taken at the university. However, the mere fact that the need hierarchy is familiar makes it no less profound (Thorlakson and Murray, 1996).

Abraham Maslow was born in Brooklyn, New York, in 1908 and received his doctorate in psychology at the University of Wisconsin. Although the years immediately following the completion of his education were tragic in the sense that he was a victim of the anti-Semitic prejudice in the United States, he managed to get a job at Columbia University working as a research assistant to the famous psychologist E. L. Thorndike. Even though jobs were almost impossible to obtain for scholars from Jewish families, it is said that Maslow resigned his position because Thorndike gave him the assignment of determining how much of behavior was caused by heredity and how much was the result of environment. Maslow sent a note to Thorndike saying the assignment was "silly" and "not worth doing" (Wilson, 1972). Fortunately, neither religious prejudice nor silly assignments discouraged Maslow from becoming one of the most widely known and recognized psychologists of the 20th century.

He was chairman of the Psychology Department at Brandeis University and a founder of humanistic psychology. Many of his writings made significant contributions, although our attention will be directed primarily toward his best known book, *Motivation and Personality* (1970). Maslow defined motivation as the "study of ultimate human goals" (p. 66).

Although all human beings have essentially the same goals, different cultures influence the ways in which goals are accomplished. It is an essential part of Maslow's theory that human beings never fully attain their objectives. When one need is satisfied or one goal is accomplished, others replace it.

Perhaps Maslow's most familiar idea relates to the way in which needs are arranged in a hierarchy of relative potency (p. 81). The basic needs at the bottom of the hierarchy, when satisfied, are replaced by higher level needs and desires. Maslow made three basic assumptions about human nature, which provide the foundation for his theory. (1) Human beings are wanting animals whose needs are never satisfied. (2) The state of dissatisfaction or unsatisfied needs motivates human action. Accord-

---

▲ Box 8-3
GIVING MEANING TO "PEOPLE FIRST"

Wainwright Industries, a manufacturer of components for the automobile and aerospace industries, uses a "people-first" strategy. The people-first strategy stresses the development of corporate strategies around employee needs. Surveys of employees indicated that the number one job concern they had was safety. Safety became the strategic priority of the company.

Trust is also an important part of Wainwright Industries' strategy. The company's books are open to all employees and there are no secrets. All employees, regardless of organizational level, participate in profit sharing. The results are impressive. Defects have been reduced by 90 percent. There has been a 35 percent reduction in production costs and lead time has been reduced from 8.75 days to 15 minutes. The external customer satisfaction index stands at 95 percent. The people-first strategy has meant increased productivity at Wainwright Industries.

Source: Wainwright (1997).

ing to Maslow, "the best way to send someone searching for love is to deny them love" (p. 113). (3) Needs are arranged in a hierarchy with the basic, lower level needs at the bottom and the higher level needs at the top.

Maslow's Hierarchy of Needs

At the base of the hierarchy are the physiological needs for food, water, clothing, and shelter. These are survival needs—without them we die. They appear early in life, in fact, at birth. As the physiological needs are satisfied, safety or social needs appear. Human beings need protection from danger and the uncertainty of the future. Food may no longer be a problem foremost in the minds of most people in industrialized nations, but there is a pressing need for protection against income loss in old age, catastrophic illness, and other dangers in the uncertain future.

Not all of our needs, however, relate to the individual, personal security, and survival. Human beings also need companionship and a sense of belongingness. Thus, the third level in the hierarchy is belongingness needs. People need to be accepted by others and feel a part of groups. Next, the esteem needs appear because all of us desire self-respect. We need to believe what we do is important and that we are honest, fair, and accepted as friends and respected as colleagues by others. When we are assured of such acceptance, our esteem needs become satisfied. At the very top of the hierarchy is the need for self-actualization—making all one can of the talents and skills he or she has developed. While other needs are often satisfied, almost no "normal" person ever completely self-actualizes. Self-actualization is a quest, a goal, not a defined accomplishment. There are always jobs to be done, relationships to mend, and opportunities to pursue.

At one point the needs in the hierarchy were globally classified by Maslow into two major categories. Deficiency needs was the label applied to the lower levels, including physiological, safety, and belongingness needs. Growth-motivated or developmental needs were represented by esteem and self-actualization. Note that the deficiency needs are satisfied by factors somewhat external to the individual, such as food, a safe environment, friends, and loved ones. Growth needs, on the other hand, are more intrinsic or internal to the individual. This realization will appear again in the forthcoming discussion of job enrichment.

Maslow illustrated the importance of maintaining favorable working conditions in his discussion of the "theory of threat." The general public and employees in an organization experience severe psychological problems when faced with threats. When an individual confronts deprivation of a life goal, undesirable outcomes result. Consider the case of "threatening conflicts" whereby an employee is forced to choose between two important yet mutually exclusive goals. The sales manager who holds a political office in her local community is required to relocate in order to progress further up the organization. A move, however, will require her resignation from the elected office. Organizational success is important as is loyalty to the voters.

Another, more serious threat is "catastrophic conflict." In this case the employee is faced only with threatening options. At least in the first incident the manager can either receive a promotion or retain a highly valued political office. The employee who has been offered early retirement may perceive his only options as leaving his life's work and sitting in a rocking chair the rest of his days, or remaining in an organization where he is not wanted. This is catastrophic conflict. In the extreme, it can lead to such violent outcomes as suicide.

Unlike many psychologists, Maslow provided insights into the healthy rather than the pathological human being. In *Motivation and Personality* a major portion of the book is devoted to the "self-actualized" personality (pp. 199–234). Maslow's subjects for his theory were friends, acquaintances, and students who he believed were motivated to self-actualize. The first important difference in this *self-actualizing personality* is the individual's attitude toward life. These people "live more in the real world of nature than in the human-made mass of concepts, abstractions, expectations, beliefs, and stereotypes that most people confuse with the real world" (p. 25). Self-actualizing people perceive what is real rather than what they wish or hope is real. They are unselfish and concerned about the welfare of others.

Even though self-actualizing personalities care about the welfare of others, they are problem centered and are often thought to be cold and aloof. However, this type of person desires an ever closer relationship with the person they love. A more complete knowledge of this "relevant other" is a constant goal. The partner's needs become the needs of the self-actualized person, and caring is an essential part of the love relationship. The picture provided by this exceedingly healthy person is one who needs privacy yet intensely loves and cares for others. The self-actualizing individual sets goals and works to accomplish them, yet is guided by a set of principles and a code of ethics that sometimes makes him or her appear so "good" that others may even come to dislike this person who so clearly provides a role model for the more "normal" people in the organization.

Revision of the Need Hierarchy

While the hierarchy of needs as presented by Maslow is popular, it is not without limitations. One of the most obvious is the inability of ordinary people to distinguish among the various levels in the hierarchy. If these levels cannot be identified and isolated, it is difficult, perhaps impossible, for managers to individualize and customize motivational programs.

In response to this criticism Clayton Alderfer (1972) proposed his existence, relatedness, and growth theory (ERG). In this theory, human needs are divided into three categories—existence, relatedness, and growth. Existence needs correspond to Maslow's physiological and safety needs; relatedness needs are similar to belongingness and internal esteem needs; and growth needs compare to external esteem and self-actualization needs.

Even though ERG theory has gained in popularity because of its relative simplicity due to fewer hierarchical levels, it is similar in most ways to Maslow's. Both recognize the existence of several needs and propose a relationship among the various types of needs that can be useful in motivating and rewarding individual behavior in organizations. However, Alderfer does not conceptualize needs in a hierarchi-

```
┌─────────────────────────────────────────────────────────────────────┐
│                                                                       │
│  ▲ Box 8-4                                                            │
│  BUILDING NEW HUMAN RESOURCE SYSTEMS                                  │
│                                                                       │
│  In 1992, Samaritan Health System was large but did not have the      │
│  profit margins ex-pected in the health care industry. The vice       │
│  president for human resources thought that one factor contributing   │
│  to the low profit margin was obsolete, reactive, and hi-erarchical   │
│  systems. He proposed changes that would enhance clinical care,       │
│  improve customer satisfaction, and reduce costs. An important        │
│  element in this plan was a compensation system that tied pay to      │
│  performance.                                                         │
│      Under the new system supervisors rate employees as               │
│  "developing," "compe-tent," or "masters." The evaluation is broken   │
│  down into two parts—how well em-ployees do the technical aspects of  │
│  their jobs and how well they perform other func-tions such as their  │
│  demeanor with customers and team members. Evaluations are also       │
│  completed by employees and peers.                                    │
│      The new system involves doing things a different way, and there  │
│  are those at Samaritan who are uncertain about the new way of doing  │
│  things. However, man-agement is committed to developing reward       │
│  systems for the future.                                              │
│                                                                       │
│  ───────────────                                                      │
│  *Source:* Moore (1996).                                              │
│                                                                       │
└─────────────────────────────────────────────────────────────────────┘
```

cal arrangement and suggests that all needs can be active at any given time. Some, such as growth needs, may actually increase in intensity the more they are satisfied (Mitchell, 1984). Even though actual research data on human needs tend to fit Alderfer's theory better, there remains a limited amount of research support. There is certainly little reason to look upon ERG theory at this time as a radical alternative to the popular and familiar theory of the need hierarchy.

McClelland's Achievement Motive

If you find need hierarchies, even simple ones like Alderfer's, unrealistic and confusing, McClelland's motivation theory is for you. This theory focuses on a single need—the need to achieve. McClelland has also done a great deal of research on the need for power, but his most significant contribution remains the achievement motive, and that will be the subject of this discussion.

David McClelland was born in Mt. Vernon, New York, in 1917. He studied languages at MacMurray College and graduated from Wesleyan University in 1938. He received his doctorate in psychology from Yale and joined the Department of Social Relations at Harvard in 1956.

When one reads the work of McClelland (1961) and McClelland and Winter (1969) it is impossible not to be impressed by the brilliance of the research designs. In his studies of economic growth and the achievement motive, McClelland artfully looks at the relationship between the *n Ach* or achievement motive evident in children's stories in one time period and the consumption of electrical power at a later time (that is, consumption of electrical power was used as a surrogate measure of economic development). The underlying theme of McClelland's research is that the achievement motive is at least partially responsible for economic growth. More specifically, the research was directed toward discovering whether or not there was a relationship between the need to achieve and the performance levels of individuals, organizations, and societies. Once this relationship was established, McClelland developed a training program designed to increase the need to achieve in managers, owners of small businesses, and other groups. To illustrate the practical significance of all this, one of his studies indicated that small business owners "trained" to possess higher achievement needs were more active in community affairs, invested more money in expanding their businesses, and employed twice as many people as a similar group that did not receive the training (McClelland, 1978).

There are many implications of McClelland's research. However, one of the more important ones relates to the motivation of entrepreneurial talent in a society at large. McClelland argued that societies with higher achievement motives produce more energetic entrepreneurs, and these entrepreneurs, in turn, produce more rapid economic growth. Entrepreneurs must take risks, and the willingness to assume moderate degrees of risk is associated with higher *n Ach*. Moreover, the data show that people with higher achievement motives believe they have a greater likelihood of success than those with low *n Ach*. People with higher achievement motives are generally more energetic, creative, and hard working. Finally, these people receive satisfaction from the knowledge that they are successful rather than from public recognition and praise.

McClelland also addressed the issue of how high achievement motives are, and can be, developed. First, it is important that parents and managers set high standards of excellence and respond warmly and promptly when children and employees perform consistently with the desired behavior standards. For countries that desire to use these findings to accelerate economic growth it is necessary to: (1) break orientations toward tradition and increase the other-directedness of the citizens; (2) increase the *n Ach* by initiating actions like insisting on excellence and setting high performance standards; and (3) provide for better allocation of existing achievement-oriented resources by channeling the most appropriate human talents into areas where they can have the greatest impact on organizational and social performance and by recognizing and rewarding the achievement-oriented people in the firm and nation.

To this point several motivation theories have been examined. All have one thing in common—they focus on the individual, the way needs are aroused, and how this aroused energy can be directed toward higher performance. Now we will shift the orientation. This shift will change our focus from the individual to the nature of work. The individual will be no less important than before. However, the importance of work and what it means to the worker should be a constant concern to all success-oriented managers.

From the Individual to the Job

Not too far from Boston, where much of Maslow's and McClelland's research was taking place in the mid-1950s, a group at the Psychological Services of Pittsburgh found the existing theory incomplete. The result of this dissatisfaction was the publication of a book by Frederick Herzberg and others, entitled *Job Attitudes: Review of Research and Opinion* (1957).

Frederick Herzberg was born in Lynn, Massachusetts, in 1923. He received his doctorate from the University of Pittsburgh, where he also earned a master's degree in public health. It was during his tenure as the research director at the Psychological Services of Pittsburgh that he and his associates published their first book on motivation. Later he was the Douglas McGregor Professor of Psychology at Case Western Reserve University and became University Distinguished Professor of Management at the University of Utah (Bedeian, 1993a). After reviewing several thousand articles on the subject of motivation, Herzberg and his colleagues concluded that much confusion existed in the field and that a *fresh approach* was needed. He thus set out to provide this fresh approach.

A Fresh Approach to Motivation

In *The Motivation to Work* (1959) Herzberg, Mausner, and Snyderman took an entirely different approach than that utilized in *Job Attitudes*. The former review of the literature convinced the authors that the major failure of prior work was the fact that it was fragmentary. Research that examined the factors affecting workers' attitudes toward work rarely looked at the effects of these attitudes. Studies of the effects of attitudes about work, on the other hand, almost never included anything about the origin of the attitudes. What was needed, according to Herzberg, was an investigation of job attitudes *in toto*, or a study that would simultaneously examine factors, attitudes, and effects. This was called the "factors-attitude-complex" (p. 12).

Armed with this need for a fresh approach, Herzberg and his associates collected data from professional employees (that is, accountants and engineers) in nine dissimilar plants in the general area of Pittsburgh. The respondents were interviewed and asked to relate incidents about times when they were extremely satisfied and dissatisfied with their work. Analysis of the results indicated something that motivation researchers had not recognized in the past—that the factors leading to job satisfaction when present were different from the things that led to job dissatisfaction when they were not present.

In other words, managers could not look at a single factor like good working conditions and assume that if employees were dissatisfied with the conditions a little expenditure on painting the facilities, providing more rest periods, and contracting with a background music company would solve the motivational problems of the company. To the contrary, it was determined that certain factors operate to increase job satisfaction and other factors only decrease it. The factors that could increase satisfaction were labeled *motivators*, while those that could only decrease satisfaction were called *hygiene factors*.

What All This Means to Managers

The results of Herzberg's initial research in *The Motivation to Work* stirred a great deal of executive interest because the implications were profound. Herzberg had illustrated that there are certain aspects of a job (he called them hygiene factors, no doubt because of his public health orientation) that are necessary but not sufficient conditions for motivation.

Factors such as company policies and administration, supervision, interpersonal relations with bosses and peers, and general working conditions provided only the basic conditions of work. Just as public drinking water systems make no one well but merely prevent people from becoming ill, these hygiene factors could not motivate people. They could only keep people from being dissatisfied. The worker expects safe surroundings, reasonable company policies, and pleasant relations with the boss and peers. If these conditions are not present, employees will be dissatisfied. If they are present, workers will not be motivated to higher performance.

The motivating factors, on the other hand, include things like an opportunity for achievement, recognition for a job well done, a chance to assume greater responsibility, advancement, and the nature of the work itself. These factors, it should be noted, address the need for a job to be a source of self-actualization and personal growth. The manager should note that the factors that only have the power to increase dissatisfaction if not present are all external or *extrinsic* to the job. They relate to the surroundings, fellow workers, and company policies.

The motivators, on the other hand, are internal or *intrinsic* to the work itself. The key to motivation, in Herzberg's view, is simple! If you as a manager want to motivate employees or other managers, give them work that provides an opportunity for achievement, advancement, recognition, and is designed in such a way as to be meaningful. This recognition clearly established the idea of *job enrichment* that has been so much a part of recent motivation theory and practice.

The third book in this trilogy by Herzberg was *Work and the Nature of Man* (1966). Here the author elaborated on techniques used in prior studies and provides citations of evidence that the theory works in a variety of settings. To a great extent the book is a defense of the earlier research, which received a great deal of criticism regarding its relatively small sample of professional employees in the general vicinity of Pittsburgh.

Perhaps the greatest contribution of Herzberg's work is that it gives managers something tangible to work on in addressing the motivation problem. This, of course, is the job itself. Advocates of job enrichment argue that work must be made more meaningful. It is not enough to merely enlarge tasks or rotate them to keep people from becoming excessively bored. Work should be fundamentally designed to provide meaning to the one performing the task.

One company that adopted many of Herzberg's ideas was American Telephone and Telegraph (Ford, 1973). The AT&T approach was based on three basic principles. (1) Defining jobs so that employees have natural areas of responsibility and logical tasks. This is called *horizontal loading* or ensuring that the job is structured in a way that is logical and sensible to the one who must accomplish it. In and of itself, however, horizontal loading results in little more than logical job enlargement not enrichment. (2) Providing employees with more control and responsibility over the job. This involves *vertical loading* and actually provides the employee with some managerial aspects of his or her own job. (3) Providing frequent performance feedback to the employee to create a sense of responsibility, achievement, and recognition. Again, this involves vertical loading since traditionally performance feedback and evaluation was considered a managerial role.

The AT&T experience, although there were isolated failures, was an overwhelmingly favorable experiment with job enrichment. The important thing to remember is that the focus in Herzberg's theory is on the task and ways to make work more meaningful. Taylor, Gantt, and Gilbreth were obsessed with defining and measuring the task; Mayo, Roethlisberger, Maslow, and other human relations writers insisted on recognizing that tasks had to be accomplished in a social setting; Herzberg, however, convincingly argued that the task must have meaning. To define and measure is fine, so is positioning work in the social arena. However, if the task does not have meaning in and of itself, it is not likely to motivate workers to high levels of excellence.

We have seen that Taylor was inclined to view human nature in somewhat primitive terms. Mayo, Maslow, and now Herzberg present a view of human beings as highly unique and "chosen" demigods. The view changes again, however, as the loop is closed in some of the most popular motivation theories discussed today. The image of the human being is once again radically altered. We are not returned to the level of oxen nor are we allowed to continue on the plane of the angels. The final two theories we will discuss are classified by Mitchell (1984) as intended choice motivation theories. We will simply refer to them as *cognitive theories* because of their emphasis on cognitive or thinking processes such as perception and learning.

Motivation and Human Choice

Intended choice or cognitive theories of motivation, which according to one writer have occupied 80 percent of recent motivation research, "involve current situations or informational factors that influence an individual's intention to choose one action over another" (Mitchell, 1984, p. 19). The first theory to be briefly discussed relates to the employee's perceptions of the outcomes that will result from various behaviors when the goal is simply to maximize one's payoff. The individual is viewed as a rational actor in search of the greatest benefit for a limited expenditure of energy.

Expectancy Theory

Expectancy theory was first introduced by Vroom (1964). To understand this theory, a few important terms must be introduced. The first is *expectancy*, which, according to Vroom, is "a momentary belief concerning the likelihood that a particular act will be followed by a particular outcome" (p. 17). *Valence* is the attractiveness or perceived value attached to the particular outcome by the individual. The magnitude of the valence is determined, in turn, by how instrumental the outcome is in obtaining something of value. To illustrate, an employee may choose to work hard because she believes that hard work will lead to higher earnings (that is, high expectancy). The valence of the higher earnings is determined by how instrumental the money is perceived to be in purchasing the new car that is needed by the employee and her family. Therefore, the *motivational force* on a person to perform a particular act or choose a particular alternative is equal to the perceived likelihood (expectancy) that the act will lead to a desired outcome times the perceived value (valence) of that outcome (p. 18). In more practical terms, the essence of Vroom's theory is summarized by Pecotich and Churchill (1981) as follows: ". . . a person's motivation to expend effort on any task depends upon: (1) expectancy—the person's perception of the probability that expending a given amount of effort on that task will lead to improved performance; (2) instrumentality—the person's perceptions of the relationship between improved performance and the receipt of certain outcomes such as more pay, a promotion, and so on; and (3) valence—the person's perception of the desirability of receiving these outcomes or rewards" (p. 214).

Vroom's expectancy theory is complex and difficult to understand. A reading of *Work and Motivation* will do little to clarify the points since the mathematical properties of the various measurements are frequently highlighted. However, we can itemize three important implications and guidelines for managers from expectancy theory (Bedeian, 1993b).

First, it is important to recognize that the anticipation of the reward is more important than is often considered. People make choices on the basis of what they think

---

▲ Box 8-5

ADDING SOME RISK TO PAY AT SATURN

It all began with great excitement—Saturn Corporation, the wholly owned subsidiary of General Motors, was to have a special partnership between GM and the United Auto Workers to train all team members, build leadership qualities, and provide fair and highly motivational rewards. The reward system developed was called *Risk and Reward* because it was argued that substantial rewards cannot be expected without the assumption of some risk.

At Saturn, total compensation is composed of base pay, risk pay, and reward pay. The base pay is lower than the market rate. Risk pay is the difference between the market rate and base pay and must be earned through the productivity of team members. The amount of risk pay increases as the team matures. Exceptional performance results in an even higher reward pay. In this manner employees are made genuine owners with rewards and risk.

Source: Overman (1995).

will happen in the future rather than on the basis of what happened in the past. Second, rewards should be closely and explicitly tied to actions that are considered desirable by the organization. The behaviors that are considered valuable should be rewarded openly, frequently, and generously. Third, remember Mayo's maxim of individual differences. People value different rewards so that some attempt should be made to match organizational outcomes with the desires of individual employees (Mitchell, 1984, p. 22). Finally, one additional point will be added that relates to fairness, even though no attempt will be made to discuss equity theory. Rewards should be equitable in terms of the effort required to accomplish the task.

Expectancy theory is not easy to apply. It is abstract and complicated in one sense but general and easy to relate to in another. All of us understand the importance of the expected outcome in determining our behavior. Expectancy theory provides an opportunity to apply what we know about ourselves to the motivation of those with whom we work.

If we characterize the implicit assumption made by expectancy theory about human nature we must describe it in one word—"rational." Human beings are viewed as calculators; even with limited information, they calculate the wisdom of a behavior now in terms of its likely outcomes in the future. The image of human beings provided by our final theory of motivation is less complimentary. In fact, the basic orientation of operant conditioning has already been introduced in our previous discussion on science and management. In the remainder of this chapter we will look at the implications of this scientific orientation in the study of motivation. This theory is radically different from the other motivation theories we have discussed to this point.

Operant Conditioning and B. F. Skinner

Operant conditioning is one of the more familiar applications of traditional science to management. Advocates of this approach owe the origins of their ideas to behaviorism in psychology and specifically to the ideas of B. F. Skinner (1974). Skinner's ideas about the proper way to study human behavior is illustrated by his abiding faith in the scientific method. He states: "The methods of science have been enormously successful wherever they have been tried. Let us then apply them to human affairs" (Skinner, 1953, p. 5). In perhaps his most challenging and to some his most frightening call, he advocates the development of a *technology of behavior* that would allow us to adjust the growth of the world's population as rapidly as we correct the course of a spaceship. This behavioral technology should be, according to Skinner, as powerful as our present physical and biological technologies (Skinner, 1971).

The most complete development of behaviorism in management is the subfield known as behavior modification, or *organizational behavior modification* (*O.B. Mod*), as it is often called (Luthans and Kreitner, 1975 and Bedeian, 1996). The theory underlying O.B. Mod is the positive reinforcement concept of Skinner. Familiar theories of motivation like that of Maslow take an internal view and concern themselves with things such as needs, desires, attitudes, and aspirations (Maslow, 1970). Approaches to motivation like that of Skinner are external in the sense that they describe and attempt to explain human motivation in terms of its consequences. The key to understanding Skinner's views and the managerial prescriptions that can be deduced from them is the schedule of reinforcement, or how desired acts are rewarded or not rewarded.

B. F. Skinner was born in Susquehanna, Pennsylvania, in 1904 and was attracted to psychology by reading the experiments of the Russian psychologist, Ivan Pavlov. In 1931, Skinner received his doctorate from Harvard University. After a period of postdoctoral research, he moved to the University of Minnesota and later to Indiana University. He returned to Harvard in 1948.

Actually, Skinner had little to do with management. None of his books deal with the subject and virtually all of his original research was done on pigeons rather than people (Skinner, 1971). Yet, the findings of his studies have been applied to the field of management so that we must concern ourselves with his views on motivation and learning. Skinner believed motivation theorists placed too much attention on the "inner being" along with related factors such as needs, motives, and desires (Hart and Scott, 1972). He therefore concentrated only on observable phenomena—stimulus and response—in presenting his theory.

Operant Conditioning: What Is It?

Learning is defined by psychologists as any relatively permanent change in an established relationship between a stimulus and a response. Learning, however, can occur in two ways. First, there is classical conditioning, where the stimulus precedes the response, as in the famous Pavlovian experiments with dogs. A second type of learning is known as instrumental or operant learning. In this type of learning, the response takes place prior to and in anticipation of the stimulus. This is the basis of Skinner's theory.

While we cannot develop the theory in its entirety, a few elements must necessarily be discussed. Skinner states that operant conditioning is the process by which behavior is altered and learning takes place. The process is facilitated by positive reinforcement of desired behaviors. A positive reinforcer is, therefore, anything that increases the frequency of the desired response when it is present. A monetary payment for a job well done is a positive reinforcer. The key to understanding Skinner's theory of motivation lies, however, with the manner in which reinforcement takes place, or the schedule of reinforcement.

Schedules of Reinforcement

To this point there is really nothing unique about operant conditioning or B. F. Skinner. Even Frederick Taylor recognized the potential motivational impact of positive reinforcement. The problem with Taylor's differential piece rate was that, in Skinner's terms, this reward system amounted to *continuous positive reinforcement*. Every time the worker introduced a unit at or below standard, the same payment was made. Even when the standard was exceeded, the reward was paid continuously. Only the rate of payment varied. This continuous reinforcement is familiar to all of us. Each time we complete a week or month at work, we receive our pay and the amount is based more on a contractual agreement than performance.

If we use the simple symbols where *O* represents the operant behavior (production of another unit of a widget or completion of another day at work) and *C* represents the consequence or receipt of the day rate or salary, we can illustrate what is meant by a continuous reinforcement schedule in the following manner:

$$O–C, \quad O–C, \quad O–C, \quad O–C.$$

Each time the behavior takes place, the consequence or payment is received. This type of reinforcement schedule encourages steady yet unenthusiastic behavior. The primary incentive is to complete the interval of time necessary for receipt of the weekly paycheck or to produce enough to keep your job.

In addition to continuous reinforcement, the manager may choose some form of *partial reinforcement*. As the name implies, with these schedules the desired consequence does not follow every iteration of the behavior. Partial reinforcement schedules may be either fixed or variable intervals or ratios. We will deal only with ratios, although the principles are the same when applied to intervals. The *fixed-ratio partial reinforcer* has the consequence occurring at predictable points. It may, for example, take three or four iterations of a task before one receives positive reinforcement. Symbolically this appears as

$$O–O–O–C, \quad O–O–O–C.$$

Every three times the task is completed, the reward or consequence follows. For example, a manager might hire a consultant and indicate that partial payments will be made when the project is 30, 50, and 100 percent complete. The incentive is to complete the project as fast as possible in order to receive a paycheck. While this is likely to result in harder and faster work, potential problems exist. What, for example, is there to discourage the consultant from working so fast that the quality of the work suffers?

The final schedule of reinforcement presented by Skinner is called *variable-ratio reinforcement*. In this schedule one cannot predict the exact iteration that will result in the desired consequence. Symbolically, this might appear as

$$O–C, \quad O–O–O–O–O–C, \quad O–O–C.$$

The best illustration of this schedule is the game of chance. No one can predict exactly when the winning poker hand will be dealt or the pull on the "one-arm bandit" that will result in the payoff. The excitement of this type of reinforcement schedule is what makes the work of the laboratory researcher rewarding. Who knows if the next iteration of an experiment will or will not result in a finding of great scientific significance. This type of schedule is considered one of the most motivating forms of reinforcement. The problem is, "how can this be applied to management?" Obviously no labor union or employee is going to allow us to pay according to a random schedule. There are, however, many examples of how operant conditioning concepts have been applied in organizations. For one innovative alternative consider the way the *Denver Post* used a variable-ratio partial reinforcement schedule to stimulate advertisement sales. The management of the *Post* became aware of a slot machine two individuals developed with a microcomputer that could be programmed to pay off according to different specifications. Employees who sold advertising space were given one chance to play the machine each time they sold a classified advertisement. Each play provided an opportunity to win up to $50, although the average payoff was 12 cents.

Obviously, the average payoff would not provide a substantial monetary incentive to work hard. However, the possibility of winning $50 for each sale and the excitement that accompanied playing the machine resulted in a tremendous increase in classified ad sales after only a few months of operation (Higgins, 1983). Additional impressive results have been reported when operant conditioning principles have been applied in small businesses such as grocery stores and video game parlors (Komaki, Waddell, and Pearce, 1977).

Emery Air Freight, for example, was one of the early business firms to receive a great deal of press coverage for the results it achieved through the practical use of positive reinforcement techniques ("At Emery Air Freight," 1973). Some estimate that Emery benefited more than half a million dollars in the first year of this program. Another, more recent example of the use of operant conditioning principles in management is an experiment by Scandinavian Airlines. The airline selected a group of reservation sales personnel and through the principles of positive reinforcement significantly increased the performance of the agents in the direction desired by the organization (Feeney, Staelin, O'Brien, and Dickinson, 1982).

The development of a successful behavior modification program relies on the skillful use of operant conditioning principles (Scott and Podsakoff, 1985). The manager first identifies the target or desired behaviors she wants to achieve. Baseline measurements are then taken to provide a reference point against which change can be measured. For example, in one case at Emery improvement in the utilization rate of containers was the goal. Managers and employees initially believed the containers were in use 90 percent of the time. Careful measurement revealed 45 percent was a more accurate figure. Care was taken to analyze the factors that led to an improved utilization rate of containers (antecedent conditions) and the consequences of a higher utilization rate. The behavior change program was implemented by providing positive feedback to dockworkers each day the utilization rate fell between 45 and 95 percent. Many companies have found that tangible rewards as well as information feedback increases the rate of progress toward target levels of accomplishment. As with all good change programs, it is important to evaluate and update the use of behavior modification programs frequently.

Although some people fear that the overzealous use of O. B. Mod and other operant conditioning programs could become a new form of social engineering, advocates point to their effectiveness as proof that scientific principles and programs can be applied with precision to human behavior in organizations.

Much has been written about management and motivation. In fact, so much has been written that managers are often confused by the volume and the conflicting prescriptions of different motivation theories. How is the manager to make sense out of a field that even the researchers cannot agree on? Managers need to focus on the underlying similarities rather than always highlighting the differences. Even though

---

▲ **Box 8-6**

BANKING ON INCENTIVES

The Union National Bank has used behavior modification principles for years. Specifically, the bank has employed positive reinforcement in the form of praise and financial reward. The rewards are as immediate as possible, even financial incentives are paid on a daily, weekly, or biweekly basis. The incentives are contingent on the performance of specific tasks, and each person controls his or her own amount of incentive. Finally, the focus is on results not process.

The results, as measured against a baseline established in the proof department, are impressive: (1) proof operators can earn 50 to 70 percent of their base pay in incentives; (2) turnover has gone from 110 percent to less than 1 percent; (3) absenteeism has dropped from 4.2 percent to 2.2 percent, overtime from 475 hours per year to 13 hours per year; and (4) staffing in the department has been reduced from 11 full-time and three part-time employees to three full-time and six part-time employees. Savings in this department alone are estimated to be about $100,000 per year.

Source: Dierks and McNally (1987)

Skinner might object, one cannot "go wrong" by carefully examining the fact that people are different—they have different experiences, they aspire to different goals, and they are motivated by different needs. Of course, even the most sensitive manager cannot design a motivation program for each employee. If she could, the organization would probably not allow it.

Managers, however, need to think of employees as individuals. They need to appreciate that the people who work with and for them all have unique talents and potentials to contribute to organizational goals.

Implications and Conclusions

This chapter has discussed far-ranging issues concerning the nature of several important theories of human motivation. The works of human relations theorists such as Mayo, Roethlisberger, and Maslow have been contrasted to the engineering-oriented views of scientific management presented earlier. More contemporary behavioral views by McClelland, Herzberg, Vroom, and Skinner have also been examined. Even though the theories differ with respect to their focus and complexity, all have important lessons for present and future managers. Hopefully, one of the most important things to be gained from this discussion is how the writers make different assumptions about human nature. Some of our more important conclusions are outlined next.

1. Motivation theory took a significant and dramatic change in direction from the engineering-oriented view of scientific management to the human relations view after the Hawthorne Studies.
2. The Hawthorne Studies are important to management because of their scope and influence.
3. The importance of individual differences is a fundamental tenet of modern psychological theories of human motivation at work.
4. Abraham Maslow's theory of human needs is one of the most influential theories of motivation primarily because of its applicability to so many areas of human performance.
5. Maslow's ideas have been expanded and applied by other need theorists such as Alderfer and McClelland.
6. Frederick Herzberg did much to alter management thinking about motivation by focusing on the nature of work and the job performed.
7. Expectancy theory, although abstract, illustrates the importance of instrumental learning as it applies to motivation.
8. B. F. Skinner's operant conditioning provides the basis for applications of behavior modification in education and industry.

Questions for Discussion

1 Why do you think the view of human nature has changed so dramatically from scientific management to today? Which view is more accurate? Explain your response.

2 Many criticize the Hawthorne Studies as unscientific. How could unscientific studies be as influential as the Hawthorne Studies have been to management thought?

3 The pig iron studies of Taylor and the mule-spinning studies of Mayo have much in common. What are some of the more important similarities?

4 What is the rabble hypothesis? Why is it important to motivation theory in management?

5 What are the similarities and differences among Maslow's, Alderfer's, and McClelland's need theories of human motivation?

6 Why is Herzberg's theory referred to as the two-factor theory of motivation? Is this an accurate description? Why or why not?

7 Why was the factor–attitude–effect complex important to the development of the two-factor theory of motivation?

8 Briefly define expectancy, instrumentality, and valence and note why each is important to a theory of human motivation.

9 Do you think operant conditioning is human engineering? Why or why not?

10 Why is the schedule of reinforcement the cornerstone of operant conditioning as a theory of motivation?

RESPONSIBILITY AND CULTURE

At the beginning of this book we defined management as the process of co-ordinating individual and group actions toward the accomplishment of organizational goals in a way that is consistent with the values of the larger society. Regardless of how efficient an organization is or how innovative and adaptive it becomes, if managers are not sensitive to the demands of the larger society, problems will develop. One study found that the price fixing scandal at Archer Daniels caused that company a $1 billion loss in the market value of its stock. Questions about race discrimination at Texaco cost them a little over $1 billion in market value, and the Valdez oil spill reduced the value of Exxon's stock by over $3 billion. In fact, the entire oil industry suffered because of the Exxon spill (Fombrun, 1997).

Chapter 9 discusses yet another responsibility of management—its responsibility to society. While it is recognized that ethical management is an extremely personal thing, individual organizations have a profound impact on society. A plant closing in a small town can cause significant suffering. However, businesses are not charitable institutions. They are economic institutions founded to create value for their owners. Managers have a difficult task ensuring that their multiple responsibilities are considered in the numerous decisions they make.

For some managers the task may be a little easier because of the culture and history of the organization. Some business firms have always made it clear that the welfare of the community was a major factor in their decision making. Ben and Jerry's, Marriot Corporation, and other businesses place a high value on ensuring that environmental, religious, and social values are considered in their actions, even if these considerations result in smaller returns for investors. Similarly, some investors are attracted to organizations that possess such values. As Chapter 10 demonstrates, the values of different organizations can often be observed in their cultures, and managers should be skilled at dealing with all aspects of organizational culture.

The final chapter attempts a retrospective view of all we have discussed throughout the book and provides a summary of some of the important lessons of management. These lessons are discussed and some speculations are offered about the future of management ideas and actions.

Managing Responsibility: Obligations and Values

"America's great achievement has been business. The business of business is to take part in the creation of the Great Society."

Henry Robins Luce
Cofounder of *Time*

It seems that things never really change. Just when it appears widely understood that business has accepted a more demanding responsibility to society, scandals develop. Tobacco firms are accused of focusing their advertising on teenagers, managers are suspected of sexually harassing employees, respected companies are said to be so demanding that executives do not have time for their families, and even *The Wall Street Journal* is found guilty of libel. The scandals have been so frequent that a writer in *Time* (May 25, 1987, p. 22) stated that "what began as the decade of the entrepreneur is becoming the age of the pinstriped outlaw." Hopefully, this is overstated. Yet, all agree that the question of the responsibilities and values of managers is as critical today as it was in the years of the environmental crisis and other social issues. Any institution that is as important as business is expected to be, at a minimum, a good citizen.

The factory system and the methods of mass production it made possible served us well economically. Even the most utopian reformer is likely to concede this point. When Babbage looked at the engines that drove the Industrial Revolution, he heard the music of prosperity. Even though Ure recognized that devils lurked in the factories, he believed the evil was the doing of the slubbers not the industrialists. However, the same factories that increased wealth and improved efficiency were too often the economic prisons of the working class. Heilbroner (1967) illustrated, in vivid terms, the horrors of mid-18th-century England. In the mines, for example, he talked of men and women working together:

> Stripped to the waist, and sometimes reduced from pure fatigue to a whimpering half-human state . . . sexual appetites aroused at a glance were gratified down some deserted shaftway; children of seven or ten who never saw daylight dur-

ing winter months were used and abused and paid a pittance and . . . pregnant women drew coal cars like horses and even gave birth in the dark black caverns (p. 29).

What Is The Business of Business?

The idea that managers have a responsibility to groups other than owners is not new. Sometimes we are tempted to believe things are simpler and fairer when we leave the market forces alone to allocate resources, even if it works to the disadvantage of a large segment of society. Babbage did not divert his energies to such philosophy, Ure was too busy defending an exploding industrial society, and classical economists were determined to make their models of reality analytically simple, even if it meant making assumptions about maximizing behavior that were empirically false. Fortunately, the by-products of industrialization, like those mentioned, did not escape the attention of everyone.

The Making of a Welfare Capitalist

Robert Owen was a contemporary of Babbage and Ure. He was born in 1771 and, by his own admission, was a "manufacturer for pecuniary profit" (Owen, 1825). Whereas Babbage was a technologist and Ure tended to see things as he wished them to be, Owen was impossible to stereotype. He sought profit, yet he disliked private property. His contempt for private property led him to advocate the formation of a "village of cooperation," which was, in reality, a commune where children were to be taken from parents and educated to ensure that they were taught the proper values. The government in the village was expected to play an active role in economic and industrial planning.

Where Babbage and Ure saw magic in the machines, Owen saw suffering. His concern became so great that he had few options except to purchase a manufacturing facility and do his best to improve the plight of the worker. This he did in New Lanark, Scotland, an industrial oasis in the wilds of Scotland. New Lanark became a tribute to a man who has since been labeled a welfare capitalist and a utopian socialist. Yet, in New Lanark the abuse of children was prohibited, child labor laws were passed and enforced, and the company built public schools and streets.

Owen, from all available evidence, was concerned about workers. Heilbroner (1967) found this and the radical difference between his ideas and those of Babbage and Ure surprising. Actually the discrepancy is not hard to understand at all. Babbage and Ure were born into prosperous, if not wealthy, families. Owen enjoyed no such accident of birth. He was born in Wales, the son of poor parents, and at the age of nine left school to become an apprentice draper. There was no university, no travel, and very little happiness in his childhood. Such a reality makes for a different perspective on machines and factories. The view from the inside out is different from that of the outside in! Babbage and Ure were the benefactors of factories, Owen, at least in his childhood, was their victim.

189

Chapter 9 ▲
*Managing
Responsibility:
Obligations
and Values*

▲ **Box 9-1**

SOCIAL CHANGE AND BUSINESS

Ben Cohen and Jerry Greenfield, founders of Ben & Jerry's Ice Cream, have been committed to social change in their business decisions from the beginning. They pay more to Vermont dairy farmers to acquire milk that is free from a potentially harmful growth hormone and changed the recipe of a popular flavor so they would not have to buy Oreo cookies from the tobacco firm RJR Nabisco. They changed their production process to use brownies purchased from a not-for-profit bakery that employed handicapped workers and have made tremendous investments in modern facilities to reduce the amount of high-fat dairy waste (a by-product of making ice cream) put back into the environment. Most impressive of all, they give away 7.5 percent of pretax profits, when the average charitable contribution for American corporations is less than 2 percent.

These policies have not been easy to initiate or maintain. In August 1992 the company's stock was selling for $32. In 1997 it was trading at less than half this figure. Ben and Jerry, like Robert Owen, have experienced a cost for their commitment to social change.

Source: Cohen and Greenfield (1997).

Through acts of fate and sensible investments Owen became a successful businessman and even managed to purchase a textile mill. Immediately he went to work making his factories a more tolerable place to work. In fact, the entire village of New Lanark was a pleasing place thanks to Robert Owen. Children received schooling rather than strappings and workers were treated kindly, even if the kindness was paternally motivated.

Owen advocated devoting more time and attention to the human being or, as he called it, the "living machine." It should be kept neat and clean, treated with kindness, and supplied with all the necessities of life. Regulated hours of work for all, child labor laws, public education, company-furnished meals at work, and industrial involvement in community projects were all part of Owen's plan. His mistake was that of many zealots—the belief that everyone would agree if they only knew the truth about injustice. In the final analysis, Owen was not only naive, but he did not understand human behavior nearly as much as he wished to improve it.

His enthusiasm about the success of New Lanark persuaded him to pursue reforms through legislation and, needless to say, he was not successful. In fact, his reforms were so firmly rejected that he decided to travel to America, where people desired freedom and cared about their fellow men and women. In New Harmony, Indiana, he attempted to replicate and improve the New Lanark experiment. Again, he misjudged the character (or lack of character) of his fellow men and women. New Harmony ended in failure and Owen returned to England, where he became involved in the organization of a national workers' union, which was no more acceptable than his village of cooperation.

Robert Owen was a strange combination—capitalist and socialist; manufacturer and organizer of unions; profit seeker and reformer. He is not remembered in management history for his successes. They were few indeed. He is remembered for his courage and his commitment to reducing the suffering of the working class. He is remembered most as the first person to seriously address the ultimate obligation of management—not just as an institution but as individuals responsible for using human and nonhuman resources in the accomplishment of corporate goals. The tradition he started is evident today in the questions asked about the ultimate responsibility of management and managers.

From Owen to Gantt

In previous chapters we have mentioned Henry L. Gantt, perhaps the most influential of Taylor's associates. A close examination of Gantt's writings reveals the tremendous influence Taylor had on his ideas and theories. However, there was a uniqueness to Gantt that went beyond the ideas of his mentor. This was particularly true relative to the responsibilities Gantt believed managers had to workers and society. In a word, Gantt appeared considerably more concerned than Taylor about issues relating to individual and social welfare.

There is no doubt that a person's experiences fashion, to a great extent, his or her philosophies. Gantt, like Owen, was not favored in matters of birth. The American Civil War turned the fortunes of the Gantt family from prosperity to privation. In the process, he came to understand the perspective of the worker. Gantt seemed always to understand the person doing the work better and, for that reason, he concentrated more on processes such as motivation, leadership, and training.

Gantt respected democracy in government and on the job. He was influenced, to the great surprise of many, by the goals of the government of Russia. Much of his writing took place around the time of the Russian Revolution and, as a consequence, he was familiar with the economic and social philosophy that led to the overthrow of the Czar. His affection for the socialist cause, it might be noted, did not endear him to business circles, but it did enable him to operate in a different manner than Taylor.

For example, one of Gantt's accomplishments was the use of beneficial aspects of Taylor's system along with elements of welfare work at firms such as Bancroft and Sons, where he served as a consultant. The responsiveness of Gantt to the wishes of the Quaker owners resulted in strained relationships with Taylor, who believed his associate was giving in too much to the desires of the proprietors (Nelson and Campbell, 1972). That, however, did not deter Gantt from proceeding in his own way and accomplishing some impressive results.

Gantt's philosophy with regard to the payment of workers also differed from that of Taylor. For example, he developed a task and bonus system whereby workers were paid a bonus in addition to their regular day's pay when they followed instructions

191

Chapter 9 ▲
*Managing
Responsibility:
Obligations
and Values*

and accomplished all their work within the time required. Foremen also shared in the bonuses of their workers and rewards were given for suggestions that resulted in increased efficiency. One of Gantt's papers, entitled "Training Workmen in Habit of Industry and Cooperation," has been praised by several writers as an extremely unique insight into the humanistic dimension of management and labor (Alford, 1934).

As important as Gantt's views about the worker were, his ideas concerning the social responsibility of business and management were even more significant. As his writings developed, Gantt became increasingly convinced that management should concentrate on its "broad obligations" to society. In his last book, *Organizing for Work* (1919), he talked of a "parting of the ways" that he feared would take place if America's free enterprise system did not find some means of reconciling the quest for profits with the welfare of society. Gantt clearly viewed business firms as institutions existing for the good of society. If, at any time, society deemed the costs excessive compared to the benefits received from sanctioning corporations, the rights of existence could be withdrawn. One gets the impression from Gantt's writings that he considered such actions possible if not probable.

In the midst of the social and economic upheavals in Europe, Gantt could see analogies to the United States. In fact, he believed that all industrial societies had to ensure the equitable distribution of returns to all the factors of production, with special emphasis on labor. Capital was entitled only to the return it rightfully earned. Anything more amounted to excess profits. He was greatly concerned about the ap-

---

▲ Box 9-2
AN ATTEMPT AT A NEW AGE

In 1985 Pepsi left South Africa to protest against apartheid. Coca-Cola decided to stay. In 1994 Pepsi returned with a $65 million investment. Three years later Pepsi was packing again, convinced that it could not compete against Coca-Cola's virtual monopoly that was firmly established in the decade of Pepsi's absence.

New Age Beverages was the name of the soft drink company that was formed to compete in South Africa. The name itself was reflective of the hope and promise of the product. However, the challenge was apparently too great and the decision was made to withdraw.

Apartheid in South Africa was an issue that went to the heart of corporate social consciousness. Some firms argued they could do more to overcome apartheid by staying and working within the system. Others, like Pepsi, thought the most effective strategy was to show their disapproval by leaving in protest. These differences illustrate the extremely different views of and approaches to social responsibility.

Source: "Farewell Pretoria" (1997).

parent desire on the part of business to emphasize profits over community service. If business did not accept its social responsibility and devote itself to service, Gantt believed, the community would "ultimately make the attempt to take it over in order to operate it in its own interest" (Gantt, 1919).

Gantt possessed a special fear of big business. He was convinced that small enterprises, because of their competitive situation, had to concentrate on service to the customer and society if they were to survive. However, in his view, as businesses become larger and control more of the market (develop monopolistic power), they become less responsive to customers and pursue excess profits through higher prices.

With Gantt we see the continuity of the concern for social responsibility that emerged in the midst of scientific management. The theme continued in Barnard and others. Gantt, perhaps because of his fascination with the Russian Revolution or the misfortune with regard to his family's wealth, possessed a zealousness that reminds us of Owen. This zealousness did not emerge again until a less well-known but highly significant contributor to the field of management appeared on the scene. His name was Ordway Tead, introduced earlier in our discussion of leadership, and his ideas were as revolutionary as those Gantt admired in Russia.

Ordway Tead: Conscience of a Developing Art

Before looking specifically at Tead, it is important to note that there was considerable interest developing in the early 1920s regarding philosophy in management. Perhaps the point of Taylor was finally being recognized—to adapt the techniques of a system such as scientific management without simultaneously adapting its philosophy could be dangerous. Unfortunately, this has been the case all too often in management. The pursuit of quick fixes has reduced many useful management concepts to mere fads and expedient measures to address immediate problems.

Oliver Sheldon, like Gantt, believed that managers had to do better than merely apply techniques to the problems of industry. According to him, combining management and ethical actions was the responsibility of all managers. Managers should adopt 3 important principles: (1) the policies, conditions, and methods of industry should be conducive to community well-being (similar to the words of Owen and Gantt); (2) management should endeavor to adopt the highest moral standards of the community as a whole in applying social justice to industrial practice; and (3) management should take the initiative in raising ethical standards and conceptualizing social justice (Sheldon, 1923, p. 284). Sheldon took the moral "high ground" and spoke academically of management and responsibility. Ordway Tead entered the trenches.

Tead was born in Massachusetts in 1891. At the time of Tead's birth, Gantt was busy perfecting his task and bonus system at Midvale Steel. Tead planned to become a minister but was disillusioned by the hypocrisy he saw in religion and chose instead business as a career. He held a variety of jobs and even worked as a management consultant before finding his true calling in 1920, when he was employed by McGraw-Hill Book Company in the area of business publishing. Within 5 years he became the editor of social and economic books at Harper and Brothers. This position provided Tead with a base or forum for developing and expanding his ideas on

193

Chapter 9 ▲
*Managing
Responsibility:
Obligations
and Values*

business, economics, and social issues. Tead was more a reformer in the tradition of Owen than an observer like Gantt.

Emergence of a Theme

Tead called his first book *Instincts in Industry* (1918). He introduced some of the more important instincts that he thought existed in all human beings. The themes of psychology and leadership continued in his writings for the next two decades (Tead, 1929, 1935). For our purposes, however, Tead made his most important statement on management and social philosophy in *The Art of Administration* (1951). This book, according to the foreword by Lawrence Appley, took advantage of all of Tead's previous writing, experience, and exposure to other authors and combined everything into his attempt to deal with the inequalities and injustice he saw in his day. In a real sense, the book is the *magnum opus* of Ordway Tead.

Tead began his analysis of social philosophy and management at the level of the individual worker. He believed there was no necessary contradiction between organizational efficiency and employee happiness and welfare. Yet in 1951, as today, many people expressed discontent with work. Something was or is missing.

This missing ingredient, according to Tead, is "the glory of inner confidence, zest, and a sense of significance." Participative management was the best means of hammering out the political, industrial, and economic order where all people could live and work with dignity and self-respect. Management was a critical factor in ensuring that this became a reality.

Management, Tead believed, was a "grave social liability" unless the human being was taken into account. Human beings should never be reduced to the level of a machine or made victims of a "soulless business world bent on mere profits." Imagine the response these ideas received in 1951. Social responsibility was not an established doctrine. Moreover, private enterprise advocates of that day, as today, saw no relationship whatsoever between business' quest for profits and the exploitation of the human resource. In fact, such advocates were likely to envision profit seeking as the ultimate defender of the rights of workers.

Tead Builds His Argument

As with any serious argument regarding social responsibility, Tead's starting point was the goals of the organization. The goals, after all, are the factors that most directly provide us insights into what a business values and the priorities it places on each value. Tead believed there are several legitimate corporate aims. The more important are legal, technical, profit making, personal, and public. Successful managers must consider all these aims if they propose to build an effective organization. Most of us assume profit making is the primary driving force controlling all business operations.

It is not! Tead stressed that without accomplishing important secondary goals the primary goals stated in the corporate charter and the quest for profits could never be realized. It is important, in fact essential, to prioritize goals. This is one of the most

---

▲ Box 9-3
NIGHTMARES AND BUSINESS RESPONSIBILITY

If ever there was a nightmare of social responsibility, it had to be the 10 million gallons of oil spilled by the Exxon Valdez in Prince William Sound in Alaska. It cost the company over $1 billion to clean up only one-tenth of the spill, and who knows what the more than 150 lawsuits will eventually cost. The damage done to the company's image is beyond measure! In spite of Exxon's attempts to blame the Coast Guard, the weather, a captain with a drinking problem, and others, the company has been consistently pictured as irresponsible in its handling of the spill.

The Exxon case illustrates the complexity of the social responsibility debate in an increasingly complex technological society. The world demands oil, yet its discovery, refinement, and distribution are dangerous to the environment and ultimately to the very individuals who demand it. Business is the institution in the middle. On one hand it discovers, makes, and delivers a dangerous product. On the other hand, it must balance the quest for profits with the responsibility it shares with all parties for minimizing the dangers inherent in modern technology.

Source: "Alaskan Oil Spill" (1990).

---

effective ways to communicate what is important to employees. If managers do not make corporate goals appealing to employees in a sustained way, they cannot obtain more than a nominal, grudging, indifferent response from their efforts to motivate workers. Tead stated:

> Managers have to be experts in the clarifying, articulating, and purifying of aims, in assuring the relative appeal of the several prevailing or possible goals, in bringing about their pervasive communication, and in supplying the supporting conditions which make acceptance of them likely throughout the organization (p. 23).

Tead, as with many social critics, thought that worker satisfaction, loyalty, and productivity can be best obtained when employees have a stake in the final outcome of business activity. For this reason, profit sharing was advocated as a way to provide workers with such a stake. This would be instrumental in building a *partnership attitude* between workers and managers. Otherwise rank and file employees would only be involved in creating profits and never allowed to share in the fruits of their labor.

Making workers stakeholders, however, does not ensure cooperation and hard work. The association between ownership and productivity is not automatic. Some

195

Chapter 9 ▲
*Managing
Responsibility:
Obligations
and Values*

businesses have been generous but paternalistic and employees have rejected such a philosophy of rewards. Paternalistic approaches sooner or later are rejected because they are regarded as "a substitute for autonomous and self-respecting participation by employees in affairs they eventually realize to be their own" (p. 36).

Tead believed that society was more complicated in 1951 than in 1900. By implication, we can infer he would think today is more complex than the 1950s. He perceived society as characterized by big corporations, big schools, big cities, and big governments. Because of the bigness and a substantial degree of mobility, people seemed less in agreement about how to achieve democracy, equality, and justice than when the economy was less urban, less industrialized, and less concentrated.

In a time of significant activism, Tead proposed that managers become proactive and spell out in some detail what the nature and aims of a democratic society are. At this point an almost radical activism is sensed on the part of Tead the social critic. However, it was his conviction that when people are working together to achieve worthy goals and the creative expression of people and the meaningfulness of life are enhanced for all, their rightful democratic claims are being satisfied.

Could it be that Tead suggested that management and managers become agents of social change? Indeed he did because of his belief that corporate aims cannot be viewed apart from democratic aims. There is no escaping the conclusion that an intrinsic purpose of management is to help organizations operate democratically. He stated the argument as follows:

> Democracy as a moral aspiration with its concomitant institutional expressions is an influence extended into the lives of all and in all areas of our activity. And good administration has a major role in helping to translate this intrinsic American aspiration into processes and procedures which promise well for the growth of robust personalities (p. 91).

Tead was idealistic but not unrealistic. He recognized the dangers of democracy. He even quoted Chester Barnard and observed that the freedoms of action, thought, and speech necessary to democratic processes require a greater sense of responsibility, initiative, and adaptability on the part of individuals.

Tead anticipated many contemporary issues and ideas like the quality of work life, which he called collective cooperation. In this system workers and managers strive in harmony for the "progressive improvement of any and all phases of operation looking to the increasing productivity of the entire enterprise" (p. 166). The conditions required as prerequisites for such cooperation are familiar—job security for workers, quality work standards, criteria for promotions, guidelines for labor-saving modernization, employee grievance procedures, job classifications, wage and salary administration, and provision for the workers' old age, safety, and death.

Tead believed that when corporations provide these conditions, employees are more likely to believe that the company and its managers care about them and they, in turn, will care more about the organization. Collective cooperation can best, perhaps only, be accomplished through coordination, which includes all managerial effort to formulate, adopt, transmit, give effect to, interpret, and oversee organizational policies. Managers, according to Tead, should ask themselves: "Do we all know what we are up to now, and are we all relating our efforts to this end in the best possible way?"

Above all, Tead believed there was a need for greater appreciation of the social and moral significance of management and its role in business and society. To him, the most profound meaning of management is "a more participative, more dynamic type of managing where organized administrative relations are democratically proposed, are mindful of the whole man (person) and are ethically sensitive" (p. 207).

Ordway Tead is rarely discussed in the history of management thought. George (1972) refers to him as a *minor* writer and Wren (1994) devotes little attention to him. Significance is, of course, a matter of judgment. Certainly, Tead does not deserve the recognition of Taylor or Barnard. He was, however, one of the first management writers of modern times to courageously advocate the social responsibility doctrine. His personal philosophy, particularly his concern for social injustice, was applied to real management issues. His implicit, and sometimes explicit, view of the role of business in solving social ills were at least 2 decades before their time. In 1950, it was unusual to suggest that business had any stake in correcting social problems, much less taking the proactive role of actually defining social problems.

Management was to hear more about social issues with the passage of time. In the 1960s, civil rights and the evils of racial discrimination were to focus on the question of employment and promotion equity. In the 1970s, the environmental crisis and the role of business in protecting the ecology of spaceship earth came to the forefront. The 1980s brought even more issues. We are fortunate to have the wisdom of Tead, Gantt, and others to guide us through these turbulent times.

Social Responsibility and Management

Steel mills emitted smoke and particulate matter into the atmosphere for years and automobile exhaust fumes filled the lungs of millions of people, yet only a few complained. What is it that has increased the interest in the social impact of business in recent years? There are at least three reasons for the growing social consciousness.

First, people have become more affluent and their needs have changed. At the turn of the 20th century the majority of people were concerned about employment and ensuring that their economic and security needs were met. The same steel mills that emitted smoke provided jobs, and employment was a more basic need than one's health status—especially since adverse health effects did not appear until 20 years later when the correlation seemed at best a little dubious. Things are different as we approach the end of the last decade of the century. Employment is important, but all of us are more aware of the ill effects of a polluted environment and increasingly we have become aware of the dangers left by a half-century of Cold War (Reed, Lemak, and Hesser, 1997).

Second, the corporate form of organization effectively separated ownership and management. Professional managers of corporations are not the owners nor are the owners the managers. The identity between managerial effectiveness and profits has become less direct as additional criteria of performance have been applied to the work

197

Chapter 9 ▲
*Managing
Responsibility:
Obligations
and Values*

of managers (Chandler, 1977). Professional (nonowner) managers are often evaluated on the basis of labor relations in the plants they manage, turnover rates, absenteeism, and sometimes the number of employees and the size of the budgets they oversee.

Third, the simple truth is that managers and the general public are more aware of social issues and their role in business decision making. The relative importance of balancing traditional economizing, power-oriented, and ecology values in business is frequently discussed in the press, and managers seem increasingly aware of the need to consider the implications of their actions on society (Frederick, 1995).

Drawing the Lines in the Controversy

The social responsibility controversy has been debated according to two extreme positions. The first is the familiar profit-maximizing argument. Theodore Levitt (1958) stated that "welfare and society are not the corporation's business. Its business is to make money." Milton Friedman (1970) stated more directly that professional managers are agents of the owner, and their social responsibility is to increase profits.

The alternative position maintains that business is a social institution and should consider the impact of its decisions on the larger social system. The corporation that hires thousands of people and affects millions with a single decision cannot, according to this argument, disregard the social impact of its operations. Robert D. Kilpatrick, Chairman of the Board of CIGNA Corporation, stated that CIGNA is part of the communities in which it operates and "shares with these communities a bond of

---

▲ Box 9-4
MAYBE WHAT WE NEED IS A VICE PRESIDENT FOR ETHICS

Columbia/HCA Healthcare Corporation has been accused of a "systematic corporate scheme" to defraud Medicare. The FBI investigator stated that a $1 million error was not reported by Basic American Medical, Inc.—a company Columbia purchased—and a reserve fund was set up to cover the error in case it was discovered. It was further alleged that the fraud continued even after the purchase of Basic by Columbia/HCA.

In response to these charges, Columbia/HCA officially agreed to allow audits rather than simply complying with search warrants and subpoenas in an effort to cooperate with investigators. The company also appointed its first senior vice president of ethics, compliance, and corporate responsibility. These efforts are part of a corporate effort to ensure that Columbia/HCA's actions are consistent with legal statutes and social expectations. For more on the position see Box 11-10.

Source: Asplund (1997).

interest and obligation." A more familiar example is J. W. Marriott, head of the Marriott Corporation, who is also a Mormon bishop and applies his faith to his business life. He is known for the attention he gives to detail and to listening to employees and customers. His entire business philosophy is summed up in the title of his book, *The Spirit to Serve* (Marriott and Brown, 1997).

Social Responsibility and Ethics

Writers often make careful distinctions between social responsibility and business ethics. There are important differences, even though historically the attention in management has been more on the former than the latter. One could speculate as to why this is the case, but the reasons for the focus on social responsibility are not particularly important. Perhaps the most likely reason is that early writers were concerned about the emergence of a new discipline and management's influence on society as a whole. Ethics ultimately is a very personal and individual thing and, therefore, related more to the personal convictions of individual managers than to the collective values of a new and important social institution.

▲ Box 9-5
DOES BEING GOOD PAY?

Is there any reward for doing good in a competitive economic system? Stockholders and decision-makers have long debated the question of whether or not there is any relationship between corporate social performance (CSP) and financial success. A study of 469 companies in 13 industries suggested that there is an association, although the relationship is very complex. It was found, for example, that the extent to which a company engages in CSP is influenced by prior financial success. More financially successful firms tend to engage in more social activities. At the same time, it appears that CSP contributed to improved financial success.

It was suggested that there may be a "virtuous circle" at work whereby CSP and positive financial outcomes interact and become mutually reinforcing. It is unclear where the circle actually begins. Does CSP actually increase the financial performance of the firms? Does positive financial performance create the slack in the organization that allows managers to engage in socially desirable activities? The precise nature of the relationship could not be determined. However, it was clear that CSP and return on assets and return on sales were positively related. Even in competitive economies, doing good works may actually be rewarded in the marketplace.

Source: Waddock and Graves (1997).

Hosmer (1987) states that the ethics of management involves the determination of what is right, proper, and just in decisions and actions that affect other people. Perhaps the most effective way to appreciate where business ethics "fits" into the overall perspective of social responsibility is with Carroll's (1991) pyramid of social responsibility. According to him, the most basic responsibility is economic—to make a profit for shareholders. Professional managers are agents of shareholders and must ensure returns are provided for investors. Without profits the organization will not survive.

The next level of responsibility is legal. Business firms and mangers are expected to adhere to the "rules of the game." Laws are developed to ensure that the overall welfare of society is protected and that no one has an unfair advantage in the marketplace. Ethical responsibilities take place at even higher levels than economic and legal responsibilities. Managers are expected to do what is right and just individually. Finally, there is the philanthropic responsibility or to be a good corporate citizen and return value to the society within which you exist.

There are no easy answers to questions of business ethics. Questions of what is right and just are extremely individual and people deal with them in different ways. Jan Baan, founder of the Dutch software firm Baan, N.V. and a devout Dutch Reformed Calvinist believes that his success in business provides an unusual opportunity and obligation to practice his religious faith in business (Grugal, 1997). In less than 3 years he built a charitable trust larger than the Rockefeller Foundation. The $2.6 billion foundation is called *Oikonomos*, meaning "steward." Many business managers base their ethical decisions on religious convictions.

Some Issues and Controversies

The responsibility of business firms and managers is questioned regularly on television and in the press. We will briefly review a few of the issues that have been the focus of a significant amount of investigation and criticism on the part of writers, politicians, and other individuals concerned with the role of business in modern society.

Executive Compensation: How Responsible Is Business in the Conduct of Internal Affairs?

In the early 1980s, labor unions and business economists began to focus on a strange phenomenon—the salaries of top executives in the United States. We cannot be sure why this issue became so popular. It might have been the fact that executives during the 1980s were asking labor unions to grant wage concessions in the interest of job security while they pocketed extremely large total salaries and worked busily preparing golden parachutes to ensure their own future welfare. It could have been because the Japanese were "eating our lunch" with executives who earn considerably less than their American counterparts. In the 1990's the problem of executive compensation has been presented as a scandal in the face of downsizing. No doubt some of the bad press resulted from the fact that, in some cases, there was little correlation between what an executive made and the performance of the company he or she managed.

Drucker (1986) referred to trends in executive compensation as the *greed effect* and philosophically dismisses it as a scandal, but not an entirely important one because only a few people are affected. Besides, he argued, the unions and the Internal Revenue Service are sure to rectify the situation in the not so distant future. The AFL-CIO, for example, has developed a Web page that provides details on executive salaries as well as information on how to file proxies and contact corporate directors. However, if anything, executive pay has increased at an increasing rate in recent years.

The magnitude of the issue is illustrated by the fact that in 1996, Lawrence Coss of Green Tree Financial was paid $102 million in salary and bonus. By comparison, Andrew Grove of Intel was paid a little over $3 million in salary and bonus and almost $95 million in long-term compensations (stock options) for a total of $97.5 million. Even a nonCEO, such as Frank Lanza at Lockheed Martin received total compensation in excess of $50 million. Some companies—Avon Products and Microsoft—performed very well compared to the pay received by their top executives. Other companies such as America Online, Digital Equipment, and Tandy did not perform well between 1994 and 1996, even though their chief executive officers received total compensation ranging from $3.8 to $33 million (*Executive Day*, 1997, p. 60).

The question, of course, from the social perspective is how such large sums can be justified. Unions complain that executives make too much compared to rank and file employees. Stockholders wonder if managers are really their agents or independent contractors working for themselves. The greed effect certainly operates, but there are legitimate defenses for the compensation packages. Perhaps the best defense relates to a comparison between executives such as Iacocca and professional athletes and rock stars. Who, one should ask, really deserves the most pay—the chief executive of a corporation that employs thousands of people and possesses assets greater than most states in the Union or the rock star, bonus baby, or free agent? The market, to a great extent, determines the economic value of all services, and surely the talents of the leaders of industries must be among the most scarce and valuable of all resources. In spite of the fact that all these salaries may be scandalous, most would cast their lot with corporate executives rather than with entertainers or athletes.

Product Liability: How Responsible Is Business in Looking Out for the Welfare of Customers?

It has been estimated that the use of tobacco products costs the American public more than $70 billion annually. Much of this cost is for health-related problems of those who use the products and those who live or work near smokers. Nonsmoking airline attendants claim that exposure to smoke in airplanes causes health problems. Young children are harmed by the second-hand smoke of their parents, and coworkers are inconvenienced by the thoughtlessness of fellow workers. It is even claimed that tobacco companies have intentionally targeted their advertising efforts toward teenagers in direct violation of the law.

Perhaps the most significant development in recent years, however, is the fact

201

Chapter 9 ▲
Managing
Responsibility:
Obligations
and Values

that individual states have examined their health care costs and determined that tax payers are paying the bill for the health problems caused by smoking. Some of the states have brought legal action against tobacco firms to recoup these expenses. At the present time, there is much debate about the most appropriate manner of prosecuting product liability cases. The diversity of the laws of individual states is one reason cited for the need for federal legislation. Proponents of new legislation also contend that punitive damages should be limited.

The social problem presented by product liability cases centers around the very heart of the private enterprise system. Critics argue that in a system of free enterprise the corporation must always see to the welfare of the customer. Never should chances be taken with the health and safety of those who trust the corporation by purchasing products or services. The temptation to cheat in the system comes when decisions are made not to report adverse effects in the tests related to drugs and other health products or to withhold vital engineering information that might suggest the unsafe nature of products such as airplanes or automobile braking systems. Such behavior, when it occurs, is usually caused by premature entry into a market for purposes of making a profit. Withholding or the misuse of information in this manner is irresponsible and unethical behavior (Duncan, 1986). It cannot be justified since it is a short-sighted approach to decision making.

Question and Response

That business firms have been the focus of criticisms relating to social responsibility is probably not surprising. But how have firms responded to the critics? Organizations respond in many different ways to the social needs that are perceived around them. Sometimes responses are defensive, as has frequently been the case in dealing with changing market demands. Software engineering, for example, has been an area dominated by males. However, Microsoft recognized that the future of the company in the area of interactive media depended to a great extent on talent availability. The ability to develop creative CD-ROMs that engage a growing market segment has created a significant demand for software engineers, and Microsoft has looked increasingly to females to meet this demand (Cushmano and Solby, 1995).

Firms usually begin responding to social issues in ways that many would classify as tokenism. Tokenism at times is merely a way of avoiding coming to grips with the real issue. At other times it may be a low-risk way of attempting to deal with social concerns. The National Association of Manufacturers states that there are more than 200 to 250 board-level committees focusing on public policy issues likely to affect business firms, whereas there were fewer than 20 such committees 2 decades ago. The concern, if not the commitment, for social issues is growing.

Sometimes important social services can be performed by businesses without tremendous commitments of financial resources. U.S. West Communications formed a disability committee with representatives from different states to improve opportunities and working conditions for employees with disabilities. Honeywell has a council of two dozen employees with disabilities. These employees represent the union as well as salaried positions and function apart for the human resources department. The role of the council is to promote awareness and accessibility for the disabled (Hall and Hall, 1994).

Perhaps the most widely discussed and debated case of social responsibility in modern times is that of General Motors' involvement in South Africa. Its ongoing significance was illustrated by the case of Pepsi presented in Box 9-2. GM's dilemma can be best appreciated by recognizing that the Company has operated continuously in the Republic of South Africa since 1926. Throughout this time apartheid, or the systematic separation of the native blacks and the white population, was the official policy of the government. As repeated attempts to convince South Africa's leadership to eliminate this policy failed, activists throughout the world suggested that economic sanctions and commercial withdrawal were the only means to effecting the desired changes. For a number of years GM resisted persistent calls for withdrawal. The justifications used for the company's continued presence were: all foreign companies, including GM, operate in South Africa as guests of the country, and the options available to influence social change are limited. GM tried, according to its statements, to influence the policy of apartheid through positive pressure on government policies. Much of this pressure has been applied with other companies through organizations like the Associated South Africa Chamber of Commerce, the Federated Chamber of Industries, and the American Chamber of Commerce.

In response to the partial embargo imposed on South Africa by the U.S. government in 1978, GM discontinued any sale to the police and the military of vehicles specially adapted for their use. All sales were not stopped because the company be-

---

▲ Box 9-6
CODES OF CONDUCT AS MANAGEMENT TOOLS

Northern Telecom, a global company with over 60,000 employees, believes codes of business conduct are important decision-making tools. If the code is relevant, it can assist employees in knowing what to do under different business circumstances. The company, however, was not sure the existing code provided the relevance necessary to aid in decision making. So it asked employees what they needed from a code of business conduct.

The employees responded with enthusiasm. The revised code provides more detail on topics that employees thought were important, such as how to avoid conflicts of interest, what should be done about offers of gifts and entertainment, bribes and kickbacks, and what are the proper ways of gathering intelligence on competitors? Involving employees in the ethics program has assisted Northern Telecom in making its Code of Business Conduct a useful tool for managers and employees.

Source: Richardson (1996).

203

Chapter 9 ▲
*Managing
Responsibility:
Obligations
and Values*

lieved that such a restriction of sales would effectively force them out of the South African market because of the bad press such an action would entail. GM engaged in a number of internal actions to reduce its participation in apartheid. Racial discrimination in hiring and promotion was reduced, all company facilities, including eating and comfort areas, were desegregated, and attempts were made to provide training that would allow the promotion of more blacks into managerial positions (General Motors Public Interest Report, 1985).

Finally, GM generally resisted disinvestment and withdrawal until 1986 because of the opinion that if all U.S. firms left South Africa, the American leadership role in the area would be reduced significantly. Many corporate officials even believed that such a move would hurt the black population because of the jobs it would eliminate. Hypothetical issues of this nature are difficult to discuss and almost impossible to solve. There would be loss of jobs and suffering caused by the withdrawal of the American firms. There would also be a reduction in the American presence and leadership there as well. At the same time, such an action might cause a "crisis of conscience" among the nation's white government. No one could say for sure what the ultimate outcome would be. That is why socially responsible decisions are so complex and multidimensional and why many managers attempt to avoid making them. Such decisions, however, must be made. The real issue is whether business or government will be the ultimate decision maker. In the case of GM, it eventually became apparent that disinvestment and withdrawal would be the only action that would satisfy the demands of the public. Other firms have reluctantly reached decisions that they would have preferred to postpone or ignore entirely. However, society expects more.

Business, many believe, is too large and important to abstain. Business decisions have never been easy. Nothing makes us believe they will be any easier in the future. The concern about management's responsibility is not new. There have been significant champions of socially responsible business for centuries. The concern is real, proper, and at least a little ironic. While one should never justify irresponsible decision making, we cannot help but wonder if business morality can be expected to exceed that of the larger society.

We live in a time when political figures are forced from high offices because of misconduct. Even religious leaders are not free from criticism. To the extent that irresponsible acts occur in business, we must wonder whether business can be rightfully expected to rise above the moral climate in general. We must opt for higher standards of conduct on the part of politicians, bureaucrats, as well as business executives. Society deserves more and, as Gantt warned, may very well demand it.

Implications and Conclusions

In this chapter we have discussed an important doctrine of management thought—the social responsibility of business. To some it is a controversial subject while to others it is merely a self-evident reality. We have attempted to provide the historical context for this issue and concluded the following.

1. Business firms, because of their real and potential impact on society, are expected to assume great responsibilities.
2. The precise responsibility of business has been viewed along a continuum of extremes ranging from no responsibility except to produce profits for investors to a champion of all social causes.
3. Gantt, the engineer and social philosopher, illustrated how extreme views can be resolved and reconciled.
4. The expression of management as a "grave social responsibility" emerged in early management thought and is not, as many suppose, the product of modern times.
5. The idea of a partnership between business and society is probably the most productive of all attitudes.
6. Discussions of social responsibility have become more accepted today because of increasing affluence, the separation of ownership and management, and generally increasing social consciousness.
7. Social responsibility today is most often expressed relative to specific issues such as executive compensation, product liability, and related topics.
8. It is important that all managers and prospective managers develop their personal philosophies regarding their obligations and responsibilities to society.

We have argued throughout this book that management is a difficult and demanding task. When executives make decisions that have social implications, and most do, the job is even tougher and more thankless. However, there is consolation. As Drucker (1986) notes, nobody in America is important except "people who don't really matter." That is one of our safeguards against tyranny. "We save our adulation for people who never become a menace—for baseball players and rock stars and movie idols who are completely innocuous" (p. 13). Decision makers should take heart. The fact that they are criticized is the best evidence that what they do is important.

Questions for Discussion

1 How could an individual such as Robert Owen see the implications of the Industrial Revolution as so much more destructive than Andrew Ure and Charles Babbage?

2 Are you surprised that Owen's ideas about the responsibility of business firms were rejected in America in the same manner they were rejected in England? Why or why not?

3 How would you explain the level of sophistication and insight achieved by Gantt in his view of the relationship between business and society during the scientific management period?

4 How does Gantt's task and bonus system demonstrate a different understanding of business and society than Taylor's differential piece rate system?

205

Chapter 9 ▲
*Managing
Responsibility:
Obligations
and Values*

5 Do you agree with Tead's assessment of the relationship between participative management and a worker's feeling of self-esteem? Why or why not?

6 Why do you think most people view the social responsibility of business as conflicting rather than mutually reinforcing? Explain your answer.

7 Are executives paid too much? What is the best way to determine the compensation level for executive decision makers?

8 What is your personal philosophy of the social responsibility of management?

Managing Culture and Quality

*"Culture is a feel-good tool, a set of behavioral blinders; it makes a corpo-
ration comfortable with its habits."*

John Sculley
Odyssey, 1987

This chapter is unlike those that have preceded it. The subjects of earlier discussions
had clear and evident origins in early management thought. However, organizational
culture and quality are products of more recent times. Culture, as we will note, is an
older concept than most writers recognize, but it is still relatively new when compared with ideas such as goal setting, decision making, authority, and efficiency. Quality likewise is a relative newcomer to the stage of management thought.

For no other reason than their lack of history, there was some reservation about
including these topics in this historical view of management ideas and actions. Culture continues to be little more than a "feel good" concept to some and the "quality
movement" is being discarded for many reasons by an increasingly large number of
organizations. In spite of the hesitations, it seems appropriate that these two topics
should be discussed because they are important parts of the thoughts and actions of
many managers and employees.

Understanding Organizational Culture

Corporate culture is discussed in academic journals and television talk shows, but
what does it mean to people in the organization? Executives read and hear about strong
cultures and wonder how to get one. Employees listen to the benefits of working for
culture-rich firms such as Microsoft, 3M, and Johnson and Johnson and wish they
could enjoy the benefits that accompany strong cultures. The uniqueness of certain
organizations when it comes to the spirit or atmosphere they are able to build and
maintain has not gone unnoticed in management thought (Peters and Austin, 1985).

However, if culture is to be a meaningful concept and to impact on the bottom line of business firms, it has to be made useful to the managers and employees who make things happen.

Origins of Organizational Culture

It always comes as a surprise when managers discover that management ideas such as organizational culture are not new. Most people in business, government, health care, and education are surprised to find out that corporate culture was not invented with the publication of Terrence Deal's and Alan Kennedy's 1982 book, *Corporate Culture*. This book, in fact, does an admirable job illustrating the importance of the concept in familiar organizations, but at the time it was written the idea of corporate culture was at least 30 years old. Maybe it was older. In 1951, the British writer Eliot Jacques published his book titled *The Changing Culture of a Factory* and defined a concept that included all the essential elements of what we now call *organization culture*. Jacques stated that an organization's culture is:

> . . . the customary or traditional way of thinking and doing things, which are shared . . . by all members of an organization and which new members must learn and at least partially accept in order to be accepted into the service of the firm" (p. 251).

No one does a better job of defining the concept than Jacques' definition of more than 4 decades ago. All useful definitions include 3 essential characteristics of organizational culture:

1. *Organizational culture is learned*: An organization's culture becomes meaningful to managers and employees by experience within the organization. Anthropologists call it assimilation. In business it is called socialization. In simple terms, the learning of culture refers to a sharing of an understanding of "how things are done" around here, of paying one's dues, or getting your "tickets punched."
2. *Culture is composed of shared values, meanings, understandings, and assumptions*: This involves conveying to managers and employees what the organization values or "believes in." Culture includes the beliefs that members of the organization share.
3. *Culture is both subjective and objective*: In addition to the more subjective aspects of values, beliefs, assumptions, and meanings, culture includes symbols, language, and artifacts. In other words, there are physical and verbal manifestations of organizational cultures such as the design and layout of office buildings, stories and myths that become intertwined with accurate company history, and heroes whose exploits have been preserved in the memory or archives of the firm (Kilmann, Saxton, and Serpa, 1996; Posner, Kouzes, and Schmidt, 1985).

▲ Box 10-1
GENDER GAP IN THE EXECUTIVE SUITE

In 1972 women held only 17 percent of managerial position in American industry. The percentage increased to almost 43 percent in 1996. However, less than 5 percent of top-level executive positions are held by women. The glass ceiling, an invisible barrier to advancement based on attitudes and organizational bias, has been blamed for this lack of progress.

One study of more than 1,000 female executives in Fortune 1000 companies revealed that there is a great difference in the perceptions of what constitutes barriers to advancement between high-ranking women and their male counterparts. Male executives thought that women did not become CEOs because they lacked general management and line experience or they had simply not been in the "pipeline" long enough. Women executives, on the other hand, blamed inhospitable work environments and male stereotypes of women.

The most feasible solution to addressing the limited upward mobility of women executives is increased understanding on the part of the people making promotion decisions in organizations. Most likely traditional barriers will be removed only by conscious attempts to address and remove the barriers that have become a part of the corporate culture of most organizations.

Source: Ragins, Townsend, and Mattis (1998).

Types of Cultures

Researchers and managers recognized that organizational cultures come in different forms. These differences have been noted in a variety of ways, but some of the most frequent classifications are noted in the following sections.

Strong and Weak Cultures

Cultures are sometimes strong and sometimes weak. Strong cultures are characterized by members who share the same values, expectations, and commitments. IBM is one of the most frequently cited examples of a strong culture company. The strength of the IBM culture is illustrated by a Brazilian executive who was being interviewed about Brazilian approaches to strategic planning. The executive made the point that much of American strategic planning theory is difficult to apply in Brazil because Brazilians do not work in groups as comfortably as Americans. He stated that he, however, was personally very comfortable working in groups. When the interviewer questioned why he worked easily in groups but many Brazilians did not, he replied that his familiarity with group processes came during his decade of employment at IBM. Everyone at IBM, according to him, was taught to work in groups. "When you finish the executive development program at IBM," he stated, "you are no longer Brazilian, Chilean, or Swiss. You are an IBMer."

The opinion was further illustrated when the same executive stated that 4 years after he resigned from IBM he was traveling in Germany and lost his passport. Instead of going to the Brazilian embassy for help, he went to the local office of IBM and explained his problem and his past affiliation with the company. The office was of immediate service in obtaining him another passport. The strength of the culture at "Big Blue" had actually become stronger that the executive's national culture.

The strength of an organization's culture can be inferred by questioning members, examining company logos, and similar measures designed to discover the intensity of the commitment typical employees have to the organization and to one another. The outstretched "helping or healing hands" of the Catholic Hospital Association convey what the organization stands for, while mottoes and slogans such as "we know the territory" build confidence in a company such as Philadelphia Electric. These are illustrations of strong cultures.

The logo of an organization can become so familiar that observers recognize the culture by its symbol. The Goodyear Wingfoot fashioned after the wings of Mercury has been used by the company since the turn of the century "as a reminder that Goodyear's future, like its past, rests on a foundation of quality."

There is no consistent evidence that a strong organizational culture actually impacts the bottom line of a business. The IBM, Goodyear, and other cases suggest that it might. However, there is evidence that American executives believe strong cultures are positive factors for an organization to possess. One survey of CEOs, for example, found that all but a very few believed that strong corporate cultures were important to the success to their organizations. More than 40 percent believed it strongly enough to "try to deal with culture in a serious manner" through the commitment of corporate resources (Gardner, 1985; Wilkins and Bristow, 1987).

Adaptive Cultures

Kotter and Heskett (1992) examined the literature in an effort to better understand the relationship between an organization's culture and its long-term performance. They found that the strength of the culture was only one factor influencing the culture–performance relationship. A more important determinant was the extent to which the culture assisted in anticipating and adapting to environmental changes. These *adaptive cultures* were most often associated with superior performance.

Adaptive cultures are those that allow managers and employees to take reasonable risks, are built on trust and a willingness to allow people to fail, and where employers display a willingness to take responsibility at all levels. Leadership, in other words, is evident throughout the organization not just at the top. Organizations with adaptive cultures tend to have less fear of failure so that all employees and managers are encouraged to initiate changes that are in the best interest of the corporation.

Subcultures and Countercultures

Although organizations develop dominant cultures, they also sometimes possess sub-cultures and countercultures. IBM, for example, may have subcultures formed around functional responsibilities such as hardware engineers, software specialists, and "marketing types." A *subculture* may enhance operations by possessing the same values as the dominant culture but in an exaggerated form. The marketing director of a large bank, for example, stated to her staff at the monthly meeting that she expected the department to be so committed to new services such as special pricing on equity lines of credit that none of them would be content until they had an account with *everyone* in the state.

Independent, nondestructive subcultures may also exist. In the literature these are referred to as *orthogonal subcultures* because the members accept the values of the dominant culture but possess their own, nonconflicting set of values (Martin and Siehl, 1983). Professional employees sometimes form this type of subculture in large corporations. The accountants, engineers, and attorneys all belong to their own professional subcultures, yet they are simultaneously able to contribute to the goals of the corporation.

More serious problems are presented by countercultures that sometimes emerge in an organization. One of the best known cases of the development of a countercul-

---

▲ Box 10-2
COMMUNICATING CULTURE INSIDE AND OUTSIDE

Leaders must be careful in communicating about organizational culture. A study of 11 public accounting firms found that the "espoused" culture does not always capture or even represent the reality employees experience in organizations, and that causes problems. Researchers found that there are very few differences in the cultures public accounting firms espouse to their clients and the public, regardless of the size of the firm.

If you read the externally circulated documents of almost any public accounting firm, you might accurately infer that "they are pretty much all the same." Thus the stereotype most people have of public accountants. However, a closer look inside would reveal substantial differences in the values and cultures of individual firms. Some are elite and bureaucratic while some are collegial and informal. Some aspire to professional leadership and value innovation and change. This "culture split" is extremely important in understanding the nature of any particular accounting firm and has profound implications for the employee in understanding and adapting to organizational cultures.

Source: Holmes and Marsden (1996).

ture was that of John DeLorean and General Motors. GM had understood policies designed to ensure respect for authority, value loyalty, and codes of dress and behavior. DeLorean did not like the values and openly ridiculed and criticized the standards that others lived by and accepted. He challenged the dress code and even used his own artifacts to make fun of those at GM. These counter cultures are often dysfunctional and can be destructive to the most cherished values of an organization (Martin and Siehl, 1983).

Evidence of Corporate Cultures

Much of what we call corporate or organizational culture is not observable to the typical manager or employee. To the trained eye and ear, however, there are "manifestations" or evidences of organizational cultures that can be seen and heard in the workplace.

Artifacts and Heroes

When Johnson and Johnson wanted to change its image to that of a progressive and dynamic technical and marketing force, one of the first things the company did was move out of its traditional surroundings to an ultramodern headquarters building (*Business Week*, May 24, 1984). The building served as a symbol of the image that Johnson and Johnson wanted for its future.

Organizational histories often provide useful insights into the nature of a firm's culture. The mere fact that people are assigned the responsibility of compiling a history, are given access to key documents, and are allowed to meet with key "actors" in the corporation demonstrates a relatively strong culture. The history of Saab-Scania, for example, presents the employee, investor, and outsider with a picture of how the company began as a manufacturer of railroad cars in 1891 and diversified into trucks and buses around the turn of the century. Its adaptability is illustrated by the decision to make airplanes under agreements with American and British firms in 1930. Then, in 1947, it entered the passenger car market, further demonstrating the company's adaptability to changing conditions. Company histories are effective ways of building and maintaining the culture of an organization.

Histories also identify heroes. Sometimes the heroes are the founders and sometimes they emerge long after companies have been founded (Schein, 1985). At Monsanto, for example, the company history pictures the founder, John Francis Queeny, standing in front of his sulfur processing plant in 1899 watching it burn to the ground. A year later, like the legendary phoenix, Monsanto Chemical Company ascended from the flames with the production of saccharin in a plant in St. Louis. The company took on the name of Mr. Queeny's wife—Olga Monsanto. That is the type of story that sends chills up the back of the loyal employee and impresses the customer with the organization's tradition and accomplishments.

Not all heroes are founders. One of the best known hero stories of this century is Lee Iacocca and Chrysler. Little can be added to the achievements of Chrysler and

Iacocca. There were reports of Iacocca being "mobbed" by his dealers at their national convention as they pushed and pressed one another to get a closer look at the boss. More spectacular perhaps was the greeting he received from workers at Chrysler's Sterling Heights assembly plant with chants of Lee! Lee! Lee! when he arrived to inspect a new line of sports sedans.

Company histories are, by and large, accurate, if slightly exaggerated, accounts of an organization's achievements. As such they are the source of many inspiring stories. These stories are narratives based on true events. Stories are not folk tales because they are based on fact and they are not sagas because they do not always involve a hero. However, organizational stories are important because they communicate information to members that may not be available from other sources.

One study challenged the view that organizational stories are mostly random accounts of unique events or specific to each organization. Instead, they often follow patterns. In fact, 7 types of stories have been identified, and each type serves an important cultural function. These stories usually follow familiar themes like "is the boss really human?" Stories arise about particular altruistic acts of the boss or how someone was really helped by this person (the boss) from whom almost everyone felt isolated. These stories usually emerge to reduce tensions among individual, organizational, and societal values, to explain paradoxes relating to quality and inequality, security and insecurity, and control versus lack of control (Martin, Feldman, Hatch, and Sitkin, 1983).

Organizational sagas are a special type of story. Sagas are accounts of historical events that involve heroic actions. These sagas are very capable of stirring the hearts of organizational members and providing them with a sense of pride. One of the very familiar organizational sagas is the experience at 3M of the invention and development of the product known as Post-it. In this saga, a 3M engineer named Arthur Fry, through his own effort and determination, converts what appeared to be a failed project, or at best marginally profitable, to a tremendous market success that has put millions of dollars of profits into the corporate bank accounts.

Organizational myths, if one can get to the point of the real lesson, can provide important insights into the organizational culture. The example of Hewlett Packard's "open lab stock" policy given by Peters and Waterman in *In Search of Excellence* (1982) is a great illustration of this point. Whether or not Bill Hewlett actually cut the lock off the storehouse door to give his permission for employees to use company property for after-work experimentation is not known. Peters and Waterman underscored the importance of these stories, however, when relating their astonishment at two young engineers at Hewlett Packard who spent an hour telling them tales about "Bill" and "Dave." The interesting point was that neither had ever met or seen the founders. Obviously, stories, myths, and folklore are important to the culture of Hewlett Packard.

The purpose of organizational myths is to justify policies that seem to be the only way of doing something. Myths follow interesting and predictable life cycles. First, the myth is developed by the individual, a department, or even society. Next, it matures and becomes a "solid myth" because of its wide acceptance. The myth then declines when challenged and closely examined. On a few occasions, it may actually disappear. More likely, the myth will shift to another myth and begin the life cycle over again in an altered form (Martin, Feldman, Hatch, and Sitkin, 1983). The irony is that although myths are not true, they assist managers and employees in dealing with the realities of the organization.

Rites, Rituals, and Ceremonies

Organizations possess many rites, rituals, and ceremonies. Some are familiar and their purpose is obvious. Others are more difficult to understand. Rites are relatively elaborate sets of planned activities such as the company's "understood" career progression process. In many organizations there is talk of "getting one's tickets punched," "paying one's dues," or adhering to the familiar "rites of passage" (Trice and Beyer, 1984). The armed services probably have the most familiar rite of career progression. Every career commissioned and noncommissioned officer can tell you precisely what activities and time are required for the next stage in the career ladder and the consequences of not measuring up to expectations.

Organizational rites, rituals, and ceremonies are useful aids in the accomplishment of certain desired organizational outcomes (Trice and Beyer, 1984). They aid in indoctrinating and socializing employees into the firm, stabilize things, and provide consistency among the behavior of all employees. This stability reduces the uncertainty that so often accompanies a new employee's entry into the organization. Consider the function and effects of the following:

1. *Rites of separation and transition:* A company's management training program is an example. Every manager knows that the recent graduate from a college or university is rarely able to enter a firm and assume a responsible management position. The management training program often assists the graduate in separating from the relatively "loose" life of college to the demanding reality of making a living. During this time the trainee is oriented into what the company expects of employees, the things the company values as important, and an idea of the firm's heritage. When trainees complete the program, they share a common inheritance with other employees, feel a part of the organization, and are relieved of much of the uncertainty of finding things out through trial and error.

2. *Rites of degradation and intimidation.* This is a less discussed rite in organizations, but it is present in many small companies and the largest corporations. Rites of degradation and intimidation require 3 essential components: (1) a rule breaker; (2) a violated rule; and (3) a denouncer who must emerge to support the traditional values and denounce the rule breaker.

3. *Ritual of intimidation:* The rite of degradation is sometimes extended into a ritual or standardized set of behaviors designed to manage anxieties of one or a few, even if they increase the anxiety of others. When this occurs, one observes a ritual of intimidation. Usually the intimidation ritual progresses through two stages. First, there is indirect intimidation, which usually involves social isolation or insults, or both. Second, direct intimidation follows. Direct intimidation is sometimes called "playing hard ball" and may go so far as to involve the defaming of a person's character and expulsion from the organization.

4. *Parting ceremonies.* Organizations and individuals cease to exist and eventually die. When they die, the lives of many people are adversely affected and people try to deal with the hurt in much the same way they deal with the loss of a loved one. One study of plant closings illustrates how people try to deal with this real and depressing problem (Harris and Sutton, 1986). In this study former employees were observed as they attended the final parting ceremony or company-sponsored "wake." The responses were similar. Initially people could not believe this was happening to them. They eventually became bitter and blamed the company, the union, and the government. Later they accepted the reality of the job loss, became philosophical, and attempted to "get on with life" while resolving to keep track of their good friends (Ginter, Swayne, Duncan, and Shelfer, 1992).

5. *Play ceremonies*: Organizations and their members also engage in play ceremonies that can be useful and productive. At Sequent Computer Systems, for example, nickels are dropped in a jar each time an organizational goal is accomplished. A red light on the assembly line comes on when a quality problem is detected and the entire line is stopped until the problem is found and corrected. Management believes this to be an effective way to reinforce the company's commitment to quality.

Bottom Line on Culture

From a management perspective, the important point about corporate culture is, "how does it affect the bottom line?" Does culture really impact on performance, satisfaction, turnover, morale, or any other relevant organizational outcome? As noted earlier, some people believe strong cultures improve organizational performance because excellent cultures stress things such as well-conceived mission statements and focus individual actions on the accomplishment of organizational goals. The presence of philosophy statements and credos facilitates planning and coordination. Fuzzy cultures, on the other hand, are typical of companies in mature industries with caretaker managers (Buno, Bowditch, and Lewis, 1985; Cartwright and Cooper, 1993; Denison, 1984).

Although culture is not a new concept in management, it appears to be an important and meaningful idea that managers need to understand and appreciate. Culture building is a practical means of ensuring commitment to the organization's mission and increasing a team spirit among groups. Although not synonymous, one topic that has been closely related to issues such as culture and excellence is quality. Total quality management (TQM) and continuous quality improvement (CQI) have become important parts of the philosophy of many managers and organizations and are deserving of some attention.

▲ **Box 10-3**

TRANSPLANTING AND PRESERVING THE CULTURE AT TOYOTA

Opening of the Georgetown plant provided an opportunity and a challenge for Toyota Motor Manufacturing Corporation. How could management open a new operation under an established parent that was the model for manufacturing excellence? Total quality management was to be the basis of the philosophy for the new operations, and values and operating principles were established based on TQM concepts.

In accepting this challenge, management recognized that: (1) all organizations develop predictable patterns of behavior, so excellence must be the guiding philosophy; (2) every business system is itself a culture, and culture can be an effective way of defining and communicating predictable behavior patterns; (3) the basis of every effective organizational culture must be individual responsibility and citizenship; (4) corporate leadership has the responsibility for ensuring individual citizenship emerges and guides behavior in the organization. When the manufacturing excellence already exists as the dominant corporate culture, the challenge is to nurture and preserve it throughout all operations and communicate its importance to all employees and managers.

Source: Allen (1995).

Getting Better at What We Do

The topics that have occupied more attention in management in the past decade are TQM and CQI. Even more than was the case with organizational culture, TQM and CQI have no real counterparts in management history. We can only speculate why quality was not discussed widely in early management thought. For one thing, America simply did not challenge nations with well-established reputations for specific products. The Swiss were generally conceded the market for mechanical watches, the Germans were acknowledged as the quality leaders in optics and consumer electronics, and no one dared to challenge the French wine makers seriously. American energies were expended in the development of relatively new products. Quality, in other words, was not the major concern of an emerging industrial society.

America also, because of its inheritance of craftspeople from around the world, enjoyed a commitment to quality in its early development. Products built in America had a reputation of quality from the beginning—automobiles, firearms, and furniture. It was not until after World War II that the reputation of American products began to suffer and serious competitors began to emerge for products produced by our core competencies.

▲ **Box 10-4**

IMPROVING GOVERNMENT

Business firms are not the only organizations faced with implementing and using newly developed management concepts. Managers of public organizations have been challenged to improve the performance of government, and tools such as strategic planning and total quality management have been offered as ways of achieving such improvements.

Unfortunately, the relationship between strategic planning and TQM is often as unclear in government as it is in private industry. Confusion exists when employees are faced with multiple demands from various management initiatives, and sometimes they are confused about where strategic planning fits in with TQM and where TQM fits in with strategic planning. Such confusion only complicates the likelihood of achieving the maximum potential of either initiative. It is critically important that leaders "weave together" a consistent image of how all cultural and managerial changes are directed toward achieving organizational excellence while preserving the unique purpose and mission of the organization.

Source: Vinzant and Vinzant (1996).

Culture and Quality

Although we can speculate about the reasons for a lack of concern for quality in early management thought, it is difficult to understand why the indifference remained in the midst of eroding quality and loss of market share. The American automobile industry, for example, appeared almost unaware of the deterioration of its quality and the incredible opportunity it created for competitors in Japan and Western Europe. Similarly, markets in consumer electronics, photographic technologies, and optics that had been captured so successfully from Western Europeans were lost to the Japanese in relatively short order. The underlying cause, many agree, was eroding quality. In spite of this, quality remained virtually unrecognized as the culprit by managers and a topic that was rarely addressed by researchers (Scholz, 1987; Stacey, 1993).

Today much of the focus has been on various approaches and the advantages and disadvantages of the ideas about quality presented by different people such as W. Edward Deming (1982, 1986), Philip Crosby (1979), and Joseph Juran (1980). Each of these individuals has offered a great deal to managers. A more important practical concern has to do with the building and maintaining of a "quality-oriented culture." Quality is more of a "way of doing things" and "what we believe in around here" than it is of any particular program or approach. Quality, if it is to be a philosophy, must be a part of every employee's and every manager's thinking process.

▲ **Box 10-5**

TQM IN THE PUBLIC INTEREST

Culture change in the direction of TQM was the goal at the Texas Department of Mental Health and Mental Retardation. The department was able to learn some important lessons from its 4 year implementation process, which are important for all managers involved in changing organizational cultures.

Perhaps the single most important thing to recognize is that senior managers must alter their way of viewing the organization and their work. The purpose of the organization must be reconceptualized in terms of customers and stakeholders rather than function. Traditional methods of coordination, policies, procedures, rules, and structures are likely to be less important than shared visions and values. Communication is critical, and the method of communication requires reexamination. Memoranda and policy manuals are rarely effective means of alerting employees and managers to changing cultures. Finally, individual responsibility requires empowerment. Empowerment requires trust and a willingness to allow people the freedom to innovate and do their jobs. This is sometimes particularly difficult in public sector organizations.

Source: Rago (1996).

Basic TQM

TQM has been described as a "powerful tool" for improving the management of organizations. It focuses on work processes, applies analytical and behavioral techniques, emphasizes integration of services, and aims to improve both processes and outcomes (Nolan, 1990). It is never complete and when working properly, all members of the organization are in the process of getting better at what they do. For this reason, TQM is difficult to reduce to a few basic concepts, and any attempt to do so ultimately oversimplifies this apparently simple but obviously demanding philosophy. However, it is safe to say that most TQM programs share certain characteristics. These include: (1) the need for top management commitment; (2) extensive communication and training; (3) customer orientation; (4) zero defects and statistical quality control; and (5) continuous improvement (Duncan and Van Matre, 1990).

Top management commitment and leadership are critical to the success of TQM programs. Top management is responsible for articulating and communicating the priorities to everyone in the organization. Therefore, it is top management's job to make it clear that quality is important, that behaviors that contribute to improved quality will be rewarded, and that the most important goal of the organization is to determine what are the right things for the organization to do and to do these things right. Remember our earlier discussions of the importance of doing the right things (effectiveness) and doing them right (efficiency).

Communication and training are essential in any successful quality program. Top management leadership and communication are essential if everyone is to be made aware of the importance of quality. Moreover, this commitment is necessary to legitimize the training needed by employees in the tools necessary to ensure that their own work meets high standards. Communication and training are essential to build ownership for the quality program among employees.

Customer orientation is the foundation of TQM. One of the problems faced by management when attempting to implement TQM is the belief by some that customers really cannot make informed judgments and that "we" really know what is best in our industry. Admittedly, few people understand the technical aspects of any particular industry, but customers pay the bill and, informed or not, they make the decisions that determine the success or failure of any corporation.

In fact, many argue that the customer is the sole judge of product or service quality. This judgment takes place relative to five dimensions, which include (Crawford-Mason and Dobyns, 1991):

- *Tangibles*—The appearance of facilities, equipment, and personnel
- *Reliability*—The ability to perform accurately and dependably
- *Responsiveness*—The "willingness" to provide prompt service
- *Assurance*—The ability to convey trust and confidence
- *Empathy*—The provision of caring attention

Organizations devoted to TQM are close to their customers. They ask them regularly what they think and how they were treated, and they act on the feedback received. They listen carefully to what customers tell them. The goal is to keep defects and problems from developing, and this is accomplished through monitoring performance with widely available and simple statistical techniques. Doing things right the first time is a basic principle behind zero defects. Deming (1986) maintained that "the central problem of management in all its aspects . . . is to understand better the meaning of variation." In other words, when people are able to distinguish between normal, routine changes in processes and unusual, abnormal changes that can be attributed to specific causes, quality can be improved and corrections in basic quality problems implemented (Berry, 1991).

Continuous improvement is the ultimate goal of TQM. It forces employees and managers to acknowledge that things can always get better and that we should learn from our experiences. Mistakes are to be looked on as learning opportunities not failures. Successes likewise are opportunities for learning and practicing what we have perfected. Focusing on mistakes and successes helps organizations and employees improve—the ultimate goal of TQM. It has been said that "finger pointing" is the least useful gesture ever created by human beings. In TQM finger pointing and the assignment of blame is not important. Getting better at what we do is the goal.

Quality and Management

TQM and CQI are concerns to managers in a variety of organizational settings. Even though the initial interest was in business, quality programs are found throughout government, education, and health care. For example, in 1992 the Joint Commission on the Accreditation of Healthcare Organizations insists on quality improvement programs in accredited facilities. At Rush-Presbyterian-St. Luke's Medical Center, a total quality program, after a 3-year implementation period, increased service, productivity, and employee morale. It was described as a "win–win" process for everyone involved (Berwick, Godfrey, and Roesner, 1990; Gaucher and Coffee, 1993).

An ongoing study conducted among hospitals listed in *100 Top Hospitals—Benchmarks for Success* (hospitals that have achieved excellence in patient care and cost containment) found that this unique group of organizations lowered expenses per discharge by 16 percent, reduced mortality by 20 percent, and raised the return on their assets by 58 percent compared to "typical" hospitals. These diverse measures of performance illustrated that cultures among the top hospitals were based on a concern for quality as well as cost. It was estimated that if all hospitals performed at the same level as the top 100, health care expenses would fall by $21 billion per year, medical complications would decrease by 17 percent, and inpatient mortality would drop by 24 percent ("Quality Watch," 1996).

▲ Box 10-6
TQM AND VARIETIES OF SNAKE OIL

A survey of more than 5,000 hospitals found that in health care, as in business, the most frequently adopted approaches to TQM are Deming, Crosby, and Juran. Deming is by far the approach most often used in hospitals regardless of size, mission (teaching versus nonteaching), and membership in larger health systems. Interestingly, almost 20 percent of the responding hospitals indicated that they used some approach other than these dominant three.

The survey illustrated, as might be expected, that smaller hospitals are more likely not to have any formal TQM program than their larger counterparts. However, the most interesting finding was the apparent disregard for adherence to any single approach and a determination to employ useful ideas regardless of their origins. To illustrate, more than 25 percent of the hospitals surveyed indicated that they used a combination of Deming, Crosby, and Juran. Hopefully, this demonstrates a willingness to use any and all ideas that assist in improving hospital performance.

Source: "The Quality March" (1993).

TQM and Its Critics

Choi and Behling (1997) point out that many managers and their organizations are having second thoughts about TQM. Florida Power and Light, which gained notoriety by winning the Deming Prize for Quality Management, reduced its quality staff from 85 to 3 and the Wallace Company, winner of the Malcolm Baldridge National Quality Award, filed for protection under Chapter 11. Surveys of American and Western European executives have found that an increasing number of managers have concluded that TQM and CQI programs have simply not produced the results they expected and have certainly not improved the organization's ability to compete globally. Original assessments by some skeptics that TQM may be a passing fad rather than a recurring theme in management appear more increasingly accurate.

On the basis of a study of 6 firms that supplied components to the automobile manufacturing industry, Choi and Behling (1997) concluded that the primary reasons

---

▲ Box 10-7

MANAGING PARADOXES IN A TOTAL QUALITY ENVIRONMENT

To have effective total quality management, 7 paradoxes must be effectively managed. These paradoxes are outlined as follows.

Paradox 1. Seek diversity, but build a shared vision.

Paradox 2. Encourage creativity, but be consistent in everything.

Paradox 3. Focus on continuous process improvement, but make breakthrough change an important part of the job.

Paradox 4. Use autonomous work groups to enhance performance, but ensure careful and uniform control of product and service quality.

Paradox 5. Build a cohesive work team, but welcome conflict when critically analyzing ideas.

Paradox 6. Set realistic, yet challenging goals for maximum performance, but use stretch targets to dramatically improve performance.

Paradox 7. Reward team effort, but create a high performance climate for individuals.

Source: Thompson (1998).

for the failure of TQM programs were not those customarily discussed—poor substitutes for real TQM practices, overly ambitious expectations, and improper implementation of sound techniques. Instead, these researchers argued that a major determinant of TQM success or failure had to do with the orientations of top executives.

Some executives in this study displayed a defensive orientation toward TQM. To them, TQM offered at least some hope of survival in a hostile world where customers made unreasonable demands. These managers generally focused on the past and the practices that made them successful. Another group of top executives possessed a tactical orientation toward TQM. They believed that responding precisely to strong and demanding customers was the only way to succeed in today's competitive world. Finally, some managers exhibited a developmental view. To these executives, TQM represented a means of "growing the company" and propelling it into an exciting future. Customers were looked at as partners with mutual interests in making the customer–supplier relationship a success.

TQM and CQI are important management concepts, but they are not the magic bullets many believed would restore American competitiveness or relieve worker malaise. Any serious observer of the implementation of quality programs can speculate about why this has been successful for some and disappointing for others. In the end, quality must be a state of mind. Taylor recognized, almost a century ago, that if scientific management is to be successful, it must be accepted as a philosophy not a technique. Histograms, fishbone diagrams, affinity charts, and upper and lower control limits are useful, but they are merely techniques.

When organizations build their culture around quality as a philosophy and a commitment on the part of everyone to "get better at what we do," significant changes can take place. No one opposes quality, but there is a substantial mistrust of quality programs. To some organizations quality became a cult. Quality advocates and experts became despots, and quality jargon was the only language allowed. Something as simple as a commitment to getting better at what we do became autocratic, bureaucratic, and ineffective.

Reengineering and "Final" Frontiers

Reengineering according to Hammer and Champy (1993) is the "fundamental rethinking and radical redesigning of business processes to achieve dramatic improvement in critical contemporary measures of performance such as cost, quality, service, and speed" (p. 3). These same authors indicate that 3 types of companies become interested in reengineering—those that are in trouble, those that are not currently in trouble but foresee problems in the future and are trying to avoid them, and companies in excellent condition but desire a more ambitious and even more successful future.

Reengineering Defined

Reengineering typically takes place in 4 phases, which include analysis, redesign, implementation, and transformation (Cross, Feather, and Lynch, 1994). Analysis strives

---

▲ Box 10-8

SPACE AGE REENGINEERING

We usually think of reengineering taking place in automobile factories and insurance companies. However, even the Marshall Space Flight Center benefited from reengineering. The objective of one reengineering project was to increase efficiency in the Spacelab mission requirements flow. This is the process that manages all the change requests from mission customers.

A team was formed to review the existing process and employed systems engineering and TQM principles. Emphasis was on eliminating rework and duplication of efforts. It was also important to see whether there were any ways to standardize work and reduce the time that change requests actually "stay in the system" before the changes are actually approved and implemented. It was believed that even the rapidly moving space program should move even faster.

Implementation of the team's recommendations resulted in a reduction in average processing time by more than 60 percent. This case study illustrated the potential usefulness of reengineering and TQM principles in high-technology environments.

Source: Watson and Tytula, 1996.

---

to obtain an in-depth understanding of the market facing the company and customer requirements. It also involves understanding standards of how work should be done and performance levels required. The analysis is essential to developing a framework for the reengineering plan as well as outcome objectives and design specifications for the reengineering project. Redesign takes place as phase 2. Redesign requires the rethinking of how to do business in a way that best serves customer needs. This redesign often involves radically changing work flow.

In phase 3 of reengineering, the redesign is implemented and the entire organization institutionalizes the new design in its day-to-day activities. This is the phase where the small-scale reengineering activities are extended to large-scale organizational changes. If all this is successful, the final phase of transformation occurs. Successful reengineering projects result in a total transformation of the organization into a more efficient and effective corporation.

Reengineering in Perspective

In order to understand reengineering we must place it in perspective. In recent years the business press has praised many forms of changes taking place in organizations. Keidel (1994), however, points out that not all attempts at change are reengineering and, in fact, reengineering is not even the most effective. He carefully differentiates among restructuring, reengineering, and rethinking.

Restructuring is merely manipulating units on an organization chart. It is commonly referred to as delayering, downsizing, or rightsizing, or in similar terms, and involves reducing the number of employees or units or the sizes of organizational units or layers in the hierarchy. Restructuring is not exclusively the product of recessions and declining business. Near the end of 1997, for example, with the stock market near all-time highs, large and powerful companies continued to announce cutbacks. Eastman Kodak announced it planned a workforce reduction of 10,000, International Paper planned to lay off 9,000 employees, as did Citicorp, and Whirlpool followed with a plan to reduce total employees by almost 5,000. Restructuring exists in the midst of prosperity. The value added from restructuring accrues only to stockholders because it is directed exclusively at improving efficiency and the bottom line.

Reengineering is more ambitious in that it is directed toward serving customers, and when this happens stockholders automatically reap benefits. Since business corporations have been designed "vertically" for all the reasons we discussed in earlier chapters, they have evolved into functional silos or stovepipes. The objective of reengineering is to encourage managers and employees to think in terms of outcomes instead of functions. The focus is on interdependencies rather than functions.

One successful implementation of reengineering is described by Hall, Rosenthal, and Wade (1993) and involved the business telephone systems sales force at AT&T. Among other things the reengineering efforts reduced the "handoffs" or number of people involved between time of sale and final installation from 12 to 3, increased customer readiness to repurchase from AT&T from a little over 50 percent to more than 80 percent, and increased the percentage of invoices paid within 30 days of installation from 31 to 71.

As important and useful as reengineering might be, employees often do not see the same value-added benefits as customers and stockholders. This suggests the need for something beyond reengineering, which Keidel (1994) refers to as rethinking.

The target of rethinking is not organizational units nor is it organizational processes. Rethinking focuses on individual members of the organization. It involves changing the ways managers and employees make sense of the world and the organization in which they live and work (Weick, 1995). Continuously rethinking about the organization in terms of "who are we," "who are our important stakeholders," and "what are our distinctive competencies and how can we best take advantage of them," are critical aspects of organizational success in highly competitive environments. Customarily we ascribe the responsibility of rethinking to high-level executives, and to some extent this is appropriate.

It has been said that executive leaders must be the architects, assimilators, and facilitators of strategic change (Gioia and Chittipeddi, 1991). Indeed, they must constantly develop and interpret new visions. They must be both sensemakers and sensegivers to rank-and-file members of the organizations. Successful organizations, however, require more than sensemakers and sensegivers. They require employees and managers who are available and ready to learn and change (Senge, 1990).

Summary and Conclusions

This chapter has discussed three important topics—organizational culture, total quality management, and reengineering. Although the topics are built on distinct concepts, they are all interrelated. All are important to getting better at what we do and building organizations that value and reward high performance. Some of the more important conclusions are listed next.

1. Contrary to popular belief, organizational culture is a topic that has been acknowledged in management for almost half a century.
2. Organizational cultures are learned, shared by large percentages of employees, and may be both objective and subjective.
3. Organizational cultures are found in a variety of forms. Sometimes they are described as strong or weak and at other times as adaptive or conventional (nonadaptive).
4. In addition to the dominant culture in a organization, there may also be countercultures and subcultures.
5. Subjective aspects of culture include shared assumptions, values, and meanings, while objective aspects include artifacts such as histories, heroes, and stories.
6. Rites, rituals, and ceremonies are also important objective artifacts of organizational cultures.
7. Total quality management and continuous quality improvement are important aspects of organizational cultures that aspire to excellence.
8. Some of the important requirements for the success of TQM and CQI programs are: (1) top management commitment and support; (2) extensive communication and training; (3) customer orientation; (4) zero defects and quality consciousness; and (5) continuous improvement.
9. In recent years organizations have employed a number of approaches to strategic change. The most familiar are restructuring, reengineering, and rethinking.
10. Rethinking is the most promising and currently least employed approach to attaining organizational excellence.

QUESTIONS FOR DISCUSSION

1 What is meant by the term "organizational culture?" Is organizational culture a new concept in management?

2 List and briefly discuss three important characteristics of organizational culture. Are all three characteristics equally important?

3 Do you think organizational culture is positively related to a corporation's bottom line? Explain your response.

4 How can subcultures and countercultures be dysfunctional to the dominant cultures of an organization? Can they perform positive functions?

5 Explain the difference between organizational myths and folklore. What role do these factors play in building and maintaining organizational cultures?

6 What is the function of parting ceremonies? Why do you think these ceremonies are so important to individuals when organizations cease to exist?

7 Is it important to differentiate among approaches to quality management such as those advocated by Deming, Crosby, and Juran? Explain why it might be important to highlight the differences. Why would it be important not to highlight the differences?

8 List and briefly discuss the primary determinants of successful TQM implementations. Are any of these determinants more or less important than others? Explain your response.

9 Why have so many companies lost confidence in the ability of TQM to improve their performance? How could these disappointments have been prevented?

10 What are the primary differences among restructuring, reengineering, and rethinking? What is the focus of each of these approaches to organizational change? Which do you think has the most likelihood of success? Why?

Lessons for Management: Prescriptions, Enigmas, and Paradoxes

"The historian always oversimplifies, and hastily selects a manageable minority of facts and faces out of a crowd of souls and events whose multitudinous complexity one can never quite embrace or comprehend."

Will and Ariel Durant
The Lessons of History (1968)

Scientists like to talk about the "big bang" of which we, according to Carl Sagan, are the most spectacular, although remote descendants. Through the big bang, the theory goes, the cosmos was created from chaos. From nothing came something! Theologians have been telling us that for thousands of years. Why do such things seem more believable coming from astronomers?

There was also a big bang of sorts in management. Things were happening in management before the beginning of the 20th century, but not very much. People were "doing management" even if they had little understanding of what they were doing and why they were doing it. Pyramids were built, garbage was removed, governments enacted and enforced laws, and things eventually made it to market. If the system was not efficient, at least it was sufficient for slower and less complicated times.

All that changed with factories, assembly lines, and standardized components. The world of work has not been the same since and never will be again. The "visible hand of managerial direction" discussed by Alfred Chandler (1977) replaced Adam Smith's "invisible hand" as the force responsible for coordinating the flow of goods from the suppliers of raw materials to the retailer and eventually to the consumer (Chandler, 1977).

Management became an established institution, and the chaos that characterized the quest for management off and on throughout the course of human history took form and became a reality. Since that time the management movement has gained momentum, increased its speed, and today seems almost in danger of destroying itself as it spins wildly toward ever-increasing amounts of knowledge and technological improvements.

The purpose of this book has been to slow things down a bit and try to make some sense out of what has been happening for the past century in management. In

227

Chapter 11 ▲
*Lessons for
Management:
Prescriptions,
Enigmas, and
Paradoxes*

doing so, we were overwhelmed with the complexity and opted to focus on only a few recurring themes. We did so to heed the advice the experienced pilot gave the apprentice steamboatman in Mark Twain's *Life on the Mississippi*. After observing the shapes the shadows of the shore cast on starlit, pitch-dark, and gray misty nights, the apprentice asked how he could keep all the thousands of variations of the river's shape in his head without becoming stoop-shouldered. The pilot replied: "You only learn the shape of the river; and you learn it with such absolute certainty that you can always steer by the shape that's in your head, and never mind the one that's before your eyes" (p. 53).

We have not argued that the recurring themes of management are absolute truths or that they are never deserving of variation. However, once learned and in the absence of compelling reasons to do otherwise, adherence to the prescriptions proclaimed by the recurring themes is not bad advice. The wisdom of the ages, even though the ages are short in the case of management, demands a certain respect—certainly more than to merely discard it by chasing after fads, fashions, and quick fixes.

We have examined the ideas of engineers, philosophers, psychologists, and executives in our search for wisdom, values, and instruction. What we have found is a collage of prescriptions, enigmas, and paradoxes. At first glance it is tempting to accept the Durants' (1968, p. 12) jest that "most of history is guessing and the rest is prejudice." A deeper look convinces us instead that we have witnessed and traced the genesis and evolution of an exciting and increasingly important field of study as well as an essential vocation. To a great extent the very fate of humanity depends on our ability to effectively manage resources, time, and energy—all of which seem in too short supply.

This chapter concludes the book by looking at a set of 10 "bipolar terms," which summarize some of the important lessons taught by early and modern management writers. The list is not exhaustive, but the lessons highlighted are recurring frequently and have remained relevant for successive generations of managers. Each lesson will be discussed and the nature of the prescription, enigma, or paradox it presents all too briefly examined.

Lesson 1: Specialization and Meaning

We began this book with the proposition that specialization of labor made possible the factory system, and the factory system led inevitably to the need for management. The logic was simple. When the family farm provided the economic unit everyone was basically self-sufficient and had relatively less need to engage in exchange. At the level of work, farmers did "logical modules" or reasonably complete tasks. As a result they took a great deal of pride in the field they planted or the prize-winning animals, vegetables, and fruits they raised.

With the division of labor came the need to coordinate diverse and sometimes distant tasks into a unified whole, culminating in a desired product or service. That was the role management was obliged to assume. This specialized approach to work has served us well. The accomplishments of the factory system allow all of us to enjoy unprecedented wealth and leisure.

But, there is a problem. With specialization comes a loss of identity with what we do. The production worker whose job it is to put hubcaps on the left side of cars moving down what seems to be an infinitely long assembly line has trouble relating to the quality of the finished product. The consequence is boredom, monotony, absenteeism, and probably job stress. The quality of work life and sometimes even productivity suffers. The lesson management theory provides is that specialization leads to tremendous increases in productivity, and for that reason it will continue to be an essential part of the ongoing drama of modern industrial life.

At the same time, we are challenged to provide job and work designs that can preserve a degree of meaning in even highly specialized tasks. The fact is that too much of a good thing, when it happens to be specialization, can be bad. As an example, consider the reorganization of McCormack and Dodge, a New England software company. The success of the company was recognized to be its entrepreneurial spirit. However, with increased specialization came the temptation to be less and less innovative. The company intentionally reorganized because it "was becoming a monster company where jobs get too small" (Watts, 1987). What a statement and what a challenge to management. Although there remains doubt about the validity of theories of job enrichment, there is considerable evidence that American workers value some things more than high wages. The excitement of the job and its meaning to them personally are valued more than the fat paycheck (Kovach, 1987).

▲ Box 11-1
JOB INTEGRATION AND MAINTENANCE SPECIALISTS

Maintaining aircraft is one of the most important jobs in the United States Air Force. After the end of the Cold War, the USAF decided to reduce its numbers by more that 25 percent. Prior to 1989 flight-line maintenance crews consisted of eight specialists in areas such as engines, hydraulics, flight controls, communications, and so on. Each specialist was highly trained in their narrow area.

The decision was made to combine or consolidate the eight specialties into general areas such as avionics and tactical aircraft maintenance. Jobs became, in other words, less specialized. Perhaps jobs became more meaningful (not measured in this study), but performance suffered. Studies of selected performance indicators clearly showed a decrease as the various skills were integrated, leading researchers to conclude that many of the benefits of specialization were lost. This was a particularly troublesome problem in view of the critical need for consistence and precision in all areas of aircraft maintenance.

Source: Dumville and Torano (1997).

Lesson 2: Efficiency and Change

Chapter 11 ▲
*Lessons for
Management:
Prescriptions,
Enigmas, and
Paradoxes*

Most of what we have discussed in this book took place during what Haber (1964) called the Progressive Era. In this era, efficiency became a secular "great awakening" and "efficient and good came closer to meaning the same thing during these years than in any other period . . ." Efficiency was the gospel of scientific management. Through the improvement of efficiency, at least for Taylor, the Gilbreths, and Emerson, the solution to society's most troubling problems could be found. Efficiency made possible a win–win solution by increasing the returns simultaneously to workers and owners. Who could refuse such a deal? The "catch" was that efficiency required order, specialization, standardization, and structure. Flexibility, adaptability, and perhaps even creativity had to take the back seat. Order and innovation rarely exist side by side. Yet, to choose either to the exclusion of the other is clearly out of touch with contemporary reality (McFarland, 1976). Efficiency remains important, but we must also preserve the ability to adapt to changes quickly and decisively.

The continuous quest for efficiency regularly exposes one of the important lessons and serious paradoxes of management theory. In competitive economies firms must be efficient to survive. Yet, the actions required to increase efficiency add structure, controls, and inflexibility when creativity demands the opposite. Thus, there appears to be, at least for the time being, a recognition that the ability to change is as important as efficiency in ensuring organizational survival.

▲ Box 11-2

SUCCEEDING BY CHANGING THE RULES

"Top companies thrive by changing the rules of the game," says Gary Hamel. Although Nike's stock bounces all around the chart, none can deny that the company has experienced tremendous success. In the 1960s, CEO Phil Knight believed joggers would pay a premium for high-quality shoes. They did, and Nike became a marketing machine. Today the company does even more. It manages golf tournaments and sells equipment and cloths as well as shoes. Between 1986 and 1997 Nike stock gained an average of 47 percent per year. Only 17 companies in the Fortune 1,000 belong to the same elite club as Nike by providing their shareholders annual returns of 35 percent or more during the same period.

Nike achieves this performance, according to Knight, by "constantly reviewing how the world has changed and how we're reacting to it." The company has followed a strategy of "continuous reinvention." Nike has not been afraid of radical change such as "deciding it was a sports company not a shoe company."

Source: Hamel (1997).

To illustrate the potential conflict consider the comments of the head of research and development at 3M Corporation, who stated that when managing creative people, you have to behave in a different way (Kiechel, 1985). Sometimes, even though you are the manager, you have to keep your mouth closed and your eyes half shut. Often the most promising project begins with unauthorized actions. You have to trust the innovators and expect them to do their best. This is far from the close controls of early management.

Waterman (1987) captured the importance of change and the manager's ability to adjust to it in what he calls the "renewal factor." According to him, successful businesses are those that understand and deal with uncertainty. Often we do not detect the changes taking place in highly successful organizations until we stop and analyze that these organizations are constantly adapting and adjusting their structures, strategies, products, and services to new demands of consumers and markets. According to Waterman, these organizations have successfully learned how to manage the "last frontier"—the challenge of renewal. Management by wandering around is important. Management by getting out of the way and allowing others to do their jobs may be even more important.

Taylor, the Gilbreths, and Emerson taught us about the importance of efficiency. Lawrence and Lorsch, Thompson, and Woodward illustrated the importance of innovation and change. The renewal factor is real, and firms that choose to deny or ignore it will put themselves in peril for the future.

Lesson 3: Coordination and Conflict

Classical writers emphasized the importance of coordination. Mooney and Reiley called it the first principle of organization and suggested that the need for coordination was the single most important factor leading to the emergence of management as a recognized occupation. Specialized jobs and divisionalized organizations demanded that someone be responsible for "putting everything together" in a grand unified design.

Management and managers emerged to assume the coordinative role. The lesson taught by early writers, however, is that coordination is not the normal state of affairs. It requires purposeful intervention, and intervention requires a plan, a goal, a purpose. Organizations, like all systems, experience entropy and will self-destruct unless managed. While it is true that conflict can lead to innovation and new ideas, it also leads to inefficiency, loss of direction, and sometimes less fun at work. In recent times, the lure of competition and the hint that conflict can bring about beneficial outcomes have led some managers and members of the public to go so far as to advocate a form of what Kanter (1987) called "cowboy management."

According to Kanter (1987), cowboy management "makes heroes out of hipshooters who fire before they aim" (p. 19). These are the rugged individualists who like to build competition among departments to keep everyone honest, manage by the "seat of their pants," and avoid goal statements because objectives restrict their freedom to pursue new opportunities. Like all real cowboys, management cowboys cre-

231

Chapter 11 ▲
*Lessons for
Management:
Prescriptions,
Enigmas, and
Paradoxes*

▲ **Box 11-3**

COOPERATION AND COLLABORATION

How to acquire and sustain a competitive advantage has been one of the most frequently discussed topics in management in recent years. Some believe that organizations that develop the ability to cooperate across various lines of business may have the answer to one important aspect of competitive advantage.

Much of the discussion of reengineering focuses on how to rethink the way organizations do business. Many inefficiencies and sources of customer discontent result from the inability of functional departments and business units in the same organization to cooperate. Collaboration and cooperation that lead to coordination has been called a meta capability of organizations. This means that successful organizations develop decision-making processes among interdependent groups that involve joint ownership of the decision and collective accountability for the results or outcomes. Many believe the critical nature of this internal partnering is greatly underestimated in modern organizations and will become increasingly important for future success.

Source: Liedtka (1996).

---

ate excitement and if we are not careful, their yearning for adventure and "rough and rowdy" ways can carry us away in the excitement. But cowboy management with its emphasis on building competition and "managing constructive conflict" is not the lesson we derive from the classics. Instead we are told that competition is for our competitors while cooperation is for our friends. Cowboy management is diametrically opposed to instructions of the early writers.

One interesting point emphasized by Deming (1986) is that cooperation created much of the Japanese economic miracle. Conflict between employers and employees, purchasers and suppliers, and so on only builds resentment, short-run orientations, and ultimately inefficiency.

A recurring lesson is the importance of cooperation. When we compete, we should do so with those who challenge us in the marketplace. Internally it is important to work as a team. Teamwork, whether in athletics, war, or business, is a sound principle of success. After all, as Durant and Durant (1968) note, "we cooperate in our group in order to strengthen our group in its competition with other groups." Perhaps the reason we as a nation have lost our ability to compete is that we have lost our will to cooperate. The enigma is that, in the process of not cooperating, we have effectively become our own worst enemy.

Lesson 4: Purpose and Fate

Managers have a choice when it comes to the future. They can do their best to shape it or they can be victims of fate. Successful executives always chose the former. Eisenberg (1987) uses the term "strategic opportunism" to define a type of behavior whereby managers focus on long term objectives while remaining flexible enough to deal with day-to-day operating problems. Strategic opportunism puts the manager in control of fate rather than merely accepting the role of servant. Missions, strategic goals, and strategies are not looked on as straight jackets that make the organization less responsive to new ideas and challenges. Instead, they provide a framework within which to concentrate energies and look for new opportunities.

Consider the task confronting AT&T in the early 1980s after divestiture. How could such a company direct more than 300,000 employees and $30 billion of assets toward any type of purposeful behavior? The first step was to take charge, formulate, and communicate a mission statement that was easy for employees to understand. In the words of an executive, AT&T's mission is "global information services; the measure is customer satisfaction. And, we are one great enterprise . . . a single great river to which all essential tributaries add their particular strength to one determined course" (Moran, 1984, p. 5).

Throughout this book frequent reference has been made to how managers really behave and how this behavior differs sometimes from the theory of effective management. Almost always we have been forced to admit that managers are "caught up" in the emergencies of day-to-day activities and miss looking, even on occasion, at the larger picture. To deal with the urgent is natural, but it is not good management. To think about, formulate, and communicate the purpose of the organization in the form of a mission statement or similar media remains sound advice from the annals of management history.

The dysfunctional obsession with the urgent is evident with regard to the erosion of quality in products and services. Interviews with managers indicate that many believe quality improvements increase costs and reduce productivity, cost cutting produces faster positive results on profits than quality improvements, and opportunities to improve productivity through quality improvements are limited (Shetty, 1986). In other words, short-term, bottom-line issues are perceived to be more important than long-term commitment to quality and productivity.

Improvement in quality requires a long-term commitment on the part of the organization and consequently its management team. Executives at firms such as Ford, Saturn, Motorola, and General Electric who have made quality improvements a part of their agendas agree on a number of points. Two of the more important are: (1) top management has to be devoted to improvements in productivity and quality and incorporate this commitment into company goals and policies (Shetty, 1986); and (2) quality improvement standards must be carefully woven into strategic planning, budgeting, control, communication, and training activities of the firm.

Quality cannot be left to the whims of fate. If things are not planned, they do not usually happen. Granted, some things happen in spite of a plan but good managers never depend on fate. Fate is fickle and cannot be depended on to produce results. The prevoyance of Fayol is still good advice. Not only should we forecast the future,

233

Chapter 11 ▲
*Lessons for
Management:
Prescriptions,
Enigmas, and
Paradoxes*

▲ **Box 11-4**

TODAY'S REALITY VERSUS TOMORROW'S HOPE

Sometimes consultants observe realities in organizations that scholars fail to see. Organizational tension may be one of these less observed and less studied aspects of corporate life. The tension between where an organization is today and where it hopes to be in the future can be a powerful motivator of performance. Many organizations experience change more as oscillations. Some progress is made and forward movement takes place. However, the momentum is quickly lost and the organization slips back in much the same way as a rocking chair rocks forward and then back.

Change relies on advancement or the continuous forward movement of the organization from its present state to the state where its owners, managers, and employees want it to be in the future. The most successful organizations and managers are those who dare to dream. Creative tension is useful in making the most ambitious dream realities. In the end, plans and structures are extremely important factors in whether or not an organization will truly advance or simply oscillate.

Source: Fritz (1996).

we should prepare for it as well. In the epic of *Beowulf* we learn that "fate often saves an undoomed warrior when his courage endures." Managers today, doomed or undoomed, need more than fate to survive. They need plans, a purpose, a reason to be.

Lesson 5: Science and Art

Arguments about whether management is an art or a science are boring at best and certainly a waste of time. The fact is that management is neither or, perhaps, it is both. We cannot deny, however, that if managers and management research are to be respectable, there must be some scientific basis for management study and practice. The early writers provide an important lesson on the role of science in management. With the possible exception of Taylor and the Gilbreths, early writers thought of science as a worthy, although not completely obtainable goal for management. Fayol apologized for using the term "principle" and cautioned that it should not be thought of in a scientific sense.

Much of management can and should be studied "scientifically." Certainly, a scientific attitude should guide all our investigations and be the basis for our actions. However, much of what the manager deals with—symbols, myths, and so on—defies scientific analysis in the conventional sense. That is why Deal and Kennedy (1983) found traditional scientific methods wanting in their application of culture to organi-

▲ **Box 11-5**

MANAGER AS ARTIST

Management ideas and actions are important to one another. Ideas of the past that have been tested and tried are perhaps our best hope for successful management actions. On the other hand, the most successful managers, like military commanders are those who dare to ignore the conventional and free themselves from precedent and policy.

In management, the people who generate ideas and the people who put them into action are, except on rare occasions, different in almost every way. Those people who generate ideas in management are engaged in a noble task, and science is their best ally. Those who get things done in organizations also have a noble calling, but science will be less useful. Their plans should be well conceived, their actions well prepared, and their motives well intended, but management is rarely scientific. Perhaps for managers to acknowledge that we have a common history at all is significant. Perhaps for researchers to acknowledge that the complexities faced by real mangers can only be partially captured in experiments, surveys, and case studies is equally sufficient to a mutually beneficial relationship between the observers and the doers of management.

zations and management. These writers assert: There is some reason to be skeptical about many of the "facts" in management research, especially the assumed relationships between elements like goals and structure. Many of the scientific theories of management simply have something wrong with them when it comes to prediction and implementation. Dealing with the human side of implementation requires an artist more than a scientist.

Some of the "outdated and situation-specific paradigms" of management appear scientifically sophisticated but are less applicable today. The newly appreciated magical, mystical, and metaphysical aspects of organizations are not suited to study by "scientific" methods. It is important to remain flexible on the issue of science and management. If we limit the boundaries of our knowledge to only those things that can be studied objectively and scientifically, we lose much of the richness of organizational phenomena.

Lesson 6: Rationality and Human Frailty

The sixth lesson management history teaches us is that human beings are frail in the face of complex decisions. Even though we are efficient information processors and outperform even the most powerful computer pound for pound, the typical manager can know relatively little about anything other than the most simple decision problems. No informed manager would debate the limits of human understanding, yet

235

Chapter 11 ▲
*Lessons for
Management:
Prescriptions,
Enigmas, and
Paradoxes*

managerial behavior testifies to the existence of a large range of responses to bounded rationality.

Some managers act as if knowledge about the situation were complete, effect closure, make decisions, and deal with the consequences with seemingly little cognitive dissonance. Others deny or excuse away information outside their limits of knowledge and suggest that the result of less than perfect knowledge is really better than what one would expect from the perfectly informed decision maker. Both responses are naive and dangerous.

Managers need to become as knowledgeable about the decisions they make as possible. Information search should be expanded until it is no longer economical or practical to explore. Even then choices should be recognized as something less than optimum. If we define rationality along with Simon as goal-oriented or purposeful, we should become more rational by setting goals and pursuing them. If, on the other hand, we look at rationality in terms of the degree of information one possesses, attempts should be made to become as informed as possible. Even though the ideal of perfect knowledge will never be realized, it is a worthy goal. If decision making is the "heart of executive activity," it should be as informed as possible.

Some companies have effectively gotten "back to basics" and focused more directly on the few things they do best (Wilkins and Bristow, 1987). Theoretically, this should make them more informed decision makers. In the 1960s many companies began to conglomerate and stray into a number of unfamiliar businesses. A few decided

---

▲ Box 11-6
THE VINCENNES DILEMMA

In July 1988 the missile cruiser U.S.S. Vincennes shot down an Iranian civilian A300 Airbus killing all 290 people on board. At the time, the Vincennes was engaged in combat with Iranian surface ships and mistook the airliner for an attacking fighter. The drill was familiar since U.S. intelligence had warned all personnel that it believed the Iranians would attempt to sink an American ship on or around the Fourth of July. When the airliner ignored repeated warnings, the training took over. Some call what happened "scenario lock in." In this case, the scenario becomes so familiar that automatic drilled behavior takes over in the absence of the information needed for rational decision making.

Weick (1995) talks about a similar situation where individuals become trapped in the rational decision-making model and coerced by technology so that when neither the time nor the data are available, it becomes impossible to override a situation that seems unlikely. Information technologies follow decision rationality and are closely followed in the absence of compelling contra evidence.

Source: Weick (1995).

to "stick to their knitting." Boeing, for example, used critical success factors to focus on the "relatively few things" it had to do right to succeed and, in doing so, continues to dominate one of the most complex and changing industries on the globe (Chung and Friesen, 1991; Friesen and Johnson, 1995).

Every generation of management deals with unique competitive and environmental challenges and respond with innovative strategies. Sometimes the strategies tempt decision makers to venture into areas where they have little experience and expertise. In the health care industry, for example, vertical integration has been a trend for more than a decade. To compete effectively, many believe, they must control the flow of patients from birth to death. Integrated health systems have acute-care hospitals to handle the most complicated delivery, and hospice services to make death as painless and comfortable as possible. No wonder vertical integration is such a risky strategy. Who can hope to master the nuances of organizations as different as those found in a vertically integrated health system?

Lesson 7: Universal and Situational

Although the early writers argued to the contrary, one of the lessons of early management thought is that management principles and prescriptions are mostly relative. Only seldom do we find something that is absolute and universally applicable to all situations and at all times. That, of course, does not satisfy our need to reduce uncertainty, but it should keep us skeptical of any apparent quick fix. While there are fundamental themes of management, managers must remember that the situation is an important factor in most management decisions.

As the world enters a new era of "globalism," situational or contingency questions become more important. We are no longer talking of situational in terms of the managerial prescription today as compared to a year ago, or of General Motors as compared to the City of New York. What we are talking about is the very important issue of the relative nature of management theory. To illustrate, Hafsi, Kiggundu, and Jorgensen (1987) presented an analysis of how state-owned enterprises are governed given alternative assumptions about the nature of the degree of freedom, the extent of political pressure, and the emphasis on accountability, and so on. The authors illustrated how organizational configurations varied with the extent of government involvement in the day-to-day operations of the state-owned corporation. The situation facing the decision maker clearly illustrated the importance of situational or contingency factors.

Perhaps one of the best illustrations of relativity in management relates to management style. Dowd (1986) praised President Reagan with an article in *Fortune* entitled "What Managers Can Learn from Manager Reagan." She stated that Reagan's style was simple: surround yourself with the best people you can find, delegate authority, and don't interfere as long as the policy you've decided upon is being carried out" (p. 33).

The philosophy sounded good, and for more than one term it served President Reagan well. Unfortunately, less than a year after the article hit the press, a top Reagan official were sitting before a Congressional hearing, and the President himself

237

Chapter 11 ▲
*Lessons for
Management:
Prescriptions,
Enigmas, and
Paradoxes*

▲ **Box 11-7**

SIMILARITIES CAN BE IMPORTANT

Just when we become convinced that the situation reigns, absolutes emerge as important. For years experts have argued that the key to business success in the global environment is to adapt business practices to local customs. To do otherwise is to risk stifling creativity and alienation of employees and customers. A study of companies in the United States, Japan, England, France, and Germany, however, found that even though there were clear differences in how businesses operated, the most successful employed similar strategies regardless of their location. Successful companies consistently based their decisions less on national cultures and more on proven multinational business practices.

All the successful companies fostered a competitive, entrepreneurial culture and a friendly climate. All placed a high value on innovation. The researchers suggested that highly autonomous management styles, free to adjust to local situations, may not be the best option for success. Organizationwide market-driven cultures may prove the best formula for success.

Source: Deshpandé, Farley, and Webster (1997).

was faced with one of the great crises of his administration. The management style that was praised a year before was being criticized with such terms as "bankrupt," "out of control," and "out of touch." In the case of foreign policy, Mr. Reagan found that another style of management was needed. Delegation could not be a trusted strategy when the stakes were as high as they were in "guns for hostages," and aid to the Contras causes. His style of "burning the midday oil" and letting his advisors and aides do their jobs appeared as inappropriate for his second term in office as it was appropriate for his first. The tragedy is that the President, like many managers, was not able to adapt his management style to changing situations.

Lesson 8: Dignity and Duty

Every person, when hired by an organization, accepts as their duty the responsibility to deliver a fair day's work for the agreed on pay. At the same time, individuals should expect to retain their dignity. Although we were shocked to see the way some early writers described and treated human beings, there was a recognition by all for the need for the preservation of human dignity. This was most evident in the concern for Taylor's prescription to select the "right person for the right job." The futility and tragedy of putting people in jobs for which they were "constitutionally unqualified" was a recognition of the need for preserving human dignity.

A good example of the importance of preserving human dignity at work is given by Irwin (1987) in a report on 2 American Motors study teams that visited 11 Japanese automobile manufacturing plants. The team members reported a number of impressions—some were surprising and some were not. With regard to surprises, it was found that there were relatively few computer applications to manufacturing processes, workers were allowed to share in the prosperity of the firm, and participation most often was indirect through representatives rather than directly from worker to manager. Most important, however, were the basic facts that: quality was an obsession with workers, it was their duty; all employees appeared engaged in the pursuit of common goals; and workers were very well trained to do the jobs they were responsible for completing. In line with Theory Y, workers were treated like intelligent adults; they were "never," under any circumstance, placed in positions that would compromise their human dignity; and all employees were treated with respect and honor. More than two decades of observing and studying the Japanese system have suggested that things are not as they seemed during the times these words were written. However, respect, honor, and duty do indeed appear to be important to both employers and workers.

Early in our history the work values built on the family farm were the type all wish to inspire. Honesty, justice, hard work, frugality, dignity, and humility were developed and reinforced. People worked for themselves, were close to the land, lived with and near their clan, and took time to enjoy life through simple pursuits. The factory was different. It is not inherently evil, but it is alienating even under the best of conditions. The dignity naturally gained by being in touch with nature had to be

---

▲ Box 11-8
GETTING ON WITH LIFE

How do organizations keep their best people on board and motivated when they have experienced downsizing? This is a critical question today as more and more organizations find staff reductions to be an appropriate response to competitive realities. Survivors seem to fall in one of three categories: (1) the *foot out the door* employees who are productive but ready to walk out if an opportunity comes along; (2) the *wait and see* employees who are sometimes confrontational and concerned about the future and its effect on their lives; and (3) the *ride it out* employees who are connected to the organization and colleagues and are the least likely to leave.

Keeping survivors on board requires an understanding of the history of the organization, good communication, change, and the nature of transition. Managing and dealing with downsizing is one of the greatest threats to dignity and duty in modern times.

Source: Caplan and Teese (1997).

239

Chapter 11 ▲
*Lessons for
Management:
Prescriptions,
Enigmas, and
Paradoxes*

worked for in the sweat shop, steamy factory, and pitch-dark mines. Yet human dignity and duty were no less important in all these places. The primary reason for the failure of welfare capitalism, well intended as it was, is easily summarized—it was paternalistic and robbed workers of their dignity. As a consequence, duty turned to dependence and dependence to distrust.

Whether we are referring to job enrichment or positive reinforcement, the second lesson is clear. People work better, harder, and take greater pride in what they do when their dignity is preserved. If one is to fulfill one's duty faithfully to perform a fair day's work the minimum cost of such achievement is the preservation of dignity at work.

Today, as we approach a new millennium, the challenge of dignity and duty has never been greater. In fact, it is more sinister because it is less obvious. The need to reform the factory and mine, in the end, could not be denied by people of goodwill. Downsizing, rightsizing, and restructuring are not seen as evils to attack but often as appropriate responses to competitive forces and years of misdirected actions that resulted in intolerable inefficiencies. However, to the victim they are no less demeaning than dark mines and sweaty factories. To the survivors they are clear signals that "I may be next" and that loyalty to myself and responsibility to my family must be valued more than duty to the employer (Stroh and Reilly, 1997).

Lesson 9: Technique and Politics

Lesson 9 reminds us that remarkably little is known about the nature of managerial work. To many, the myth of the manager as the "reflective calculator" is discarded forever. Others are not so sure. No one seriously doubts that managers have limited time for planning. The fact that time is limited may assist us in understanding why managers plan so little, but it does not justify the fact that planning, in the best sense of the term, does not take place at all. The importance of traditional functions of management like planning, organizing, and controlling is illustrated by what some believe are signs that firms can no longer support futuristic exercises. Actually, the evidence shows just the opposite. For example, when *Business Week* (September 17, 1984) published its article on "The New Breed of Strategic Planner" and pointed out how major corporations are trimming their planning staffs, many concluded this was evidence of the "death of strategic planning."

A closer reading of the article, however, made it clear that only detached planning staffs (planocrats as they were called) are dying. This is happening because corporations are rediscovering that planning is part of the task of every line manager. To put planning in the air-conditioned executive suite was a mistake. The challenge was to "reinfranchise" line managers to plan more not less.

This is not to deny that management also involves politics. The best formulated plans will accomplish little unless there are managers capable of providing leadership in the implementation stage. Not only must managers know the techniques of management, they must also understand political reality within the organization if they are to be successful (Bartolome and Laurent, 1986). Managers are studies in paradox. They appear to approach things systematically and to be in perfect control of situa-

▲ **Box 11-9**
POLITICS OF MANAGEMENT

A few people have always argued that management is really politics and that Machiavelli is a better instructor than Drucker. Now a new twist—women too should learn from Machiavelli if they want to survive and prosper amid the intrigue of modern corporations. The lesson to be learned is that life is war and war is unkind to the weak.

Most women play by the rules, it is argued, but in order to prosper you must be dangerous. Why should "in your face" tactics be limited to basketball players, Jack Welsh, and a few other males? Winners in corporations are the ruthless and the cunning. Sometimes, according to this argument, it is better to create chaos than it is to make peace.

The picture painted about life in the modern corporation is similar to that of the jungle, and the winning prescription is to get "down and dirty." However, one must remember that research has shown Machiavellianism is self-limiting and ultimately destructive for males. Will it prove the same for females?

Source: Rubin (1997).

tions, yet research tells us that most of the activities they perform take less than 10 minutes. Almost never do they work on something for an hour. At the same time, they are able to direct thousands of employees and distribute millions of dollars to uses that contribute to goal accomplishment.

The fact is that managers are rarely in control. Their job demands that they build strong networks of supporting relationships. At work this is done by delegating authority, careful personnel selection, and honest communication. All these actions have the potential of making the manager look as if she were not in control of the events. Actually, such actions are taken only by those managers who are self-reliant enough to give opportunities to others, let them make mistakes, and hold them accountable for achieving results (Quick, Nelson, and Quick, 1987).

Lesson 10: Responsibility and Compromise

If you believe the social responsibility controversy is something new, you are in for a surprise. In spite of Watergate, the Iran Contra Affair, insider trading scandals, and tax evasion in high places, organizational societies and democracies, for that matter, are built on trust. When people, especially managers, break the rules, the entire system is in peril. At least a few have always recognized the peril, written about it, and offered better ways to do business.

241

Chapter 11 ▲
*Lessons for
Management:
Prescriptions,
Enigmas, and
Paradoxes*

When corporations become large and complex individuals get lost, and sometimes it is difficult to appreciate the significance of a single employee, managerial or nonmanagerial, to the overall functioning of the organization. An individual, for example, can easily ruin the reputation of a firm with a few misguided actions. For that reason, Vernon Loucks, Jr. (1987), chief executive officer of Baxter Travenol Laboratories, Inc. offers four specific guidelines to protect the corporation against socially irresponsible behavior. First, the right people should be hired. People with a history of dishonest or irresponsible behavior are greater ethical risks. Second, standards of responsible behavior should be set and communicated and less attention should be placed on rules. Individual employees are mature human beings and should understand the need for responsible action. Third, managers should never allow themselves to be isolated from the everyday reality of the organization. Irresponsible actions are more likely when managers are out of touch with the employees, competitors, and other groups with whom they interact. Finally, managers should (must) provide the role models. If responsibility is to be anything other than lip service, top management must provide the role models of how things are expected to be done.

In discussing "why good managers make bad ethical choices," Gellerman (1986) offered similar suggestions. Managers violate ethics, and sometimes the law, when organizations do not: (1) establish a code of ethics for all employees; (2) stress formally and regularly that loyalty does not mean always doing what the organization says; (3) teach managers guidelines like "when in doubt don't." What is important to recognize is that the question of the appropriate responsibility of management is as

---

▲ Box 11-10
ARE COMPLIANCE COPS THE ANSWER?

They have been described as part cop, part priest, part confidante, and part snitch. These are the compliance officers who are emerging to help managers do the right things. Columbia/HCA is in ethical and legal trouble for its Medicare billing practices, and one of its actions includes hiring a senior vice president for ethics, compliance, and corporate responsibility. To find the right person, they hired the director of the Defense Industry Initiative on Business Ethics and Compliance. Whether or not the presence of a compliance officer, even at a high level, will lead to more responsible decision making remains to be seen. The greatest benefit of a senior vice president for ethics and social responsibility may be symbolic. Senior vice presidents add a lot of overhead. Clearly, the presence of such a high-level officer sends the message that ethics and social responsibility are important priorities of the firm. Ethics and social responsibility are issues that modern organizations must address and resolve if they are to live up to the expectations of all social institutions.

Source: Dunn (1997).

old as the field itself. There is nothing fundamentally different about today's managers, organizations, or society that makes us more concerned about the impact of managerial decisions on the larger society. The question is simply a continuing one that derives from the complex relationship between business and society.

The lesson for managers in classical writings is that management is an economic institution and responsible for building efficiency and ultimately profitability. However, management is part of a larger society and as such must be responsive to its demands. Business and management, therefore, exist at the pleasure of society, and if they are not socially responsive, they may cease to exist in their present form. Gantt, Barnard, Dennison, Tead, and others clearly recognized this reality, and today's managers can do no less.

Toward Professionalism in Management

Our survey of selected recurring themes in management thought is complete. There are many comments one could make about this review. With all of the possible summaries, one can only hope that present and prospective managers have been made increasingly aware of the wealth they have available to them in the form of classic books in the field. The classic books of the field vary in length, sophistication, and content, but all have contributed significantly to what we know about management as a field of study and honorable occupation. Hopefully this honorable occupation will realize the full potential of its legacy and arrive soon at the recognized and deserved status of a profession.

Follett maintained that there are two basic qualifications for a profession. It must be founded on science and its knowledge must be used in the service of others. Management cannot withhold its information from society at large and use it in its own service. Both of these requirements are being met with the passage of time, and society has reaped benefits from the increased professionalism of management and managers. Much remains to be accomplished, but no one associated with the field of management needs "bow his head in shame." The accomplishments of managers and management have been great. Because of it society's economic resources are better allocated, and the influence of the field is rapidly becoming felt in less traditional areas like health care and education. The future is bright indeed.

As for now, it is important that managers and management researchers/teachers continue the quest that others have so admirably started. The era of the classics will not end with the close of the 20th century. There is a need for more and better works that will provide a deeper understanding of the economic and social institution of management. As we go into the future confident in our knowledge of the past we must continue to build new ideas and concepts and insure that society has the benefit of the best available management knowledge.

The legacy we have is greater than that of Taylor, Mayo, and even Maslow and Woodward. It is our heritage that makes continued progress possible. We should remember, as the Durants (1968) have shown us: "If progress is real despite our whining, it is not because we are born healthier, better, or wiser . . . but because we are born to a richer heritage. . . . The heritage rises, and man [woman] rise in proportion as he [she] receive it" (p. 102).

243

Chapter 11 ▲
*Lessons for
Management:
Prescriptions,
Enigmas, and
Paradoxes*

Summary and Conclusions

This chapter attempted to summarize the contributions of the early writers in management in 10 not so easy lessons. The legacy of management is great when we objectively examine the influence managers have on the allocation of resources around the globe. We hear of the work of managers in newspapers, primarily when there is a layoff, a mistake, or an indiscretion. Increasingly, we hear of the good works of managers. Managers can be and actually are named men and women of the year in various polls because of the positive impact many have on society. In this chapter we have attempted to discuss a variety of recurring themes. Some of the important implications are as follows.

1. Specialization is a sound economic principle and is as valid today as in the days of Adam Smith. Too much specialization, however, can remove much of the meaning of work. Sometimes, with highly specialized tasks, it is difficult to see what contribution the job has to the total product or service.
2. Efficiency and change demand different actions. In almost all cases the actions that contribute to efficiency reduce an organization's ability to change. The reverse is also true.
3. Coordination is one of the most fundamental concepts in management thought. Many writers increasingly agree that a reasonable amount of conflict can have the positive effect of stimulating innovation. Reductions in coordination brought about by conflict also reduce efficiency. A balance is required.
4. Goals are critical to the success of individuals and managers. In fact, one of the important reasons for managers is to become proactive and not to be victims of fate.
5. Management has both scientific and artistic aspects. The scientific attitude is important for management, but often the success of a decision is more a matter of art and intuition.
6. Human beings, at their best, are ill informed. Managers in particular have difficulty dealing with the complexity of their environment. A critical determinant of a manager's success is her or his ability to search for the essential amount of information needed to make decisions.
7. The controversy continues about the universal or situational character of management concepts. Indeed there are generally applicable principles of management. The insightful manager will, however, always think of the situation or environment within which decisions are implemented.
8. In an era of downsizing, managers have a particular challenge maintaining the dignity of employees. Dignity is not only rightfully deserved by all people, it is the essential ingredient needed to ensure that employees adhere to their sense of duty in doing their jobs.
9. Management techniques are important and useful to managers. Business corporations, like all other human institutions, also possess a political dimension that must be understood by managers and employees.
10. Business firms are important social institutions, and the decisions of managers affect millions of people. Social consciousness is an essential ingredient of management decision making.

QUESTIONS FOR DISCUSSION

1 Is it possible to overcome the seemingly inherent conflict between specialization and meaning in jobs? If not, why are highly specialized tasks such as heart surgery considered so emotionally as well as financially rewarding?

2 In today's organizational world, is efficiency or change most important? Explain your answer.

3 Have computers made it possible for managers to become more rational? Do you think they will make it possible for managers to actually become objectively rational?

4 Why is coordination such a fundamental concept of management? In corporations emphasizing change does coordination become less important? Why or why not?

5 How important is organizational politics? Can politics really make the difference between success and failure in modern organizations?

"A Conversation with Roberto Goizueta and Jack Welch," *Fortune* Dec. 11, 1995, 62.

Abrahamson, Eric, "Management Fashion," *Academy of Management Review,* 21(1), 1996, 254–285.

Ackoff, Russell L., *The Democratic Corporation.* New York: Oxford University Press, 1994.

Adams, Bruce, "The Limitations of Muddling Through: Does Anyone in Washington Really Think Anymore?," *Public Administration Review,* 39, Nov.–Dec. 1979, 545–552.

Aharoni, Yair, *The Evolution and Management of State Owned Enterprises.* Cambridge, MA: Ballinger, 1986.

"Alaskan Oil Spill," *Management Review,* Apr. 1990, 14–21.

Alderfer, C. P, *Existence, Relatedness, and Growth: Human Needs in Organizational Settings.* New York: Free Press, 1972.

Alford, L. P., *Henry Laurence Gantt: Leader in Industry.* New York: American Society of Mechanical Engineers, 1934.

Allen, J. H., "The Realities of Culture Change and How It Worked at Toyota," *Employment Relations Today,* 22, Spring 1995, 29–40.

Anderson, John P., and W. Jack Duncan, "The Scientific Significance of the Paradox in Administrative Theory," *Management International Review*, 17, 1977, 99–106.

Arnold, W. J., "Extending the Scientific Gospel," in *Milestones of Management,* vol. 2. New York: McGraw-Hill/Business Week, 1966, 4–5.

Asplund, Jon, "Columbia 'Welcomes' FBI Evidence as Fodder for Internal Inquiry," *AMA News,* Oct. 13, 1997, 1.

"At Emery Air Freight: Positive Reinforcement Boosts Performance," *Organizational Dynamics*, Winter 1973.

Babbage, Charles, *On the Economy of Machinery and Manufactures.* London: Charles Knight, 1982 (reprint).

Bailey, R. H., *The Home Front: U. S. A.* New York: Time-Life Books, 1977.

Bamberger, Peter, and Avi Fiegenbaum. "The Role of Strategic Reference Points in Explaining the Nature and Consequences of Human Resource Strategy," *Academy of Management Review,* 21(4), 1996, 926–958.

Banta, Martha, *Taylored Lives: Narrative Productions in the Age of Taylor, Veblen, and Ford.* Chicago, IL: University of Chicago Press, 1993.

Barnard, Chester I., *The Functions of the Executive.* Cambridge, MA: Harvard University Press, 1938.

Bartlett, Christopher A., and Sumantra, Ghoshal, "Changing the Role of Top Management beyond Systems to People," *Harvard Business Review,* 73, May/June 1995, 132–143.

Bartolome, Fernando, and Andre Laurent, "The Manager: Master and Servant of Power," *Harvard Business Review*, 64, Nov./Dec. 1986, 77–81.

▲ *REFERENCES*   Bass, Bernard M., *Bass and Stogdill's Handbook of Leadership*. New York: Free Press, 1990.

Bass, B. M., and B. J. Avolio, "Transformational Leadership: A Response to Critiques," in M. M. Chemers and R. Ayman (Eds.), *Leadership Theory and Research: Perspectives and Directions*. San Diego, CA: Academic Press, 1993, 49–80.

Bavelas, Alex, "Leadership: Man and Function," *Administrative Science Quarterly*, 5, 1960, 448–455.

Bedeian, Arthur G., *Management Laureates: A Collection of Autobiographical Essays*, I. Greenwich, CT: JAI Press, 1991.

——, *Management Laureates: A Collection of Autobiographical Essays*, II. Greenwich, CT: JAI Press, 1993a.

——, *Management Laureates: A Collection of Autobiographical Essays*, III. Greenwich, CT: JAI Press, 1993b.

——, *Management Laureates: A Collection of Autobiographical Essays*, IV. Greenwich, CT: JAI Press, 1996.

Bennis, Warren G., *On Becoming a Leader*, Reading, MA: Addison-Wesley, 1989.

Bergquist, William, *The Postmodern Organization: Mastering the Art of Irreversible Change*. San Francisco: Jossey-Bass, 1993.

Berkwick, D. M., A. B. Godfrey, and J. Rossner, *Curing Health Care: New Strategies* for *Quality Improvement*. San Francisco: Jossey-Bass, 1990.

Berry, L. L., "Five Imperatives for Improving Service Quality," *Sloan Management Review*, 31(4), Summer 1991, 29–38.

Biddle, Wayne, "What Destroyed Challenger?," *Discover*, 7, Apr. 1986, 40–47.

Blake, R. R., and J. S. Mouton, *The Managerial Grid*. Houston, TX: Gulf Publications, 1964.

Bluedorn, A. C., T. L. Keon, and N. M. Carter, "Management History Research: Is Anyone out There Listening?," *Proceedings of the Academy of Management*, Aug. 1985, 130–133.

Boddewyn, Jean, "Frederick Winslow Taylor: An Evaluation," in Paul Dauten (Ed.), *Emerging Concepts in Management*. Boston, MA: Houghton Mifflin, 1962, 31–39.

Bolman, Lee. G., and Terrance E. Deal, *Modern Approaches to Understanding and Managing Organizations*. San Francisco, CA: Jossey-Bass, 1984.

Bolton, A. A., C. Toftoy, and D. Chipman, "Relay Assembly Productivity Factors," *Proceedings of the Southern Management Association*, 1987, 214–216.

Brandenburger, A. M. and B. J. Nalebuff, "The Right Game: Use Game Theory to Shape Strategy," *Harvard Business Review*, 73, July/Aug. 1995, 57–61.

Breeze, John D., "Administration and Organization of the Commercial Function by J. Carlioz," in K. H. Chung (Ed.), *Proceedings of the Academy of Management*, 1982, 112–116.

——, "Harvest from the Archives: The Search for Fayol and Carlioz," *Journal of Management*, 11, 1985, 43–54.

Breeze, John D., and Arthur G. Bedeian, *The Administrative Writings of Henri Fayol: A Bibliographic Investigation*, 2nd ed. Monticello, IL: Vance, 1988.

Bryant, K. L., and H. C. Dethloff, *A History of American Business*. Englewood Cliffs, NJ: Prentice-Hall, 1983.

Buno, A. F., J. L. Bowditch, and J. W. Lewis, III, "When Cultures Collide: The Anatomy of A Merger," *Human Relations*, 5, March, 1985, 477–500.

Burke, James, *Connections*. Boston, MA: Little, Brown, 1978.

——, *The Day the Universe Changed*. Boston, MA: Little Brown, 1985.

Caplan, Gayle, and Mary Teese, *Survivors: How to Keep Your Best People on Board after Downsizing*. Palo Alto, CA: Davies-Black, 1997.

Carroll, Archie B., "The Pyramid of Corporate Social Responsibility: Towards a Moral Management of Organizational Stakeholders," *Business Horizons*, 34(4), 1991, 39–48.

Carroll, Stephen J. and Henry L. Tosi, Jr., *Management by Objectives*. New York: Macmillan, 1973.

Carson, Paula P., Kerry D. Carson, and Ronald R. Heady, "Cecil Alec Mace: The Man Who Discovered Goal Setting," *International Journal of Public Administration,* 17(9), 1994, 1679–1708.

Carter, Nancy M., "Review of General and Industrial Management," *Academy of Management Review*, 11, 1986, 454–456.

Cartwright, S. and C. L. Cooper, "The Role of Culture Compatibility in Successful Organizations," *Academy of Management Executive,* 7(2), 1993, 57–71.

Cass, E. L., and F. G. Zimmer, (Eds.), *Man and Work in Society*. New York: Van Nostrand Reinhold, 1975.

Chamberlain, Neil W., *Enterprise and Environment*. New York: McGraw-Hill, 1968, chaps. 2, 3.

Chandler, Alfred C., *Strategy and Structure*. Cambridge, MA: M.I.T. Press, 1962.

Chandler, Alfred D., Jr. *The Visible Hand: The Managerial Revolution in American Business*. Cambridge, MA: Harvard University Press, 1977.

Choi, T. Y. and O. C. Behling, "Top Managers and TQM Success: One More Look After All These Years," *Academy of Management Executive,* 11(1), 1997, 37–47.

Chung, K. H., and M. E. Friesen, "The Critical Success Factor Approach to Management at Boeing," *Journal of Management Systems,* 3(2), 1991, 27–40.

Clark, Wallace, *The Gantt Chart: A Working Tool of Management*. New York: Ronald, 1922.

Cochran, D. S., F. R. David, and C. K. Gibson "A Framework for Developing an Effective Mission Statement," *Journal of Business Strategies*, 2, 1986, 4–17.

Cohen, Ben, and Jerry Greenfield, *Ben & Jerry's Double Dip*. New York: Simon and Schuster, 1997.

Cohen, M. D., and J. G. March, *Leadership and Ambiguity*. New York: McGraw-Hill, 1974.

Cohen, M. D., J. G. March, and J. P. Olsen, "Garbage Can Model of Decision Making," *Administrative Science Quarterly*, 17, 1972, 1–25.

Combs, James G., "An Analysis of the Administrative Profiles of the First Two Mass Production Systems in America," *International Journal of Public Administration,* 18, 1995, 987–1006.

Cooke, Morris L., *Our Cities Awake*. New York: Doubleday, 1918.

Copley, F. B., *Frederick W. Taylor: Father of Scientific Management*, vols. 1 and 2. New York: Harper and Brothers, 1923.

Crawford-Mason, C. and L. Dobyns, *Quality or Else*. Boston: Houghton Mifflin, 1991.

Crosby, Alfred W. *The Measure of Reality: Quantification and Western Society*. New York: Cambridge University Press, 1996.

Crosby, Philip, *Quality Is Free: The Art of Hassle-Free Management*. Milwaukee, WI: American Society for Quality Control, 1979.

Cross, K. F., J. J. Jones, and R. L. Lynch, *Corporate Renaissance: The Art of Reengineering*. Cambridge, MA: Blackwell Publishing, 1994.

Cushmano, M., and R. Solby, *Microsoft Secrets*. New York: Free Press, 1995.

Cyert, Richard, "Herbert Simon," *Challenge*, 22, Sept.–Oct. 1979, 62–64.

Dansereau, F., G. B. Graen, and W. Haga, "A Vertical Dyad Linkage Approach to Leadership in Formal Organizations," *Organizational Behavior and Human Performance,* 13(1), 1975, 46–78.

Deal, T. E., and W. A. Jenkins, *Managing the Hidden Organization*. New York: Warner Books, 1994.

Deal, T. E., and A. A. Kennedy, "Culture: A New Look through Old Lenses," *Journal of Applied Behavioral Science*, 19, 1983, 498–505.

▲ REFERENCES   Deal, T. E. and A. A. Kennedy, *Corporate Culture: The Rites and Rituals of Corporate Life.* Reading, MA: Addison Wesley, 1982.

De Bono, Edward, *Serious Creativity.* New York: Harper Business, 1992.

Dechant, Kathleen, and Barbara Altman. "Environmental Leadership: From Compliance to Competitive Advantage," *Academy of Management Executive,* 8(3), 1994, 7–16.

De Geus, Arie, *The Living Company: Habits for Survival in a Turbulent Business Environment.* Boston, MA: Harvard University Press, 1997.

Demarie, L. B., and E. W. Keats, "Deregulation, Reengineering, and Cultural Transformation at Arizona Public Service Company," *Organizational Dynamics,* 23, Jan. 1996, 70–76.

Deming, W. Edward, *Out of Crisis.* Cambridge, MA: MIT Center for Advanced Engineering Study, 1982.

Deming, W. E., *Out of Crisis.* Cambridge, MA: MIT Center for Advanced Study, 1986.

Denison, D. R., "Bringing Corporate Culture to the Bottom Line," *Organizational Dynamics,* 12(2), Autumn 1984, 5–22.

Dennison, Henry S., *Organization Engineering.* New York: McGraw-Hill, 1931.

Deshpandé, Rohit, John Farley, and Frederick Webster, "Factors Affecting Organizational Performance: A Five-Country Comparison," Marketing Science Institute *Insights,* MSI Rep. 97-108, Fall 1997, 1–2.

Diebold, J. T. *Automation: The Advent of the Automatic Factory.* New York: Van Nostrand, 1952.

Dierks, Wayne, and Kathleen McNally, "Incentives You Can Bank On," *Personnel Administrator,* 32(3), Mar. 1987, 61–64.

Donaldson, Gordon, *Corporate Restructuring: Managing the Change Process from Within.* Boston, MA: Harvard Business School Press, 1994.

Donleavy, G. D., "Evaluating the Potential of Office Robots," *Long-Range Planning,* 27(2), 1994, 119–127.

Dowd, Ann R., "What Managers Can Learn from Manager Reagan," *Fortune*, Sept. 15, 1986, 33–41.

Dror, Y., "Muddling through: Science or Inertia?," *Public Administration Review*, 24, 1964, 16–25.

Drucker, Peter F., *The Practice of Management.* New York: Harper and Row, 1954.

——, *Management: Tasks, Responsibilities, Practices.* New York: Harper and Row, 1973.

——, *Innovation and Entrepreneurship.* New York: Harper and Row, 1985.

——, *The Frontiers of Management.* New York: Talley Books, 1986.

——, *The New Realities.* New York: Harper and Row, 1989.

Drury, Horace B., *Scientific Management: A History and Criticism.* New York: Longmans, Green, 1922.

Dumville, James C., and Francisco A. Torano, "Division of Labor, Efficient? Empirical Evidence to Support the Argument," *S.A.M. Advanced Management Journal,* 62(2), 1997, 16–20.

Duncan, W. Jack, "The History and Philosophy of Administrative Thought: A Societal Overview," *Business and Society*, 11, Spring 1971, 24–30.

——, "Ethical Issues in the Development and Use of Business and Management Knowledge," *Journal of Business Ethics*, 5, 1986, 391–400.

——, "When Necessity Becomes a Virtue: The Case for Taking Strategy Seriously," *Journal of General Management*, 13, Winter 1987, 28–42.

——, *Great Ideas in Management.* San Francisco, CA: Jossey-Bass, 1989.

Duncan, W. Jack, Peter M. Ginter, and Stuart A. Capper, "General and Functional Level Health Care Managers: Neither Manage Very Much," *Health Services Management Research,* 7(2), 1994, 91–98.

Duncan, W. Jack, Peter M. Ginter, and W. Keith Kreidel. "A Sense of Direction in Public Organizations: An Analysis of Mission Statements in State Health Departments," *Administration & Society,* 26(1), 1994, 11–27.

Duncan, W. Jack and C. Ray Gullett, "Henry Sturgis Dennison: The Manager and the Social Critic," *Journal of Business Research*, 2, 1974, 133–146.

Duncan, W. J. and J. G. Van Matre, "The Gospel According to Deming: Is It Really Different,? *Business Horizons,* 33, July/Aug. 1990, 3–9.

Dunn, Philip, "Officer Do Right," *American Hospital Association News,* Nov. 10, 1997, 7.

Durant, Will, and Ariel Durant, *The Lessons of History.* New York: Simon and Schuster, 1968.

Eisenberg, Daniel J., "The Tactics of Strategic Opportunism," *Harvard Business Review*, 65, Mar./Apr. 1987, 92–97.

Emerson, Harrington, *Efficiency as a Basis for Operations and Wages,* 4th ed., revised and enlarged. Easton, PA: Hive Publishing, reprint 63, 1976. (Original publication 1908).

——, *The Twelve Principles of Efficiency.* New York: Engineering Magazine, 1913.

"Executive Pay," *Business Week,* Apr. 21, 1997, 58–66ff.

"Factory Robots: Bodybuilding without Tears," *The Economist,* Apr. 21, 1990, 94–95.

Fairhurst, Gail T., and Robert A. Sarr, *The Art of Framing: Managing the Language of Leadership.* San Francisco, CA: Jossey-Bass, 1996.

"Farewell Pretoria," *Newsweek*, June 23, 1997, 58.

Farkas, Charles M., and Philippe De Backer, *Maximum Leadership.* New York: Henry Holt, 1996.

Fayol, Henri, *General and Industrial Management*, Trans. Constance Storrs. London: Pitman, 1949.

Feeney, E. J., J. R. Staelin, R. M. O'Brien, and A. Dickinson, "Increasing Sales Performance among Airline Reservation Personnel," in R. M. O'Brien, A. M. Dickinson, and M. P. Rosow (Eds.), *Industrial Behavior Modification: A Management Handbook.* New York: Pergamon, 1982, 141–158.

Felder, R., J. Savory, K. Margrey, J. Holman, and J. Boyd, "Development of a Robotic Near-Patient Testing Laboratory," *Archives of Pathology and Laboratory Medicine,* 119(10), 1995, 948–951.

Ferris, Timothy, *Coming of Age in the Milky Way.* New York: Morrow, 1988.

Fiedler, Fred E., *A Theory of Leadership Effectiveness.* New York: McGraw-Hill, 1967.

——, "The Contingency Model: New Directions for Leadership Utilization," *Journal of Contemporary Business*, 3, 1974, 65–80.

——, "Life in a Pretzel-Shaped Universe," in Arthur G. Bedeian (Ed.), *Management Laureates: A Collection of Autobiographical Essays.* Greenwich, CT: JAI Press, 1992, 303–333.

Fiegenbaum, Avi, Stuart Hart, and Dan Schendel, "Strategic Reference Point Theory," *Strategic Management Journal,* 17(3), 1996, 219–235.

Floyd, Steven W., and Bill Wooldridge, "Dinosaurs or Dynamos? Recognizing Middle Management's Strategic Role," *Academy of Management Executive,* 8(4), 1994, 47–57.

Follett, Mary Parker, *Creative Experience.* New York: Longmans, Green, 1924, 101–102.

Fombrun, Charles, "Is There a Financial Benefit to a Good Corporate Reputation?," *Stern Business,* 4(2), 1997, 9–11.

Ford, Robert N., "Job Enrichment Lessons from AT&T," *Harvard Business Review*, 51, Jan./Feb. 1973, 95–99.

Frangos, Stephen J., and Steven J. Bennett, *Team Zebra.* Essex Junction, VT: Oliver Wright, 1993.

Frederick, William C., *Values, Nature, and Culture in the American Corporation.* New York: Oxford University Press, 1995.

French, John R. P., and Bertram H. Raven, "The Bases of Social Power," in Darwin Cartwright (Ed.), *Studies in Social Power.* Ann Arbor, MI: University of Michigan, Institute for Social Research, 1959.

▲ *REFERENCES* Frey, L. W., "The Maligned F. W. Taylor: A Reply to His Many Critics," *Academy of Management Review*, 1, 1976, 124–139.

Friedman, Georges, *The Anatomy of Work*. Glencoe, IL: Free Press, 1961.

Friedman, Milton, "The Social Responsibility of Business Is to Increase Its Profits," *New York Times Magazine*, Sept. 13, 1970, 32–33, 122–126.

Friesen, Michael E., and James A. Johnson, *The Success Paradigm*. Westport, CT, 1995.

Fritz, Robert, *Corporate Tides*. San Francisco, CA: Barrett-Koehler, 1996.

Froehlich, L., "Babbage Observed," *Datamation*, 31(6), 1985, 119–124.

Frost, Peter J., Special Issue on Organizational Symbolism: Introduction, Peter J. Frost (Guest Ed.), *Journal of Management*, 11, 1985, 5–12.

Gallerman, Saul, "Why Good Managers Make Bad Ethical Choices," *Harvard Business Review*, 64, July/Aug. 1986, 85–90.

Gantt, H. L., *Work, Wages, and Profits*. New York: Engineering Magazine, 1910.

——, *Organizing for Work*. New York: Harcourt, Brace, Jovanovich, 1919.

Gardner, M., "Creating A Corporate Culture for the Eighties," *Business Horizons,* 27, Jan./Feb. 1985, 59–63.

Gates, Bill (with Nathan Myhrvold and Peter Rinearson), *The Road Ahead*. New York: Penguin, 1996.

Gaucher, E. and R. J. Coffee, *Total Quality in Healthcare*. San Francisco: Jossey-Bass, 1993.

General Motors Public Interest Report. Detroit, MI: General Motors, May 15, 1985.

George, Claude S., Jr., *The History of Management Thought*, 2nd ed. Englewood Cliffs, NJ: Prentice-Hall, 1972.

Georgiou, Petro, "The Goal Paradigm and Notes Towards a Counter Point," *Administrative Science Quarterly*, 18, 1973, 291–310.

Gilbreth, Frank B., "Motion Study," in *Scientific Management Course. A Landmark Series of Lectures Given at the YMCA*, (Worchester, MA), 1912, p. 3. (Reprinted as no. 77 in the Hive Management History Series, 1980.)

Gilbreth, Frank B., and Lillian M. Gilbreth, *Applied Motion Study*. Sturgis and Walton, 1917. (Reprinted as no. 28 in the Hive Management History Series, 1973.)

Gilbreth, F. B., Jr. and E. G. Carey, *Cheaper By the Dozen*. New York: Crowell Publishing, 1948.

Gilbreth, Lillian M., *The Psychology of Management*. Easton, PA: Hive Publishing, 1973a. (Original publication 1914.)

——, *The Quest for the One Best Way: A Sketch of the Life of Frank Bunker Gilbreth*. Easton, PA: Hive Publishing, 1973b (Reprint).

Ginter, P. M., A. C. Rucks, and W. J. Duncan, "Planners' Perceptions of the Strategic Management Process," *Journal of Management Studies*, 22, 1985, 581–596.

Ginter, P. M., L. E. Swayne, W. J., Duncan, and A. G. Shelfer, "When Merger Means Death: Organizational Euthanasia and Strategic Choice," *Organizational Dynamics,* 20(3), 1992, 134–141.

Gioia, D. A. and K Chittipeddi, "Sensemaking and Sensegiving in Strategic Change Initiation," *Strategic Management Journal,* 12, 1991, 433–448.

Goodman, Paul S., and Eric D. Darr, "Exchanging Best Practices through Computer-Aided Systems," *Academy of Management Executive,* 10(2), 1996, 7–18.

Graedel, T. E., and B. R. Allenby, *Industrial Ecology*. Englewood Cliffs, NJ: Prentice-Hall, 1995.

Graen, G. B., and M. Uhl-Bien, "Relationship-Based Approach to Leadership: Development of Leader-Member Exchange (LMX) Theory of Leadership over 25 Years," *Leadership Quarterly,* 6(2), 1995, 219–247.

Graham, Pauline (Ed.), *Mary Parker Follett—Prophet of Management: A Celebration of Writings from the 1920's*. Cambridge, MA: Harvard Business School Press, 1995.

Greenwood, Ronald G., Alfred A. Bolton, and Regina A. Greenwood, "Hawthorne Half Century Later," *Journal of Management*, 9, 1983, 217–231.

Greenwood, Ronald G., and Charles D. Wrege, "The Hawthorne Studies," in D. Wren (Ed.) and J. A. Pearce, II (Associate Ed.), *Papers Dedicated to the Development of Modern Management*. Academy of Management Centennial Commemorative Volume, 1986, 24–35.

Greenwood, Royston, and C. R. Hining, "Understanding Radical Organizational Change: Bringing Together the Old and New Institutionalism," *Academy of Management Review,* 21(4), 1996, 1022–1054.

Grove, Andrew S., *High Output Management.* New York: Vintage Books, 1985.

Grugal, Robin M., "Hotelier J. W. Marriott: Developing the Knack for Running a Service Business," *Investor's Business Daily,* Oct. 30, 1997a, A1, A9.

——, "Baan N.V.'s Jan Baan: Using His Business' Stelar Profits to Serve the Almighty," *Investor's Business Daily,* Dec. 12, 1997b, A1, A12.

Grundstein, Nathan D., *The Managerial Kant.* Cleveland, OH: Weatherhead School of Management, Case Western Reserve University, 1981.

Guest, R. H., "On Time and the Foreman," *Personnel*, May 1956, 478–480.

Gulick, Luther, and Lyndall Urwick (Eds.), *Papers on the Science of Administration*, 2nd ed. New York: Institute of Public Administration, 1947.

Haber, Samuel, *Efficiency and Uplift: Scientific Management in the Progressive Era 1890–1930*. Chicago, IL: University of Chicago Press, 1964.

Hafsi, Taieb, Moses N. Kiggundu, and Jan J. Jorgensen, "Strategic Apex Configurations in State-Owned Enterprises," *Academy of Management Review*, 12, 1987, 714–730.

Halberstam, David, "Robots Enter Our Lives," *Parade*, Apr. 10, 1983, 19.

Hales, C. P., "What Managers Do: A Critical Review of the Evidence," *Journal of Management Studies*, 23, Jan. 1986, 88–115.

Hall, Francine S., and Elizabeth L. Hall, "The ADA: Going beyond the Law," *Academy of Management Executive,* 8(1), 1994, 17–26.

Hall, G., J. Rosenthal, and J. Wade, "How to Make Reengineering Really Work," *Harvard Business Review,* 71, Jan./Feb. 1993, 119–131.

Hamel, Gary, "Killer Strategies: That Make Shareholders Rich," *Fortune,* June 23, 1997, 70–84.

Hamel, Gary, and C. K. Prahalad, "Competing in the New Economy: Managing out of Bounds," *Strategic Management Journal,* 17(1), 1996, 237–242.

Hamel, Ruth, "Robots Steer Automaking into the Future," *USA Today*, July 2, 1984, 1B.

Hammer, M. and J. Champy, *Reengineering the Corporation: A Manifesto for Business Revolution.* New York: Harper and Row, 1993.

Handy, Charles, *The Age of Paradox.* Boston, MA: Harvard Business School Press, 1994.

——, *Gods of Management.* New York: Oxford University Press, 1995.

Harper, Stephen C., "The Challenges Facing CEOs: Past, Present, and Future," *Academy of Management Executive,* 6(3), 1992, 7–25.

Harris, Douglas H. (Ed.), *Organizational Linkages: Understanding the Productivity Paradox.* Washington, DC: National Academy Press, 1996.

Harris, S. G. and R. I. Sutton, "Functions of Parting Ceremonies in Dying Organizations," *Academy of Management Journal,* 29, 1986, 5–30.

Hart, D. K., and W. G. Scott, "The Optimal Image of Man for Systems Theory," *Academy of Management Journal*, 15, 1972, 530–537.

Hart, Stuart L., "A Natural-Resource-Based View of the Firm," *Academy of Management Review,* 20(4), 1995, 986–1014.

Hartley, Robert F., *Management Mistakes and Successes*, 3rd ed. New York: Wiley, 1991.

Hayakawa, S. I., "On Motivation," *Etc.*, Spring 1958, 26–27.

▲ *REFERENCES*   Heilbroner, Robert L., *The Worldly Philosophers*, 3rd ed, newly revised. New York: Simon and Schuster, 1967.

Herzberg, Frederick, *Work and the Nature of Man*. Cleveland, OH: World Publishing, 1966.

Herzberg, Frederick, B. Mausner, R. O. Peterson, and F. Capwell, *Job Attitudes: Review of Research and Opinion*. Pittsburgh, PA: Psychological Services of Pittsburgh, 1957.

Herzberg, Frederick, B. Mausner, and B. Snyderman, *The Motivation to Work*. New York: Wiley, 1959.

Herzlinger, Regina A, *Market-Driven Health Care: Who Wins, Who Loses in the Transformation of America's Largest Service Industry*. Reading, MA: Addison-Wesley, 1997.

Hickson, D., D. Pugh, and D. Pheysey, "Operations Technology and Organization Structure: An Empirical Reappraisal," *Administrative Science Quarterly*, 14, 1969, 378–397.

Higgins, Kevin, "Computerized Slot Machines Motivating Employees to Improve Their Productivity," *Marketing News*, 17, 1983, 1–10.

Hill, Linda A., *Becoming a Manager: Mastery of a New Identity*. Boston, MA: Harvard Business School Press, 1992.

Hoagland, John H., "Management before Taylor," in Paul M. Dauten (Ed.), *Emerging Concepts in Management*. Boston, MA: Houghton Mifflin, 1957, 19–39.

Holmes, S. and S. Marsden, "An Exploration of the Espoused Organizational Culture of Public Accounting Firms," *Accounting Horizons*, 10(3), Sept. 1996, 26–53.

Holmstrom, J., and P. Aavikko, "Achieving a Management Breakthrough in Inbound Logistics by Improving the Efficacy of Operational Decisions," *Production and Inventory Management Journal*, July 1994, 1–8.

Hoskisson, Robert E., and Michael A. Hitt, *Downscoping: How to Tame the Diversified Firm*. New York: Oxford University Press, 1994.

Hosmer, LaRue T., *The Ethics of Management*. Homewood, IL: Richard D. Irwin, 1987.

House, Robert J., and Terence R. Mitchell, "Path-Goal Theory of Leadership," *Journal of Contemporary Business*, 3, 1974, 81–97.

Hughes, R. L., R. C. Ginnett, and G. J. Curphy, *Leadership: Enhancing the Lessons of Experience*. Homewood, IL: Richard D. Irwin, 1993.

Irwin, Otis, "Observations of the Japanese Automotive Industry: Lessons for American Managers," *Industrial Management*, 29, May/June 1987, 5–8.

Ivancevich, John M., "A Longitudinal Assessment of Management by Objectives," *Administrative Science Quarterly*, 17, 1972, 119–127.

Ivancevich, John M., and Timothy MaMahon, "The Effects of Goal Setting, External Feedback, and Self-Generated Feedback on Outcome Variables," *Academy of Management Journal*, 25, 1982, 359–372.

"Jack Welch's Encore," *Business Week*, Oct. 28, 1996.

Jackofsky, Ellen F., John W. Slocum, Jr., and Sara J. McQuaid, "Cultural Values and the CEO: Alluring Comparisons?," *Academy of Management Executive*, 2(1), 1988, 39–50.

Jackson, Tim, *Inside Intel: Andy Grove and the Rise of the World's Most Powerful Chip Company*. New York: Dutton, 1997.

Jacques, E., *The Changing Culture of A Factory*. London: Tavistock Institute, 1951.

Johnson, Leonard W., and Alan L. Frochman, "Indentifying and Closing the Gap in the Middle of Organizations," *Academy of Management Executive*, 3(2), 1989, 107–114.

Jonas, Harry S., III, Ronald E. Fry, and Suresh Srivastva, "The Person of the CEO: Understanding the Executive Experience," *Academy of Management Executive*, 3(3), 1989, 205–215.

——, "The Office of the CEO: Understanding the Executive Experience," *Academy of Management Executive*, 4(3), 1990, 36–48.

Juran, J. M. and F. M. Gryna, Jr., *Quality Planning and Analysis*. New York: McGraw-Hill, 1980.

Kahn, W. A. and K. E. Kram, "Authority At Work: Internal Models and Their Organizational Consequences," *Academy of Management Review,* 19, Jan. 1994, 17–50.

Kakar, Sudhir, *Frederick Taylor: A Study in Personality and Innovation.* Cambridge, MA: MIT Press, 1970.

Kanigel, Robert, *The One Best Way: Frederick Winslow Taylor and the Enigma of Efficiency.* New York: Viking, 1997.

Kanter, Rosabeth, "The Case against Cowboy Management," *Management Review,* 76, Feb. 1987, 19–21.

Kantrow, Alan M., "Why History Matters to Managers," *Harvard Business Review,* 64, Jan./Feb. 1986, 81–88.

Katz, Robert L., "Skills of an Effective Administrator," *Harvard Business Review,* 33, Jan./Feb. 1955, 33–42.

Keenan, William, "A Gift for Rewards," *Sales and Marketing Management,* 147(3), pt. 1, 1995, 35–36.

Keidel, Robert W., "Rethinking Organizational Design," *Academy of Management Executive,* 8(4), 1994, 12–30.

Kerr, Steve, "On the Folly of Rewarding A, While Hoping for B," *Academy of Management Journal,* 18(4), 1974, 769–783.

Kiechel, Walter, III, "Managing Innovators," *Fortune,* Mar. 4, 1985, 181–182.

Kilmann, R. H., *Beyond the Quick Fix.* San Francisco, CA: Jossey-Bass, 1984.

Kilmann, R. H., M. J. Saxton, and R. Serpa, "Issues in Understanding and Changing Culture," *California Management Review,* 28(2), 1986, 87–94.

Kirkpatrick, S. A., and E. A. Locke, "Leadership: Do Traits Matter?," *Academy of Management Executive,* 5(1), 1991, 48–60.

Knouse, Stephen B., Paula Phillips Carson, and Kerry D. Carson, "W. Edwards Deming and Frederick Winslow Taylor: A Comparison of Two Leaders Who Shaped the World's View of Management," *International Journal of Public Administration,* 16(10), 1993, 1621–1658.

Komaki, J., W. M. Waddell, and M. G. Pearce, "The Applied Behavioral Analysis Approach and Individual Employees: Improving Performance in Two Small Businesses," *Organizational Behavior and Human Performance,* 25, 1977, 337–352.

Kotter, John P., *The General Managers.* New York: Free Press, 1982.

——, *A Force for Change: How Leadership Differs from Management.* New York: Free Press, 1990.

——, *Leading Change.* Boston, MA: Harvard University Press, 1996.

Kotter, J. P. and J. L. Haskett, *Corporate Culture and Performance.* New York: Free Press, 1992.

Kovach, Kenneth A., "What Motivates Employees? Workers and Supervisors Give Different Answers," *Business Horizons,* 30, Sept.–Oct. 1987, 58–65.

Kraut, Allen I., Patricia R. Pedigo, Douglas D. McKenna, and Marvin D. Dunnette, "The Role of the Manager: What's Really Important in Different Management Jobs?," *Academy of Management Executive,* 3(4), 1989, 286–293.

Kronman, A. T., *Max Weber.* Palo Alto, CA: Stanford University Press, 1983.

Krupp, Sherman, *Pattern in Organizational Analysis: A Critical Examination.* New York: Holt, Rinehart, and Winston, 1961.

Kuhnert, K. W., "Transforming Leadership: Developing People through Delegation," in B. M. Bass and B. J. Avolio (Eds.), *Improving Organizational Effectiveness through Transformational Leadership.* Thousand Oaks, CA: Sage, 1994, 10–25.

Kunitoshi, J., "Application of Expert Systems for Coal Blending Design at Mizushima Works," *Iron and Steel Engineer,* 72, Aug. 1995, 39–43.

Lacey, Robert, *Ford: The Men and the Machine.* Boston, MA: Little, Brown, 1986.

▲ *REFERENCES*   Laverty, Kevin J., "Economic 'Short-Termism': The Debate, the Unresolved Issues, and the Implications for Management Practice and Research," *Academy of Management Review,* 21(9), 1996, 825–860.

Lawrence, Paul, and Jay Lorsch, *Organization and Environment.* Boston, MA: Graduate School of Business Administration, Division of Research, Harvard University, 1967.

Lee, James A., *The Gold and the Garbage in Management Theories and Prescriptions.* Athens, OH: Ohio University Press, 1980.

Lee, T. W., Locke, E. A., and S. H. Phan, "Explaining the Assigned Goal-Incentive Interaction: The Role of Self-Efficacy and Personal Goals," *Journal of Management,* 23(4), 1997, 541–560.

Levine, David I., *Reinventing the Workplace: How Business and Employees Can Both Win.* Washington, DC: Brookings Institution, 1995.

Levinson, Harry, "Between CEO and COO," *Academy of Management Executive,* 7(2), 1993, 71–81.

Levitt, Theodore, "The Dangers of Social Responsibility," *Harvard Business Review*, 36, Sept./Oct. 1958, 46–50.

——, *Thinking about Management.* New York: Free Press, 1991.

Liedtka, Jeanne M., "Collaborating across Lines of Business for Competitive Advantage," *Academy of Management Executive,* 10(2), 1996, 20–34.

Likert, Rensis, *New Patterns of Management.* New York: McGraw-Hill, 1961.

——, *The Human Organization.* New York: McGraw-Hill, 1967.

Likert, Rensis, and Jane G. Likert, *New Way of Managing Conflict.* New York: McGraw-Hill, 1976.

Lindblom, Charles E., "The Science of 'Muddling Through,' " *Public Administration Review*, 19, 1959, 79–88.

——, "Still Muddling, Not Yet Through*,*" *Public Administration Review*, 39, 1979, 517–526.

Locke, E. A., "The Ideas of Frederick W. Taylor: An Evaluation," *Academy of Management Review*, 7, 1982, 14–24.

Locke, E. A., and G. P. Latham, *Goal Setting for Individuals, Groups, and Organizations.* Chicago, IL: Science Research Associates, 1984.

Locke, E. A. and G. P. Latham, *Theory of Goal Setting and Task Performance.* Englewood Cliffs, NJ: Prentice-Hall, 1990.

Locke, Edwin A., Karyll N. Shaw, Lise M. Saari, and Gary P. Latham, "Goal Setting and Task Performance: 1969–1980," *Psychological Bulletin*, 90, 1981, 125–152.

Lombard, George F. F., "Relativism in Organizations," *Harvard Business Review*, 49, Mar./Apr. 1971, 55–56.

Loucks, Vernon, Jr., "A CEO Looks at Ethics," *Business Horizons*, 30, Mar./Apr. 1987, 2–6.

Luthans, Fred, "Successful vs. Effective Real Managers," *Academy of Management Executive,* 2(2), 1988, 127–132.

——, "A Common Man Travels back to the Future," in Arthur G. Bedeian (Ed.), *Management Laureates: A Collection of Autobiographical Essays,* vol. 4. Greenwich, CT: JAI Press, 1996, 153–199.

Luthans, Fred, Richard M. Hodgetts, and Stuart Rosenkrantz, *Real Managers,* Cambridge, MA: Ballinger, 1988.

Luthans, Fred, and Robert Kreitner, *Organizational Behavior Modification.* Glenview, IL: Scott, Foresman, 1975.

Luthans, Fred, S. A. Rosenkrantz, and H. W. Hennessey, "What Do Successful Managers Really Do? An Observation Study of Managerial Activities," *Journal of Applied Behavioral Science*, 21, 1985, 255–270.

Maccoby, Michael, *The Leader.* New York: Ballantine, 1981.

Mantz, Charles C., and Henry P. Sims, Jr., *Business without Bosses,* New York: Wiley, 1993.

March, James G., "The 1978 Nobel Prize in Economics," *Science,* 202, Nov. 24, 1978, 851–860.

March, James G., and Herbert A. Simon, *Organizations.* New York: Wiley, 1958.

"Marriott: Crusader for a Moral America," *Business Week,* Jan. 21, 1985, 75.

Marriott, J. W., Jr. and K.S. Brown, *The Spirit to Serve.* New York: Harper Collins, 1997.

Martin, J., M. S. Feldman, M. J. Hatch, and S. B. Sitkin, "The Uniqueness Paradox in Organizational Stories," *Administrative Science Quarterly,* 28, 1993, 438–453.

Martin, J. and C. Siehl, "Organizational Culture and CounRercultures: An Uneasy Symbiosis," *Organizational Dynamics,* 11, Autumn 1983, 52–64.

Maslow, Abraham, *Motivation and Personality,* 2nd ed. New York: Harper and Row, 1970.

Matsui, T., A. Okada, and O. Inoshita, "Mechanism of Feedback Affecting Task Performance," *Organizational Behavior and Human Performance,* 31, 1983, 114–122.

Mayo, G. E., *The Human Problems of an Industrial Society,* 2nd ed. Boston, MA: Division of Research, Harvard Business School; later published by Macmillan, New York, 1933.

——, *The Social Problems of an Industrial Society.* Boston, MA: Graduate School of Business Administration, Harvard University, 1945.

——, *The Political Problems of an Industrial Society.* Boston, MA: Graduate School of Business Administration, Harvard University, 1947.

McClelland, D. C., *The Achieving Society.* New York: Free Press, 1961.

——, "Managing Motivation to Expand Human Freedom," *American Psychologist,* 33, 1978, 201–210.

McClelland, D. C., and D. G. Winter, *Motivating Economic Achievement.* New York: Free Press, 1969.

McConkey, D. D., *How to Manage By Results.* New York: AMACON, 1983.

McFarland, Dalton E., "Whatever Happened to the Efficiency Movement?," *Conference Board Record,* 13, June 1976, 50–55.

McGregor, Douglas M., *The Human Side of Enterprise.* New York: McGraw-Hill, 1960.

McKean, Kevin, "Decisions, Decisions," *Discover,* 6, 1985, 22–27.

——, "They Fly in the Face of Danger," *Discover,* 7, Apr. 1986, 48–58.

McNamara, Robert S., *In Retrospect: The Tragedy and Lessons of Vietnam.* New York: Time Books, 1995.

Melohn, Thomas H., "Build Trust with Team Members," *Executive Excellence,* 12(6), 1995, 11–12.

Meyer, H. H., Emanuel Kay, and J. R. P. French, "Split Roles in Performance Appraisal," *Harvard Business Review,* 43, Jan./Feb., 1965, 123–129.

Mintzberg, Henry, *The Nature of Managerial Work.* New York: Harper and Row, 1973.

——, "The Manager's Job: Folklore and Fact," *Harvard Business Review,* 53, July/Aug. 1975, 49–61.

——, "Twenty-Five Years Later . . . The Illustrative Strategy," in Arthur G. Bedeian (Ed.), *Management Laureates: A Collection of Autobiographical Essays,* vol. 2. Greenwich, CT: JAI Press, 1993, 323–374.

Mirvis, Philip H., "Human Resource Management: Leaders, Laggards, and Followers," *Academy of Management Executive,* 11(2), 1997, 43–56.

Mitchell, T. R., *Motivation and Performance.* Chicago, IL: Science Research Associates, 1984.

Mitroff, Ian I., *Business Not as Usual.* San Francisco, CA: Jossey-Bass, 1987.

Mooney, J. D. and A. C. Reiley, *Onward Industry.* New York: Harper and Brothers, 1931.

——, *The Principles of Organization.* New York: Harper and Brothers, 1947.

Moore, J. Duncan, "Samaritan's Revolution," *Modern Healthcare,* July 29, 1996, 27–34.

Moran, Len, "Setting Sail with One Enterprise, One Mission, One Measure," *AT&T Magazine,* 1(1), 1984, 2–7.

▲ REFERENCES

Morita, Akio, with E. M. Reingold and Mitsuko Shimomura, *Made in Japan: Akio Morita and Sony*. New York: E.P. Dutton, 1986.

Morris, Betsy, "Big Blue," *Fortune,* Apr. 14, 1997, 68–81.

Morris, B., "The Wealth Builders," *Fortune,* Dec. 11, 1995, 15.

Moseley, Maboth, *Irascible Genius: A Life of Charles Babbage, Inventor*. London: Hutchinson, 1964.

Munsterberg, Hugo, *Psychology and Industrial Efficiency*. Boston, MA: Houghton Mifflin, 1913.

Murrin, T. T., "Productivity Needs a Game Plan." *Enterprise*, 7, October, 1984, 14.

Myers, Randy, "The Art of Partnering," *CFO: The Magazine for Chief Financial Officers,* Dec. 1995, 26–34.

Nadler, David A., Robert B. Shaw, A. Elise Walton, and Associates, *Discontinuous Change*. San Francisco, CA: Jossey-Bass, 1995.

Naisbitt, John, *Megatrends: Ten New Directions Transforming Our Lives*. New York: Warner Books, 1984.

Nelson, Robert B., *Empowering Employees through Delegation*. Burr Ridge, IL: Richard D. Irwin, 1994.

Nelson, Daniel, and Stuart Campbell, "Taylorism versus Welfare Work in American Industry: H. L. Gantt and the Bancrofts," *Business History Review*, 46(1), 1972, 1–16.

Neuhaus, C., "A Simon Who Is Not So Simple," *Discover*, 2, June 1981, 42 ff.

"Nintendo Wakes Up," *Economist,* Aug. 3, 1996, 55–56.

Noaker, Paula A., "The Search of Agile Manufacturing," *Manufacturing Engineering,* Nov. 1994, 40–43.

Nolan, T., "Understanding Variation," *Quality Progress,* May 1990, 70.

Northcraft, Gregory B., Terri L. Griffith, and Christina E. Shalley "Building Top Management Muscle in a Slow Growth Environment: How Different Is Better at Greyhound Financial Corporation," *Academy of Management Executive,* 6(1), 1992, 76–88.

Northhouse, Peter G., *Leadership: Theory and Practice*. Thousand Oaks, CA: Sage, 1997.

"One Tough [Expletive]," *Newsweek*, June 1, 1998, 50.

Overman, Stephenie, "Saturn Teams Working and Profiting," *HRMagazine,* 40(3), Mar. 1995, 72–74.

Owen, Robert, *A New View of Society*. New York: E. Bliss and White, 1825.

Ozkarahan, I., "Allocation of Surgical Procedures to Operating Rooms," *Journal of Medical Systems,* 19(4), 1995, 333–352.

Parker, J., *Cross-Functional Teams*. San Francisco, Jossey-Bass, 1994.

Pearce, John A., II, and Fred David. "Corporate Mission Statements: The Botton Line," *Academy of Management Executive*, 1, 1987, 109–116.

Peck, M. Scott, *A World Waiting to Be Born*. New York: Bantam, 1993.

Pecotich, Anthony, and G. A. Churchill, Jr., "An Examination of the Anticipated Satisfaction Importance Valence Controversy," *Organizational Behavior and Human Performance*, 27, 1981, 210–215.

Perrow, Charles, *Normal Accidents: Living with High Risk Technology*. New York: Basic Books, 1984.

Peters, Tom, and Nancy Austin, *A Passion for Excellence*. New York: Random House, 1985.

Peters, T. J. and R. H. Waterman, *In Search of Excellence*. New York: Harper and Row, 1982.

Peterson, P. B., "Correspondence from Henry L. Gantt to an Old Friend Reveals New Information about Gantt," *Journal of Management*, 12, 1986, 339–350.

Pfeffer, Jeffrey, *Power in Organizations*. Marshfield, MA: Pitman, 1981.

Pfiffner, J. M. and F. P. Sherwood, *Administrative Organization*. Englewood Cliffs, NJ: Prentice-Hall, 1960

Pitcher, Patricia, *The Drama of Leadership*. New York: Wiley, 1997.

Pitt, Barrie, *The Battle of the Atlantic*. Alexandria, VA: Time-Life, 1977.

Poindexter, Joseph, "Voices of Authority," *Psychology Today*, Aug. 1983, 53–61.

Posner, B. Z., J. M. Kouzes, and W. H. Schmidt, "Shared Values Make A Difference: An Empirical Test of Corporate Culture," *Human Resource Management,* 24(3), 1985, 293–309.

Pugh, D. S., D. J. Hickson, C. R. Hinings, and C. Turner, "Dimensions of Organizational Structure," *Administrative Science Quarterly,* 13, 1968, 65–91.

"Quality Watch," *Hospital & Health Networks,* February 5, 1996, 14.

Quick, Jonathan D., Debra L. Nelson, and James C. Quick, "Successful Executives: How Independent?," *Academy of Management Executive*, 1, 1987, 139–145.

Quinn, James B., "Strategic Change: Logical Incrementalism," *Sloan Management Review*, 20(1), 1978, 7–22.

——, "Managing Strategic Change," *Sloan Management Review*, 21(4), 1980a, 3–20.

——, *Strategies for Change: Logical Incrementalism*. Homewood, IL: Irwin, 1980b.

Ragins, B. R., B. Townsend, and M. Mattis, "Gender Gap in the Executive Suite: CEOs and Female Executives Report on Breaking the Glass Ceiling," *Academy of Management Executive,* 12(1), 1998, 28–42

Rago, W. V., "Struggles in Transformation: A Study of TQM, Leadership, and Organizational Culture In A Government Agency," *Public Administration Review,* 56(3), May/June 1996, 227–235.

Raia, A. P., *Management by Objectives*. Glenview, IL: Scott Foresman, 1974.

Rathe, A. W. (Ed), *Gantt on Management*. New York: American Management Association, 1961.

Reed, Richard, David J. Lemak, and W. Andrew Hesser, "Cleaning up after the Cold War: Management and Social Issues," *Academy of Management Review,* 22(3), 1997, 614–642.

Reichers, Arnon E., John P. Wanous, and James T. Austin, "Understanding and Managing Cynicism about Organizational Change," *Academy of Management Executive,* 11(1), 1997, 48–59.

Richardson, Nigel, "Business Ethics," *Management Accounting,* 74(7), 1996, 60–61.

Ritzky, Gary M., "Incentive Pay Programs that Help the Bottom Line," *HRMagazine,* Apr. 1995, 68–74.

Roach, John, "Simon Says: Decision Making Is a 'Satisficing' Experience," *Management Review*, 68, Jan. 1979, 8–17.

Robinson, Edward A., "Frogs, Bears, and Orgasms: Think Zany If You Want to Reach Today's Customers," *Fortune,* June 9, 1997, 153–156.

"Robotics: Artificial Workers Are Making a Comeback," *The Economist,* Sept. 28, 1996, 122.

"Robotics: Right Rx for Drug Errors," *Hospital and Health Networks,* 1995, 20.

——, *Man-In-Organizations*. Cambridge, MA: Harvard University Press, 1968.

Roethlisberger, F. J., *Management and Morale*. Cambridge, MA: Harvard University Press, 1941.

——, *The Elusive Phenomena*. Boston, MA: Division of Research, Harvard Business School, 1977.

Roethlisberger, F. J., and W. J. Dickson, *Management and the Worker*. Cambridge, MA: Harvard University Press, 1939.

Rommel, Gunter, Jurgen Kluge, Rolf-Dieter Kempis, Raimund Diederichs, and Felix Burck, *Simplicity Wins: How Germany's Mid-Sized Industrial Companies Succeed*. Boston, MA: Harvard Business Press, 1995.

Rosenberg, N. *The American System of Manufacturers, 1854–5*. Edinburgh: University of Edinburgh Press, 1969.

Rubin, Harriet, *The Princess: Machiavelli for Women*. New York: Doubleday/Currency, 1997.

Schein, E. H., *Organizational Culture and Leadership*. San Francisco: Jossey-Bass, 1985.

▲ *REFERENCES* Schlender, Brent, "On the Road with Chairman Bill," *Fortune,* May 26, 1997, 72, 81.

Schoenberger, Richard J., *World Class Manufacturing: The Next Decade.* New York: Free Press, 1996.

Scholz, C., "Corporate Culture and Strategy: The Problem with Strategic Fit," *Long-Range Planning,* 20(8), Aug. 1987, 80–90.

Schriesheim, Chester A., and Barbara J. Bird, "Contributions of the Ohio State Studies to the Field of Leadership," *Journal of Management,* 5, 1979, 135–145.

Schwartz, H.S., "The Postmodern Organization: Mastering the Art of the Irreversible," *Academy of Management Review,* 20(1), Jan. 1995, 215–222

Schwartz, Peter, *The Art of the Long View.* New York: Doubleday/Currencies Publishing, 1991.

Scott, W. E., Jr., "The Development of Knowledge in Organizational Behavior and Human Performance," *Decision Sciences,* 6, 1975, 142–165.

Scott, W. E., Jr., and P. M. Podsakoff, *Behavioral Principles in the Practice of Management.* New York: Wiley, 1985.

Scott, William G., *Chester I. Barnard and the Guardians of the Managerial State.* Lawrence, KS: University of Kansas Press, 1992.

Scott-Morgan, Peter, *The Unwritten Rules of the Game.* New York: McGraw-Hill, 1994.

Sculley, John, *Odyssey.* New York: Harper and Row, 1987.

Senge, Peter M., *The Fifth Discipline.* New York. Currency Doubleday, 1990.

Shartle, Carrol L., "Early Years of the Ohio State University Leadership Studies," *Journal of Management,* 5, 1979, 127–134.

Sheldon, Oliver, *The Philosophy of Management.* London: Sir Isaac Pitman, 1923.

Sheriff, Don R. *Administrative Behavior: A Quantitative Case Study Six Organizations.* Monograph 12, Center for Labor and Management, University of Iowa, Jan. 1969.

Sherman, Strat, "Stretch Goals: The Dark Side of Asking for Miracles," *Fortune,* 132. Nov. 1995, 231–233.

Shetty, Y. K., "Quality, Productivity, and Profit Performance: Learning from Research and Practice," *National Productivity Review,* 5, Spring 1986, 166–174.

Shrivastava, Paul, "Ecocentric Management for a Risk Society," *Academy of Management Review,* 20(1), 1995, 118–137.

Simon, Herbert A., "The Proverbs of Administration," *Public Administration Review,* 6, 1946, 53–67.

——, *The New Science of Management Decision.* New York: Harper and Brothers, 1960.

——, *Administrative Behavior,* 3rd ed. New York: Free Press, 1976. (Original publication 1946.)

——, "Making Management Decisions: The Role of Intuition and Emotion," *Academy of Management Executive,* 1, Feb. 1987, 57–64.

Sims, Henry P., and Charles C. Manz *Company of Heroes.* New York: Wiley, 1996.

Skinner, B. F., *Science and Behavior.* New York: Free Press, 1953.

——, *Beyond Freedom and Dignity.* New York: Alfred A. Knoff, 1971.

——, *About Behaviorism.* New York: Alfred A. Knoff, 1974.

Slocum, John W., "Opel Eisenach GmbH—Creating a High-Productivity Workplace," *Organizational Dyanmics,* Spring 1996, 80–85.

Smart, T., "Jack Welch's Encore," *Business Week,* Oct. 28, 1996, 26.

Smiddy, Harold, "Wallace Clark's Contribution to International Management," *Advanced Management Journal,* 23, Mar. 1958, 17–26.

Smith, Adam, *An Inquiry into the Nature and Causes of the Wealth of Nations.* New York: Modern Library, 1937. (Original publication 1776.)

Sowell, Thomas, *Knowledge and Decisions.* New York: Basic Books, 1980.

Spriegel, W. R., and C. E. Myers (Eds.), *The Writings of the Gilbreths*. Homewood, IL: Richard D. Irwin, 1953.

Stacey, R., "Strategy As Order Emerging from Chaos," *Long- Range Planning,* 26(1), 1993, 10–17.

Stewart, Rosemary, "The Nature of Management: A Problem for Management Education," *Journal of Management Studies*, 21, 1984, 323–330.

Stogdill, Ralph M., "Personal Factors Associated with Leadership: A Survey of the Literature," *Journal of Psychology,* 25(1), 1948, 35–71.

——, *Handbook of Leadership: A Survey of Theory and Research.* New York: Free Press, 1974a.

——, "Historical Trends in Leadership Theory and Research," *Journal of Contemporary Business*, 3, Autumn 1974b, 1–17.

Stroh, Linda K., and Anne H. Reilly, "Loyalty in the Age of Downsizing," *Sloan Management Review,* 38, Summer 1997, 83–86.

Sunoo, Brenda P., "Company Gifts Say You Care about Your Employees," *Personnel Journal,* 74(10), 1995, 149–150.

Taylor, F. W., "A Piece-Rate System, Being a Step Toward Partial Solution of the Labor Problem," *Transactions of the American Society of Mechanical Engineers*, 16, 1895, 856–883.

——, *Shop Management.* New York: Harper and Brothers, 1903.

——, *The Principles of Scientific Management.* New York: Harper and Brothers, 1914.

Tead, Ordway, *Instincts in Industry: A Study of Working Class Psychology.* Boston, MA: Houghton Mifflin, 1918.

——, *Human Nature and Management.* New York: McGraw-Hill, 1929.

——, *The Art of Leadership.* New York: McGraw-Hill, 1935.

——, *The Art of Administration.* New York: McGraw-Hill, 1951.

"The Quality March: National Survey Profiles Quality Improvement Activities," *Hospital & Health Networks,* Dec. 5, 1993, 55.

Thompson, James D., *Organizations in Action.* New York: McGraw-Hill, 1967.

Thompson, K. R., "Confronting the Paradoxes In A Total Quality Environment," *Organizational Dynamics,* 26(3), 1998, 62–74.

Thorlakson, Alan J. H., and Robert P. Murray, "An Empirical Study of Empowerment in the Workplace," *Group and Organizational Management,* 21(1), 1996, 67–83.

Tichy, Noel, and S. Sherman, *Control Your Destiny or Someone Else Will,* New York: Doubleday, 1993.

Towne, H. R., "The Engineer As Economist," *Transactions of the American Society of Mechanical Engineers,* 7, 1886, 428–429.

Trice, M. M. and J. M. Beyer, "Studying Organizational Culture through Rites and Ceremonies," *Academy of Management Review,* 9(4), 1994, 653–669.

Trombely, Kenneh E., *The Life and Times of a Happy Liberal: Morris Llewellyn Cooke.* New York: Harper and Row, 1954.

Twain, Mark, *Life on the Mississippi.* New York: Harper and Brothers, 1899.

Ure, Andrew, *The Philosophy of Manufactures: On an Exposition of the Scientific, Moral, and Commercial Economy of the Factory System of Great Britain.* London: Charles Knight, 1835.

Urwick, L., "The Functions of Administration: With Special Reference to the Work of Henri Fayol," in Luther Gulick and L. Urwick (Eds.), *Papers on the Science of Administration.* New York: Institute of Public Administration, 1947.

Urwick, Lyndall F. *Elements of Administration.* London: Harper and Brothers, 1944.

——, *Freedom and Coordination: Lectures in Business Organization by Mary Parker Follett.* London: Pitman, 1949.

▲ *REFERENCES*

——, *Notes on the Theory of Organization.* New York: American Management Association, 1952.

——, "Papers on the Science of Administration," *Academy of Management Journal,* 8, 1972, 362–364.

——, (Ed.), *The Golden Book of Management.* London: Newman Neame, 1956.

Van de Ven, Andrew H., and Marshall S. Poole, "Explaining Development and Change in Organizations," *Academy of Management Review,* 20(3), 1995, 510–540.

Van Fleet, David D., "The Ralph M. Stogdill Memorial Symposium," *Journal of Management,* 5, 1979, 125–126.

Van Velsor, Ellen, and Jean Brittain Leslie, "Why Executives Derail: Perspectives across Time and Cultures," *Academy of Management Executive,* 9(4), 1995, 62–72.

Vinzant, J. C. and D. H. Vinzant, "Strategic Management and Total Quality Management: Challenges and Choices," *Public Administration Quarterly,* 20(2), Summer, 1996, 201–219.

Vroom, Victor H., *Work and Motivation.* New York: Wiley, 1964.

Vroom, Victor H., and A. G. Jago, "Decision Making as a Social Process: Normative and Descriptive Models of Leader Behavior," *Decision Sciences,* 5, 1974, 743–769.

Vroom, Victor H., and P. W. Yetton, *Leadership and Decision Making.* Pittsburgh, PA: University of Pittsburgh Press, 1973.

Waddock, S. A. and S. A. Graves, "The Corporate Social Performance-Financial Performance Link," *Strategic Management Journal,* 18(4), 1997, 303–309.

Wainwright, Arthur D., "People-First Strategies Get Implemented," *Strategy & Leadership,* 6(1), Jan./Feb. 1997, 12–17.

Waterman, Robert H., *The Renewal Factor.* New York: Bantam, 1987.

Watson, L. A. and T. P. Tytula, "Process Improvement: Reengineering Spacelab Mission Requirements Flow," *Engineering Management Journal,* 8(1), March 1996, 21–27.

Watts, Patti, "Streamlining to Get Closer to the Customer," *Management Review,* 76, Nov. 1987.

Weber, Max, *The Theory of Social and Economic Organization.* C. Henderson and T. Parsons (Eds. and Transl.). New York: Free Press, 1947.

Weick, Karl E., *Sensemaking in Organizations,* Thousand Oaks, CA: Sage, 1995.

Weisbord, Marvin R., *Productive Workplaces: Organizing and Managing for Dignity, Meaning, and Community.* San Francisco, CA: Jossey-Bass, 1991.

Weiss, R. M., "Weber on Bureaucracy: Management Consultant or Political Theorist," *Academy of Management Review,* 8, 1983, 242–248.

Wells, Stuart, *From Sage to Artisan: The Nine Roles of the Value-Driven Leader.* Palo Alto, CA: Davies-Black, 1996.

Wheelwright, S. C., and R. H. Hayes, "Competing through Manufacturing," *Harvard Business Review,* 63, Jan./Feb. 1985, 99–109.

Whitsett, D. A., and Lyle York, *From Management Theory to Business Sense: The Myths and Realities of People at Work.* New York: AMACOM, American Management Association, 1983.

Wilkins, Alan L., and Nigel J. Bristow, "For Successful Organizational Culture: Honor Your Past," *Academy of Management Executive,* 1, 1987, 221–229.

Wilson, Colin, *New Pathways in Psychology: Maslow and the Post Freudian Revolution.* New York: New American Library, 1972, 1–2.

Wishart, Nicole A., Joyce J. Elam, and Daniel Robey, "Redrawing the Portrait of a Learning Organization: Inside Knight-Ridder, Inc.," *Academy of Management Executive,* 10(1), 1996, 7–20.

Wolf, William B., "The Barnard-Simon Connection," *Journal of Management History,* 1(4), 1995, 88–99.

Woodward, Joan, *Industrial Organization: Theory and Practice.* London: Oxford University Press, 1965.

Wooldridge, Bill, and Steven W. Floyd, "The Strategy Process: Middle Management Involvement and Organizational Performance," *Strategic Management Journal,* 11(2), 1990, 231–241.

Worthy, James C., in David G. Moore and Ronald G. Greenwood (Eds.), *Lean but Not Mean: Studies in Organization Structure,* Urbana, IL: University of Illinois Press, 1994.

Wrege, Charles D., and Ronald G. Greenwood, *Frederick W. Taylor: The Father of Scientific Management.* Homewood, IL: Business One Irwin, 1991.

Wrege, C. D., and A. G. Perroni, "Taylor's Pig Tale: A Historical Analysis of Frederick W. Taylor's Pig Iron Experiment," *Academy of Management Journal,* 17, 1974, 6–27.

Wrege, C. D., and A. M. Stotka, "Cooke Creates a Classic: The Story behind F. W. Taylor's Principles of Scientific Management," *Academy of Management Review,* 3, 1978, 736–750.

Wren, Daniel A., "Scientific Management in the U.S.S.R. with Particular Reference to the Contribution of Walter N. Polakov," *Academy of Management Review,* 5, 1980, 1–11.

——, "Was Henri Fayol a Real Manager?," in L. R. Jauch and J. L. Wall (Eds.), *Proceedings of the Academy of Management.* (San Francisco, CA), 1990, 138–142.

——, "The Nature of Managerial Work: A Comparison of Real Managers and Traditional Management," *Journal of Management Issues,* 4, Spring 1992, 17–30.

——, *The Evolution of Management Thought,* 4th ed. New York: Wiley, 1994.

Yoshimura, Noboru, and Philip Anderson, *Inside the Kaisha: Demystifying Japanese Business Behavior.* Boston, MA: Harvard Business School Press, 1997.

Zand, Dale E., *The Leadership Triad.* New York: Oxford University Press, 1997.

Zwerman, William L., *New Perspectives on Organization Theory.* Westport, CT: Greenwood, 1970.

Ability. *See* Power
A. C. Gilbert Company, 3
Academy of Management, 19
Acceptance theory, 154
Accountability, 152
Ackoff, R. L., 69
Achievement motive, 171–72
Activities, managerial, 23
Adams, B., 136
Adaptability, 70
Administrative organization, 24
AFL/CIO, 200
Alderfer, C. P., 170
America Online, 200
American Airlines, 147
American Motors Corporation, 238
American Society of Mechanical Engineers,
    19
American System of Manufacture, 10
American Telephone & Telegraph (AT&T),
    163, 174–75, 223, 232
Analysis, 121
Apartheid, 191, 202
Apple Computer, 15
Appley, L., 193
Area of acceptance, 156
Arizona Public Service Company, 65
ASEA of Sweden, 15
Assembly line. *See* Moving assembly line
Aston researchers, 81
Authority,
    and accountability, 152
    classical concept of, 152
    delegation of, 152
    functional, 148
    and human relations, 156
    as illusion, 148

legitimate, 146
and linking pin, 157
as rights, 158
and power, 158–59
Automated Healthcare Company, 13
Avon Products, 200

Baan, J., 199
Babbage, C., 7, 79, 188
Bank Wiring Observation Room, 164
Barnard, C., 21, 70, 122, 126, 144, 195, 242
    and acceptance theory, 154
Baxter Travenol Laboratories, 241
Bedeian, A. G., 177
Behavioral-descriptive theory of decision
        making, 131–32
Behling, O., 220
Ben and Jerry's, 151, 189
Bethlehem Steel Company, 51
Black and Decker Company, 126
Body Shop, 82
Boeing, 236
Bolton, A. A., 154
Brandeis, L., 51
Bureaucracy, ideal, 129
Burke, J., 3, 11
Business ethics, 198

Cadillac Automobile Company, 11, 15
Carroll, A., 199
Caterpillar Company, 15
Catholic Hospital Association, 209
Centennial of Management, 19
Challenger tragedy, 137
Champy, J., 221

Chandler, A. D., Jr., 81–82, 167, 226
Change, and efficiency, 70–71
Charismatic authority, 148
Chipman, D., 163
Choi, T. Y., 220
Chrysler Corporation, 211
CIGNA Corporation, 197
Citicorp, 223
City manager, 21
Clark, W., 66
Coca-Cola Company, 191
Codes of ethical conduct, 202
Columbia/HCA Healthcare Corporation, 197, 241
Commonwealth Edison, 163
Conceptual skills, 33
Contingency theory. *See also* Situational theory
  of leadership, 111
  of organization, 76–82
Control, span of, 75
Conflict, 230
Continuous quality improvement, 215
Continuous reorganization, 78
Cooke, M.L., 64–66
Coordination, 144, 230
Coordinative principle, 125
Corporate social performance (CSP), 198
Coss, L., 200
Cowboy management, 230
Crandall, R., 147
Creative Staffing Company, 165
Crosby, P., 216, 219
Culture, organizational, 206
  artifacts of, 211
  characteristics of, 207
  and ceremonies, 213–14
  and heroes, 211
  origins, 207
  and myths, 212
  and rites, 213–14
  and rituals, 213–14
  and sagas, 212
  and stories, 212

Deal, T. E., 207, 233
Decision making,
  hierarchy of , 130
  and leadership, 112–13

  and logical incrementalism, 134
  nonrational, 129–138
  and rationality, 128–29
Delegation. *See* Authority
DeLorean, J., 211
Deming, W. E., 216, 219, 231
Dennison, H. S., 21, 77, 124, 242
Denver Post, 179
Departmentalization, 75
Dickson, W. J., 163
Differentiation, 85
Division of labor. *See* Specialization of labor
Doctrine, 126
Domination, 146
Drucker, P. F., 19, 21, 24, 126, 200, 240
DuPont, 81
Durant, A., 226, 227, 231, 242
Durant, W., 226, 227, 231, 242

Eastern Rate Case, 53
Eastman Kodak, 60, 223
Ecologically sustainable organizations, 82
Economies of scale, 14
Edison, T.A., 163
Efficiency, 47, 70, 229
Efficiency management, 47
Eisenhower, D.D., 26
Electronic Data Systems Corporation, 14
Emerson, H., 52–64, 229, 230
  on efficiency engineers, 58
  twelve principles of efficiency, 59–63
Emery Air Freight, 180
Ethics. *See* Business ethics
Existence, relatedness, and growth, (ERG) theory, 170
Expectancy theory, 175–77
  and expectancy, 176
  and instrumentality, 176
  and motivational force, 176
  and path-goal theory of leadership, 113–14
  and valence, 175
Exxon Valdez, 194

Factors-attitude-effect (F-A-E) complex, 173
Failure mode and effects analysis (FMEA), 138
Fayol, H., 21, 23, 72, 124, 129, 232
Ferris, T., 3

Fiedler, F. E., 109
Finest type of ordinary management, 50
Florida Light and Power Company, 220
Follett, M. P., 76, 124, 149–50
    and authority, 148
Ford, H., 3
Ford Motor Company, 11, 15, 26, 50, 232
Formality of structure, 84
French, J.R.P., 159
Friedman, M., 197
Fujitsu Fanuc Company, 13

Gantt, H. L., 51, 190–92, 242
Garbage can model, 132
Gates, B., 20, 94
General Electric (GE), 11, 18, 56, 96, 126,
    140, 163, 232
General Motors (GM), 14, 15, 81, 105, 176,
    202, 236
George, C. S., 196
Gerstner, L. J., 147
Gilbreth, F. B., 229, 230, 232
Gilbreth, L. M., 121, 122, 140, 229, 230, 233
Goal setting, 119
    and administrative organization, 124
    and feedback, 141
    and performance improvement, 139
Goodyear Tire and Rubber Company, 209
Graen, G., 108
Greed effect, 200
Greenwood, R.A., 164
Greenwood, R. G., 164
Greyhound Financial Corporation, 33
Grove, A.S., 22, 109, 200
Growth needs. *See* Existence, relatedness,
    and growth (ERG) theory
Gulick, L., 73

Haber, S., 47, 229
Hales, C.P., 28
Hamel, G., 94, 229
Hamer, M., 221
Harvard Business School, 163–64
Hawthorne studies, 163
Hayakawa, S. I., 162
Heilbroner, R.L., 187–88
Herzberg, F., 173
Hewlett Packard, 212

Hitachi, 12, 15
Hosmer, L., 199
Hygiene factors, 173
    as extrinsic factors, 174

Iacocca, L, 211
Individual differences, maxim of, 166
Industrial Revolution, 6
Integration, 85
International Business Machines (IBM), 3,
    18, 74, 82, 147, 209, 210
International Paper Company, 223
Intel, 22, 109, 200
Interchangeable parts, 10
Iron law of responsibility, 153
Ivancevich, J. M., 141

Jacques, E., 156, 207
Job enrichment, 174
    and horizontal loading, 175
    and vertical loading, 175
John Deere, 15
Johnson and Johnson, 82, 211
Joint Commission on the Accreditation of
    Healthcare Organizations, 219
Juran, J., 216, 219

Kaiser, H, 12
Kakar, S., 52
Kanter, R.M., 230
Katz, R.L., 32
Kennedy, A.A., 207, 233
Kerr, S., 127
Kilpatrick, R.D., 197
Knight, Phil, 229
Knight-Ridder, 78
Kotter, J. P., 36, 89, 96, 209
Kreitner, R., 177

Lanza, Frank, 200
Labor, division of. *See* Specialization of
    labor
Large-batch technology, 79
Latham, G. P., 121, 139
Lawrence, P. R., 83–85, 230
Leader-Member-Exchange theory (LMX),
    108–9

Leadership,
  assumptions, 104
  contingency theory of, 111
  and decision making, 112–13
  effectiveness, 109
  leader-follower relations, 110
  linking-pin function of, 106–7
  Ohio State University Studies, 102
  position power, 109–10
  styles, 111
  task complexity, 110
  traits, 99, 101–2
  transformational, 114
  versus management, 96–97
Learning organizations, 31
Least preferred co-worker (LPC), 110
Leland, H., 11
Likert, J.G., 157–58
Likert, R., 106–8, 157–58
Likert's organizational systems, 106–7
Lindblom, C.E., 133–34
Line and staff, 57
Linking-pin concept, 106
Locke, E.A., 120–21, 139
Lockheed Martin Company, 200
Logical incrementalism (LI), 134–36
Lorsch, J., 83–85, 230
Loucks, V., Jr., 241
Lowell, F. C., 6
Luce, H. R., 187
Luthans, F., 177

McCallum, D., 7
McClelland, D. D., 171–72
McGregor, D. M., 103, 156
McMahon, T., 141
McNamara, R. S., 26–27
Mace, C. A., 120
Malcom Baldridge National Quality Award, 220
Management,
  activities, 23
  defined, 20
  fashion, *xiii*
Management-by-objectives (MBO), 126–28
  elements, 126
  and goal setting, 138
Management of initiative and incentives, 50
Managers,
  CEOs, 37
  functional, 34
  general, 36
  myths about, 30
  real, 40
  as reflective calculators, 24
  research on, 28
  roles, 28
  supervisors, 34
Marriott, J. W., 198
Mary Kay Cosmetics, 165
Maslow, A., 167–68, 177, 242
Maslow's need hierarchy,
  assumptions, 168
  deficiency needs, 169
  growth-oriented needs, 169
  self-actualizing personality, 170
  threatening conflicts, 169
  theory of threat, 169
Matsushita Electric, 12
Mausner, B., 173
Mayo, G. E., 164–67, 242
Means-ends relationship, 122
Microsoft, 200, 201, 206
Mintzberg, H., 30, 136
Mission, organizational, 122
Mizushima Works of Kawasaki Steel, 8
Monsanto Chemical Company, 211
Monsanto, Olga, 211
Mooney, J. D., 71, 124, 125, 126, 144, 160, 230
Morita, A., 128
Morton Thiokol, 138
Motivators, 173
  as intrinsic factors, 174
Motorola Corporation, 232
Moving assembly line, 12
Muddling through, 133
  process, 133–34
  rational comprehensive model, 133
  successive limited comparisions, 133
Munsterberg, H., 141

NASA, 137
National Association of Manfacturers, 201
National Research Council, 163
New Jersey Bell Telephone System, 158
New United Motor Manufacturing, Inc., 153
New York and Erie Railroad, 7
Nike, 229

Nintendo, 139
Nissan, 13
Nonrational decision making, 136–38
Normal accidents, 137
North American Tool and Die Company, 163
Northern Telecom Company, 202

Objectives. *See* Goal setting
Oldsmobile Motor Company, 11
Olin Corporation, 82
One master. *See* Unity of command
Opel Eisenach, 53
Operant conditioning, 177–81
Organizational behavior modification (O.B.
    Mod.), 177
Organized anarchies, 132
Organizational purpose. *See* Mission
Owen, R., 188, 190

Paper theory of organization, 156
Participation, in goal setting, 140–42
Partnership attitude, 194
Path-goal theory, 113
Peck, M. S., 4
Penney, J. C., 3
Pepsi Cola, 191
Perot, R., 105
Peters, T., 212
Pfiffner, J. M., 119
Philadelphia Electric Company, 209
Planned organizational change, 86
Planocrats, 239
Postmodern organization, 91
Power, 144
    as ability, 158
    coercive, 150
    expert, 159
    legitimate, 159
    power over, 150
    power with, 150–51
    referent, 159
    reward, 159
Prevoyance, 24
Principle of integration (McGregor), 104
Principle of supportive relationships, 106
Principle of the objective, 124
Principles of management, 73, 75
Process of organizational change, 88–89

Procter & Gamble, 82
Product liability, 127
Purex, 127
Purpose. *See* Mission

Quality. *See* Total quality management
Quinn, J.B., 134

Rational authority, 145–46
Rational-comprehensive model, 133
Rationality, 234
    bounded, 131
    objective, 130
    subjective, 130
    and Weber, 129
Raven, B. H., 159
Reagan, R., 236
Reengineering, 221
    defined, 221–22
    origins of, 222–23
Reiley, A. C., 73, 124, 125–26, 160
Relatedness needs. *See* Existence,
    relatedness, and growth (EGR) theory
Relationship-motivated leaders, 106
Relay assembly experiments, 164
Restructuring, 223
Rethinking, 223
Reorganization, continuous. *See* Continuous
    reorganization
Responsibility, social. *See* Social
    responsibility
RJR Nabisco, 189
Roethlisberger, F.J., 163–64
Roles, of managers, 28–30
Rules of the game, 199
Rush-Presbyterian-St. Luke's Medical Center,
    219

Saab-Scania, 211
Saab-Valmet, 131
Sadler report, 10
Sagan, C., 226
Samaritan Health System, 171
Santayana, G., 3
Satisficing, 131
Saturn Corporation, 176, 232

Schedules of reinforcement, 178–80
  continuous positive reinforcement, 178
  partial reinforcement, 179
    fixed-ratio partial reinforcement, 179
    variable ratio partial reinforcement, 179
Schwartz, P., 18
Schwarzkopf, N. H., 26, 94
Sculley, J., 206
Sensemaking, 39, 235
Self-actualization. *See* Maslow's need
  hierarchy
Self-fulfilling prophesy, 104
Selective adaptation, 105
Servomanipulators, 15
Sequential search, 131
Sears, Roebuck and Company, 71, 81
Sheldon, O., 192
Sherwood, F. P., 119
Silicon Graphics, 19
Simon, H. A., 75, 129, 235
  and Barnard, 155–56
Situational, law of, 148
Situational theory. *See* Contingency theory
Skinner, B. F., 162, 177
Slater, S., 6
Slubbing, 10
Small-batch technology, 79
Smith, A., 7, 226
Snyderman, B., 173
Social responsibility, 198
Sony Corporation, 128
South Essex studies, 79
Span of control, 75
Specialization, of labor, 7, 74, 227
Standard Oil of New Jersey, 81
Stogdill, R. M., 94, 101–2
Stora, 72
Strategic opportunism, 232
Stretch goals, 127
Successive limited comparison (SLC), 134
Supervisors,
  as go between, 166
  as person in the middle, 166
Synthesis, 121

Tandem Computers, 61
Tandy Corporation, 200
Task, 120
Task management, 121–22

Taylor, F. W., 20, 48–49, 52, 142, 162, 164,
  178, 190, 192, 229–30, 233, 237, 242
Taylor system, 51
Tead, O., 98–100, 192–96, 242
Teamwork, 125
Technical skills, 33
Technology, and organizational design, 79–82
Texas Department of Mental Health and
  Mental Retardation, 217
Theories X and Y, 103–4, 156, 238
Thompson, J. D., 82, 84, 230
Thorndike, E. L., 168
3M Corporation, 149, 206, 212, 230
Tiffany and Company, 165
Toftoy, C., 164
Tokenism, 201
Total quality management (TQM), 214–16
  basics of, 217–18
  critics of, 220–21
  and management, 219
  paradoxes of, 220
Towne, H., 19
Toyota Motor Manufacturing Company, 215
Toys R Us, 139
Traditional authority, 148
Transferability of management skills, 26
Transformational leadership, 114–15
Turner Brothers Trucking Company, 63
Twain, M., 227

Union Carbide Company, 137
Union National Bank, 181
Unity of command, 75
Unity of spirit, 126
Universality of management functions, 26
Ure, A., 9, 79, 188
Urwick, L. F., 73, 124
  on authority, 151–52
U. S. West Communications, 201

Virtual organizations, 18–19
Vroom, V., 112–13, 175–77
Vroom and Yetton Model of Leadership,
  112–13

Wainwright Industries, 168
Wall Street Journal, 187

Wal Mart, 139
Waterman, R. H., 212, 230
Weber, M., 128
  on authority, 146
Weick, K. E., 235
Welch, J., 20
Welfare capitalism, 188
Western Electric Company, 163
Woodward, J., 79–80, 230, 242

Work, J. M., 71
Wren, D. A., 121, 196

Yale and Towne Manufacturing Company, 19

Zones of indifference, 135